THE CATHOLIC BIBLICAL QUARTERLY

MONOGRAPH SERIES

13

THE BEGINNINGS OF CHRISTIAN PHILOSOPHY: THE EPISTLE TO THE HEBREWS

by

James W. Thompson

THE BEGINNINGS OF
CHRISTIAN PHILOSOPHY:
THE EPISTLE TO THE HEBREWS

by

James W. Thompson

The Catholic Biblical Association of America
Washington, DC 20064
1982

THE BEGINNINGS OF CHRISTIAN PHILOSOPHY:
THE EPISTLE TO THE HEBREWS
by James W. Thompson

©1982 The Catholic Biblical Association of America
Washington, DC 20064

PRODUCED IN THE UNITED STATES

Library of Congress Cataloging in Publication Data

Thompson, James W. 1942-
   The Beginnings of Christian Philosophy.

   (Catholic Biblical quarterly: Monograph series; 13)
   Bibliography: p.
   Includes index.
   1. Bible. N.T. Letters. Hebrews, 2nd—Criticism, interpretation, etc.
I. Title. II. Series.
BS1825.2.D67   299'.73   81-12295
ISBN 0-915170-12-4   AACR2

TABLE OF CONTENTS

This monograph is the result of a project which has developed over a period of several years. The approach to Hebrews used in this study was originally employed in a dissertation presented to Vanderbilt University in 1974, entitled, "*That Which Abides*": *Some Metaphysical Assumptions in the Epistle to the Hebrews*. After some of the results of that study were published in journal articles, the same approach was applied to other sections and themes of Hebrews and presented in additional articles on Hebrews. The final stage in this project came during a year of research at the University of Tübingen, when I had the necessary time for research to complete this monograph. The monograph includes both studies which have appeared in articles and exegetical work which was done in Tübingen during the school year 1979-1980. Many people have cooperated at various stages of this study, whose help I gratefully acknowledge.

I wish to express my gratitude to the publications which have given me the permission to publish material in this study which has appeared previously. Some of the chapters of this work present material unchanged from previous journal articles, while in other cases slight revisions have been made. Chapters III and VI are based on works previously published in the *Journal of Biblical Literature*. Chapter III is a revision of "'That Which Cannot Be Shaken': Some Metaphysical Assumptions in Heb 12:27," *JBL* 94 (1975). Chapter VI presents in unchanged form the article, "Hebrews 9 and Hellenistic Concepts of Sacrifice," *JBL* 98 (1979). Chapters VIII and IX originally appeared in the *Catholic Biblical Quarterly*. Chapter VIII is from "The Structure and Purpose of the Catena in Hebrews 1:5-13," *CBQ* 38 (1976). Chapter IX is from "Outside the Camp: A Study of Hebrews 13:9-14," *CBQ* 40 (1978). Chapter VII is from "The Conceptual Background and Purpose of the Midrash in Hebrews 7," *NovT* 29 (1977). A shorter version of Chapter II appeared in *Christian Teaching*, Everett Ferguson, editor (Abilene: ACU Bookstore, 1981).

I wish also to express my appreciation to the two institutions which made possible the completion of this project. The European Evangelistic Society extended the invitation to me to serve as director of the Institut zur Erforschung des Urchristentums in Tübingen during the school year 1979-1980. Through their gracious support of my research, I had the freedom to pursue this project. I am also grateful to the faculty and board of the Institute for Christian Studies in Austin, Texas, for granting me the leave-of-absence to spend the year doing research.

I am grateful also to the editorial board of the Catholic Biblical Quarterly Monograph Series for accepting this work into the series. Rev. Bruce Vawter's careful attention to the details of editing the manuscript has been invaluable.

My family has also assisted me in many ways in the development of this monograph. I appreciate the assistance and encouragement provided by my wife, Carolyn, my son, Philip, and my daughter, Eleanor. I am grateful to Carolyn and Philip for their help with the typing, and to Eleanor for asking more questions than I could answer.

CHAPTER I

THE RIDDLE OF HEBREWS

In scholarship on the Epistle to the Hebrews, it has become common-place to refer to "the riddle of Hebrews." The book appears to the interpreter "wie ein melchizedekisches Wesen ohne Stammbaum," according to Franz Overbeck.[1] E. Grässer, describing the book in language drawn from Hebrews itself, suggests that Hebrews is a λόγος δυσερμήνευτος (Heb 5:11).[2] The strangeness of Hebrews is to be seen, on the initial level, in the absence of information concerning the identity of the author and readers, the time of composition, and the situation which evoked the writing of the document. These unresolved questions make Hebrews an exegetical riddle and evoke an almost unlimited variety of proposed solutions.

When describing Hebrews as a riddle, many scholars are concerned primarily with the unusual literary character of the document which dis-tinguishes it from the rest of the NT.[3] The book is unique in its structure, its combination of a rhetorical introduction and epistolary ending, and in its command of an extraordinarily sophisticated Greek style throughout. Indeed, the rhetorical style is so impressive that A. Deissmann described it as the beginning of a Christian world literature.[4] P. Wendland[5] and E. Norden[6] have both pointed to the command of Greek, the plays on words, and parallelism which demonstrate that Hebrews belongs to a literary sphere unequalled in the NT.[7] It is thus undisputed that Hebrews is a unique form of early Christian literature.

The character of Hebrews as a riddle is not limited to questions of rhetoric. A more fundamental question for the exegete has been the problem of ascertaining the intellectual and spiritual background of the author and his method of argumentation. It is undeniable that the strangeness of

---

[1] F. Overbeck, *Zur Geschichte des Kanons*, 1.

[2] E. Grässer, "Hebrews 1:1-4. Ein exegetischer Versuch," in *Text und Situation*, 182.

[3] Cf. W. Wrede, *Das literarische Rätsel des Hebräerbriefes*; E. Grässer, "Der Hebräer-brief 1938-1963."

[4] A. Deissmann, *Licht vom Osten*, 181.

[5] Paul Wendland, *Die urchristlichen Literaturformen*, 307.

[6] E. Norden, *Agnostos Theos*, 386.

[7] Wendland, 307.

Hebrews consists not only in its structural and rhetorical characteristics, but also in the pattern of argumentation as well. Thus the "riddle" consists in the background which would allow one to understand the presuppositions of the author. As H.-M. Schenke has written,[8]

> So, wie die Dinge im Hebr nun einmal liegen, ist die Frage aber allein sinnvoll und fruchtbar, wenn man unter 'Hintergrund' die geistigen und theologischen Voraussetzungen, die der Verf. mitbringt, versteht.

Scholarship on the Epistle to the Hebrews has traditionally been based on the assumption that the book can be understood only when the author's intellectual and theological assumptions are brought into focus. Schenke observes that the argument of Hebrews moves in a totally different direction from Paul's normal argumentation and asks: if Paul is a Pharisee converted to Christianity, is the author of Hebrews a Sadducee?[9] The question is only rhetorical, as Schenke is certain that a converted Sadducee would have possessed a more exact knowledge of the Jerusalem temple than is demonstrated in Hebrews. Nevertheless, Schenke's question suggests a recognition that the author of Hebrews possesses presuppositions which make the pattern of argumentation a "riddle" when compared to other NT literature. Present research is sharply divided in its attempt to solve this riddle.

The Gnostic Interpretation of Hebrews

Although a Gnostic background for Hebrews had been presupposed as early as 1931 in Hans Windisch's *Der Hebräerbrief*,[10] E. Käsemann's monograph *Das wandernde Gottesvolk*[11] was the first to give a thoroughgoing interpretation of the epistle based on Gnostic motifs. Käsemann attempted to explain both obscure references and the dominant themes of the book against the Gnostic background. Such characteristic themes of Hebrews as κατάπαυσις, καταπέτασμα, and the high priestly christology of Hebrews are explained against the Gnostic background. Käsemann concludes, after his analysis of the various motifs,

> dass sowohl die Konzeption des Gesamtthemas wie insbesondere die Christologie unseres Briefes nur auf einem von Gnosis vorbereiteten Boden möglich war.[12]

---

[8]   H.-M. Schenke, "Erwägungen zum Rätsel des Hebräerbriefes," 425.

[9]   Schenke, 26.

[10]   H. Windisch, *Der Hebräerbrief.* In the *Vorwort* to the second edition, Windisch suggests the importance of the Mandaean literature for understanding Hebrews.

[11]   E. Käsemann, *Das wandernde Gottesvolk.*

[12]   Käsemann, 110.

This brief monograph remains a remarkable achievement, even if its conclusions at many points must now be considered inadequate. Käsemann correctly perceives the "strangeness" of the argumentation of Hebrews. He recognizes also that this document, which is the most consistently midrashic in the NT, approaches the OT in an unusual way. He argues correctly that the author of Hebrews comes to his text with definite presuppositions that determine the result of the interpretation. Thus, for instance, the Melchizedek speculation of Hebrews is not simply derived from the author's use of Psalm 110:4 and Genesis 14; these passages serve as a basis for affirmations which the author wanted to make.[13] Käsemann also correctly notices the pervasiveness of the theme of being "on the way" which appears not only in Hebrews 3:7-4:11, but elsewhere in the book (cf. 11:8-16; 12:12). He recognizes that the goal of pilgrimage, described under various images (κατάπαυσις, πατρίς, πόλις), is the heavenly world. Thus Käsemann often refers to the consistent dualism of Hebrews by which the people of God are reminded that their "rest" cannot be found on earth. The argument of Hebrews, as Käsemann correctly observes, is "in kosmisch-metaphysische Spekulation eingebettet."[14]

While Käsemann's insights into Hebrews remain useful, especially in his recognition of the motifs of dualism and pilgrimage, the understanding of Gnosticism in *Das wandernde Gottesvolk* is inadequate, as subsequent research has shown. On two important points Käsemann's interpretation cannot be supported. In the first place, one cannot argue that such themes as the ἀρχηγός speculation, the κατάπαυσις motif, or the description of the high priest are particularly Gnostic, as these themes were developed widely in various contexts. A second criticism follows naturally from the first: Käsemann's view of Gnosticism is heavily dependent on the work of Reitzenstein and Bousset, in which the myth of the redeemed redeemer and *Himmelsreise der Seele* were central Gnostic features underlying works in antiquity. Pre-Christian Gnosticism was thus reconstructed out of a variety of sources, including Philo, apocalyptic literature, and later Gnostic materials (excluding, of course, the Nag Hammadi literature). Thus Käsemann, writing before the Nag Hammadi discoveries, lacks clarity concerning his identification of material that is specifically Gnostic. As H.-M. Schenke says, Käsemann's identification of Gnosticism with a general spirit of late antiquity allows him, "sozusagen alles in einem Topf zu werfen."[15]

Although Käsemann's work has been subjected to close scrutiny and widely rejected, his central thesis is still affirmed by some who have written in

---

[13] Käsemann, 134.
[14] Käsemann, 43.
[15] H.-M. Schenke, 423.

the post-Nag Hammadi period. Erich Grässer has consistently maintained that the Nag Hammadi discoveries have supported Käsemann's interpretation.[16] Grässer demonstrates that such concepts as "wandering," "Himmelsreise," "rest," and "perfection" are attested in the Nag Hammadi writings.[17] Furthermore, other motifs in Hebrews, including the "Urbild-Abbild" theme, have been discovered in the Mandaean and Manichaean writings. Thus, concludes Grässer,[18]

> Angesichts dieser ganzen Sachlage wird man sagen können, dass Käsemanns einstige These vom gnostische vorbereiteten Boden des Hb durch die seitherige [religionsgeschichtliche] Forschung eher bestätigt als widerlegt wurde und darum eine gesteigerte Aktualität gewonnen hat.

Gerd Theissen, in *Untersuchungen zum Hebräerbrief*, is more cautious in his support of Käsemann's interpretation than E. Grässer. Indeed, he offers a solid criticism of Käsemann's interpretation when he questions Käsemann's use of parallels which are not indisputably Gnostic. "Es genügt also innerhalb dieses Arbeitsganges nicht, neben den Hb viele gnostische Paralleln zu stellen; entscheidend ist ihre traditionsgeschichtliche Beurteilung."[19] Theissen correctly observes that Käsemann's major themes (pilgrimage, the relationship between the son and the sons, the high priest christology) are reconstructions from various sources, and thus of doubtful value in describing Gnosticism. Thus, according to Theissen, the important issue for determining Hebrews' relation to Gnosticism is the view of creation in the epistle. Theissen concludes that Hebrews' view of creation as "eo ipso nicht heilvoll"[20] is closer to Gnosticism than to apocalyptic.

While Theissen correctly identifies a pervasive dualism in Hebrews, which includes a negative view of all earthly existence (p. 122), such a dualism is not *a priori* Gnostic. Because one can describe Gnosticism, Platonism, and apocalyticism under the category of dualism, the term must be more carefully defined before one can describe the dualism of Hebrews as Gnostic. It is not always clear how Gnostic and Platonic dualism are to be distinguished, especially in view of the Gnostic use of Platonic metaphysics.[21]

---

[16] E. Grässer, *TRu*, 185. Cf. Grässer, *Text*, 199: "E.Käsemann's These, dass der Hebräerbrief sein Leitmotiv unter Anziehung gnostischer Motive entfaltet, hat sich aufs Ganze bestätigt, bedarf aber aufgrund der veränderten Forschungslage der differenzierten Betrachtung."

[17] Grässer, *TRu*, 185.

[18] Grässer, *TRu*, 186.

[19] G. Theissen, *Untersuchungen zum Hebräerbrief*, 117.

[20] Theissen, 121. Cf. Heb 12:27.

[21] H. Jonas (*Die Gnosis und der spätantiker Geist*, 1. 45) contrasts Gnostic and Platonic dualism, arguing that Gnostic dualism contains a more negative attitude toward creation than Platonic dualism. Cf. E. R. Dodds, *Pagan and Christian in an Age of Anxiety*, 13, for a similar

The attempt to account for the categories and themes of Hebrews against the background of Gnostic presuppositions has not succeeded, despite the valuable contributions of Käsemann, Grässer, and Theissen. To point to specific categories, such as "rest," "curtain," or "pilgrimage" does not demonstrate a Gnostic presupposition, especially since these themes are developed elsewhere. To argue that the dualism of Hebrews is Gnostic is not convincing without a closer analysis of dualism. The positive contribution of these interpreters has been in recognizing a pattern of argumentation which distinguishes Hebrews from other NT writers. This pattern of argumentation consists, at least partially, in the dualism of heaven and earth and the notion of being a stranger and pilgrim on earth.

The Eschatological Interpretation of Hebrews

It has long been recognized that, although Hebrews abounds in phrases derived from Hellenistic rhetoric and philosophy, the book contains an eschatological element. B. Klappert,[22] O. Hofius,[23] O. Michel,[24] and C. K. Barrett[25] have insisted on the strong eschatological element of Hebrews. The determining feature in the thought of the author, according to C. K. Barrett, "is the eschatological element."[26] In contrast to Käsemann, Barrett interprets the "rest" (Hebrews 3-4) and "city" as concepts shaped by an eschatological consciousness. Even where Platonic language is used in Hebrews, according to Barrett, the terminology is placed in the service of a consistent eschatological view. The "shadow" of 8:5 is, in fact, a "foreshadowing." The readers of Hebrews experience the same tension between the "now" and the "not yet" as in the Pauline literature.

Otto Michel's important commentary on Hebrews concedes that Hebrews reflects a complex rhetorical and intellectual background originating in "the intellectual sphere of the Hellenistic synagogue."[27] Thus Michel, who describes the situation of the synagogue as one in which there was both assimilation and rejection of ideas from the environment, concedes the presence of both philosophical and Gnostic categories in Hebrews.[28] Neverthe-

---

view. Nevertheless, the distinction is not always clear, for the Gnostics were indebted to Platonism for their view of the structure of the universe. See P. Boyance, "Dieu et Dualisme," *Le Origini dello Gnosticismo* (Leiden: Brill, 1967) 340.

[22] B. Klappert, *Die Eschatologie des Hebräerbriefs.*

[23] *Katapausis.*

[24] *Der Brief an die Hebräer.*

[25] "The Eschatology of the Epistle to the Hebrews."

[26] Davies, 366.

[27] Michel, 35.

[28] Michel, 96 (Heb 1:2); 142-143 (Heb 2:10-11); 256 and 262 (Heb 7:1-3); 306 (Heb 9:8); 345 (Heb 10:19). Cited in Hofius, *Katapausis*, 158 (note 73). Cf. also Michel, 35.

less, Michel is convinced that the structure of thought in Hebrews stands closer to rabbinic and apocalyptic reflection than to Philo or Gnostic thought. Thus Hebrews, according to Michel, takes Hellenistic categories into an apocalyptic structure of thought.[29]

As an example of Michel's interpretation, the description of the end in Heb 12:26-28 is interpreted against the background of eschatology and apocalyptic. The contrast between the transitory earth and that which remains is interpreted in totally eschatological terms.[30]

> Das endzeitliche Drama, dass in Hebräerbrief 1:10-12 nur angedeutet ist, wird in Hebräerbrief 12:26-29 näher ausgeführt. Der Hebräerbrief nimmt also die alttestamentliche Eschatologie wieder auf und betrachtet das Ende der Zeiten durchaus mit dem Realismus israelitischer Prophetie, nicht mit griechisch-hellenistischer Kosmosverehrung. Das eigentümlich Undramatische griechisches Weltbild ist ihm fremd geblieben. Man konnte höchstens vermuten, dass der Blick auf das 'Unbewegliche' (τὰ μὴ σαλευόμενα) und das unerschütternde Königreich (βασιλεία ἀσάλευτος, 12:28) der Eschatologie unseres Briefes ein besonderes Gepräge gibt.

O. Hofius' *Katapausis* and *Der Vorhang vor dem Thron Gottes*[31] are both challenges to Käsemann's attempt to interpret Hebrews against a Gnostic background. While Hofius is successful in demonstrating that the categories of "rest" and of the "curtain" separating heaven and earth are not limited to Gnostic texts, he overevaluates the importance of the apocalyptic conceptual framework in his interpretation of Hebrews.[32] For example, Hofius sees a definite parallel between 4 Ezra and Heb 12:26-28. Both writers, according to Hofius, expect a "Weltuntergang" and a transformation of the creation. Thus, according to Hofius, "If one takes the eschatology of Hebrews seriously, it cannot be doubted that he (the author) does not share the Hellenistic 'Jenseitsglauben.'"[33] Consequently, Hofius' monograph scarcely notices the significant parallels between the themes of Hebrews and Philo. In addition, he does not recognize the significant differences between the eschatology of Hebrews (for example, 12:26-28) and that of 4 Ezra. Thus Hofius underestimates the parallels between Hebrews and Philo and overestimates the significance of 4 Ezra.

It is necessary to offer here the same methodological critique of those

---

[29] Michel, 62-65.
[30] Michel, 121.
[31] O. Hofius, *Der Vorhang vor dem Thron Gottes.*
[32] This criticism is made correctly by Theissen, 129.
[33] Hofius, *Katapausis*, 181.

who argue that Hebrews is fundamentally drawn from an apocalyptic world view as was given of Käsemann's interpretation. Hofius, Michel, and others allow their parallels to dictate their reading of Hebrews, thus ignoring the differences between Hebrews and the apocalyptic texts. While it is undeniable that there is an eschatology in Hebrews, one must ask if the existence of parallels with 4 Ezra and *2 Apoc. Bar.* indicates precisely the same kind of eschatological expectation. There is, for example, an emphasis on stability in Heb 12:27-28 and a dualism that distinguishes it from the eschatological parallels. To say that a text is "eschatological" is not very precise, for eschatological concepts were handled with a variety of intellectual presuppositions in early Christianity. Both Gnostics and Platonists inherited and reshaped eschatological traditions. In the Gnostic texts of Nag Hammadi, the Gnostic apocalypses frequently combined Platonic metaphysics with an expectation of the end of the world.

The discovery of 11QMelch at Qumran has suggested that the intellectual and spiritual home of the author of Hebrews is with the Qumran sect.[34] Undoubtedly the discovery of this fragment is useful in demonstrating the importance of Melchizedek in the speculation of the period. Nevertheless, it is necessary to recognize the assumptions which were used in the Melchizedek speculation before concluding that 11QMelch is of decisive importance for interpreting Hebrews.

It is unquestionable that Hebrews has inherited eschatological traditions. Nevertheless, the author's handling of these traditions is not to be identified with any other NT writing. The essential question is, as E. Grässer has shown,[35] how the author takes up and interprets these traditions. The eschatological passages do not account for the "riddle" of Hebrews. One must observe the assumptions with which the author interprets his text.

Philo as the Key to Hebrews

That Philo is the essential key for a resolution of the riddle of Hebrews has been affirmed, in one form or another, since Hugo Grotius posited a Philonic influence on Hebrews in 1644.[36] In the twentieth century, C. Spicq's great commentary of 1952 is the most outstanding example of a work built on the premise that the author of Hebrews was directly dependent on Philo. The author of Hebrews was "un philonien converti au christianisme."[37] Spicq devotes more than fifty pages to the parallels between the two authors in order to show that the writer of Hebrews knew Philo personally and had

---

[34] See Helga Rusche, "Die Gestalt des Melchisedek," 238-244.

[35] *Text*, 210.

[36] Annotation in Nov. Test, II, 1646, 811. Cited in Grässer, *TRu*, 177.

[37] C. Spicq, *L'Épître aux Hébreux*.

perhaps listened to his exposition of the Hebrew Scriptures in the synagogues of Alexandria (I 39-91).

As one might expect from Spicq's exhaustive survey of parallels, some
of his parallels are more convincing than others. Nevertheless, Spicq has
brought together a remarkable collection of parallels between Philo and
Hebrews. They include a comparison of Greek style, vocabulary, exegetical
traditions, and themes which have an extraordinary similarity between the
two writers. It is doubtful if a comparison between Hebrews and any other
literature could produce such an important collection of verbal parallels.

The weakness of Spicq's presentation is probably that he claimed too
much. No collection of parallels could demonstrate that the author of
Hebrews was a "philonien converti au christianisme." Spicq has succeeded in
demonstrating that the author of Hebrews used the vocabulary of educated
Hellenistic Jews. The verbal parallels do not necessarily show that words are
used in the same way by the two authors. Nevertheless, Spicq's contribution
has been especially helpful in showing that there is some relationship
between the two writers. Furthermore, while verbal parallels demonstrate
neither literary dependence nor a common intellectual horizon, they provide
the necessary tools for a more serious comparison of the two writers.
Repeated and extensive parallels suggest strongly that two writers share a
common background, even if they may disagree at points. One can hardly
ignore Philo's works in looking for the intellectual roots of Hebrews. Even if
Spicq has claimed too much, the extensive parallels which he has demonstrated for Philo and Hebrews suggest the importance of Philo for understanding the presuppositions of Hebrews.

The massive work of Ronald Williamson, *Philo and the Epistle to the
Hebrews*,[38] is a major challenge to Spicq's thesis that the author of Hebrews
is "un philonien converti au christianisme." An examination of Williamson's
book demonstrates, however, that the book is not an important challenge to
the conviction that Philo is important for the interpretation of Hebrews, for
Williamson's undertaking was extremely modest in scope. The issue which
Williamson chooses to debate is Spicq's suggestion of a literary dependence
of Hebrews on Philo, not the more complex issue of a common milieu.
The entire book is devoted to an examination of Spicq's discussion of the
Philonisms in Hebrews. In each comparison of terms which are similar in
Philo and Hebrews, Williamson concludes that the similarity is only formal,
not conceptual. Like a refrain throughout the book, there are the words,
"There is no decisive proof that the author of Hebrews borrowed any of his
terminology from Philo."[39] In some instances, Williamson agrees that the

[38] R. Williamson, *Philo and the Epistle to the Hebrews.*
[39] Williamson, 492; cf. 276, 431.

author of Hebrews shared with Philo a common Alexandrian milieu.

> He almost certainly lived and moved in circles where, in broad general terms, ideas such as we meet in Philo's works were known and discussed; he drew upon the fund of cultured Greek vocabulary upon which he (Philo) drew.[40]

Williamson consistently insists that the similarities are only formal, thus maintaining that the two writers share only a fund of verbal similarities without sharing a common intellectual horizon.

In confining his presentation to Spicq's argument, Williamson divides his book into three sections. Part I is a study of the *hapax legomena* of Hebrews, of which many have parallels in Philo. Williamson affirms that the appearance of common words in the two writers only demonstrates that the author of Hebrews was acquainted with the LXX, as Philo was, and that he knew the language of educated Hellenistic Jews.

The major part of the book (part II, pp. 137-495) is an examination of themes treated by Philo and Hebrews. In each instance, Williamson argues that the treatment of the theme in question is different in the two writers. Hebrews has, he affirms, an eschatological perspective and messianism not found in Philo. The dualism of Hebrews is the dualism of the two ages, while in Philo it is the dualism of two spheres of reality. The two authors have similar statements about the efficacy of sacrifice, but greater differences. The Melchizedek speculation and the distinction between the two levels of instruction (cf. Heb 5:11-14), despite formal similarities, are distinguished by the metaphysical and philosophical interests of Philo, which are absent in Hebrews.

The final section of the book is a study of the two writers as interpreters of Scripture. Williamson argues that Philo and Hebrews depend on different passages of the Hebrew Scriptures, and that Philo is allegorical while Hebrews is typological in approach.

Although Williamson is probably correct in disputing Spicq's argument that the author of Hebrews was a converted Philonist, his study is particularly disappointing, especially in his exegesis of Hebrews. In each of the three sections of his book, Williamson exaggerates the differences between Philo and Hebrews. For example, in the first section his use of linguistic data is extremely dubious. He notes, for example, that ἄθλησις (Heb 10:32) appears only five times in Philo, and never in contexts of persecution as in Hebrews. He does not observe, however, that the athletic metaphor in general is extremely important to Philo, and that it was used in contexts describing the necessary suffering of the sage. A similar misuse of linguistic data is

---

[40] Williamson, 493.

to be seen in Williamson's arguments concerning such words as ἀγενεα-λόγητος and ἀκλινῆ.[41] Williamson has not demonstrated that the two writers do not belong to a common conceptual world.

Williamson's treatment of themes discussed by the two writers is so filled with oversimplifications as to exaggerate totally the differences between the two writers. The fact that the author of Hebrews depends on traditions not found in Philo does not diminish the importance of Philo as a possible background to Hebrews. The author of Hebrews, as a Christian, would obviously depend on traditions not found in Philo. Nevertheless, Williamson oversimplifies the matter greatly when he argues that Hebrews is eschatolog-ical, while Philo is metaphysical and philosophical. To argue that Philo thinks spatially while Hebrews thinks temporally is likewise an oversimplifi-cation (cf. pp. 194-150). When Williamson distinguishes between πίστις in Philo and Hebrews, arguing that Philo's view has a dualistic, world-disparaging character not found in Hebrews, he likewise has overlooked the dualism of Heb 11:7, 38, where faithful people demonstrated that they were not at home in the κόσμος.

In distinguishing Philo and Hebrews, Williamson frequently overlooks the very nuances in the argument of Hebrews which distinguish it from other NT writings and suggest an affinity to Philo. These are the dualistic assump-tions which shape the argument throughout the book. Throughout the epistle, those things which are "touchable" (12:18), "hand-made" (9:11), and "worldly" (9:1) are inferior to their heavenly counterparts. Thus when Williamson says that Philo has a metaphysical nature not in Hebrews, he greatly exaggerates and oversimplifies.

A similar kind of oversimplification occurs in the third section of the book, where Williamson argues that Philo is allegorical, while Hebrews is typological in approaching the OT. There is, of course, a partial truth in Williamson's claim, as Philo both employs and lauds the allegorical method, while Hebrews has elements which might be called typological. Nevertheless, it is an oversimplification to speak of the interpretation in Hebrews simply as typological. U. Luz has argued correctly that Hebrews has a much more radical antithesis between the old and new covenants than does Paul. There is in Hebrews, according to Luz, an ontological thinking in the comparison of the two covenants in addition to the historical typology characteristic of

---

[41] Williamson shows that ἀγενεαλόγητος (Heb 7:3) does not appear in Philo in connec-tion with Melchizedek. He does not point out that the category is known to Philo, who says (*de Congress.* 43-45) that the OT narrative of Abraham's two wives is concerned with ideal types, οὐκ ἱστορικὴ γενεαλογία. Ἀκλινῆ in Hebrews 10:23, as Williamson shows, is not used in precisely the same way in Philo. Nevertheless, Philo often describes the stability of the one who stands by God (*de Som.* II. 237). Thus it is inadequate to look at the linguistic data without also recognizing the broader categories of the writers.

the apocalyptic literature.[42] In addition, the interpretation of the OT as παραβολή is hardly typological.[43] There is, as Luz and Herbert Braun have shown,[44] a metaphysic which consistently shapes Hebrews' use of the OT.

There is a very clear statement at the conclusion of Williamson's book which indicates that an important concern of his has led to the exaggeration of the differences between Philo and Hebrews. He argues that his study has shown

> the *Jewish*-Christian character of the epistle and its readers. It invites us to think of the Epistle to the Hebrews as in the mainstream of Christian theology, not as somewhere off-centre, deflected from the central stream of early Christian thinking by extraneous philosophical doctrines.[45]

Thus the denial of a philosophical element is, according to Williamson, the rescue of Hebrews for the mainstream of primitive Chrisitan theology. Such a rescue, in my opinion, hardly depends on the question of the presence of philosophical categories, for this question must be resolved by other criteria.[46] Williamson has tried to rescue Hebrews by ignoring the features which distinguish it from other literature of the NT and ancient Judaism.

The question of the relationship between Philo and Hebrews remains open, as neither Spicq nor Williamson has given a convincing solution. Williamson has pointed to significant differences, but has exaggerated them. The relationship between Philo and Hebrews is probably too complex to be reduced to a matter of literary dependence. Neither Williamson nor Spicq has pursued the "formal similarities" to the point of explaining the world-view and assumptions accompanying these "formal similarities."

Towards a Solution

The present impasse in scholarship on the Epistle to the Hebrews in-

---

[42] U. Luz, "Der alte und der neue," 331-333.

[43] The term is used frequently in antiquity in connection with the allegorical method. Cf. Philo, *de Conf. Ling.* 99; *Barn.* 6, 10; 17, 2. Cited in Luz, 330.

[44] H. Braun, "Die Gewinnung der Gewissheit in dem Hebräerbrief," 327.

[45] Williamson, 579-580.

[46] The place of Hebrews in the canon and within early Christianity is the subject of an important discussion initiated by Herbert Braun and continued by E. Grässer. Braun has argued that the introduction of metaphysical arguments into Hebrews as the basis of Christian certainty is a radical break from the "canon within the canon" to be seen in Jesus' friendship with sinners and Paul's doctrine of justification. Braun, "Gewissheit," 330. Cf. also H. Braun, "Das himmlische Vaterland," 326. E. Grässer has, in two articles, demonstrated that the christology of Hebrews is consistent with the Pauline teaching on justification, even if Hebrews employs categories other than δικαιοσύνη: "Rechtfertigung im Hebräerbrief," and "Zur Christologie des Hebräerbriefes."

dicates that criteria have not been established for determining the conceptual world which shapes the argumentation of the book. The use of parallels from apocalyptic and Gnostic sources, as well as from Philo, has demonstrated the need for extreme care in the handling of parallels. The fact that Hebrews shares a speculation concerning angels, Melchizedek, the cult, or the heavenly rest with a given body of material does not argue convincingly for a conceptual relationship. For example, Melchizedek speculation was known both in Qumran and in Philo. Indeed, the very nature of the references to Melchizedek in Psalm 110 and Genesis 14 invite the speculation which appears in the later literature, for the biblical references are themselves obscure. It is necessary, therefore, to observe the intellectual framework with which the authors approached their material.

An analysis of the intellectual presuppositions of the author necessitates that one distinguish between tradition and redaction more carefully than has been done in previous scholarship. It is likely that the author of Hebrews employed various traditions which he reshaped for the needs of his audience. Thus a particular parallel may only show the tradition which the author was using.

Ronald Williamson has shown that the author of Hebrews employed, for the most part, different texts from those which Philo used in his interpretation of Scripture. This fact indicates that the author of Hebrews inherited a Christian tradition which emphasized certain sections of the OT, particularly the Psalms. The decisive issue here is not over which passages the author used, but the assumptions with which he handled his texts. For example, it is well known that Ps 110:1, a text which had no particular messianic significance at Qumran or in the apocalyptic literature, is the most frequently cited OT text in the NT. It is also known that Ps 110:1 is interpreted in various ways throughout the NT, depending on the issues which were involved for the respective authors. The text, which is primarily used to describe the exaltation of Christ, is also of major importance to Hebrews, where Ps 110:4 ("Thou art a priest forever, after the order of Melchizedek") is also used. Undoubtedly the text is handled with different assumptions in Hebrews from the usage in other NT books.

Other motifs belong to the tradition which Hebrews inherited from the early church. The phrase ἐπ' ἐσχάτου τῶν ἡμερῶν τούτων (1:2) was inherited from the early church.[47] Undoubtedly at least part of the proemium of Hebrews (1:1-3) was inherited from the tradition. Similarly, the humiliation-exaltation motif of Heb 2:5-18 has echoes in the Pauline literature. It is likely, as G. Theissen has shown, that the Melchizedek speculation has been

---

[47] Grässer, *Text*, 210-211.

developed from early Christian literature.[48] An analysis which accounts for the distinction between tradition and redaction would provide methodological clarity in the use of parallels.

The research of this century has shown the inconclusiveness of explaining the thought world of Hebrews on the basis of a comparison of discrete traditions or categories, as these traditions were appropriated in various ways in the literature of antiquity. Therefore the issue is not, for example, to be seen in whether the description of the sanctuary in Hebrews is identical with the description of the sanctuary in Philo or Qumran. The important issue is to be seen in the assumptions which go into a particular argument. Despite the fact that Hebrews appears to be a collection of disparate midrashim which have no connection with one another, there is a consistent pattern of argumentation and set of metaphysical assumptions which shape the author's interpretation of Scripture. Hebrews employs frequent value judgments to reinforce conclusions in a way that is unusual in the NT. Certain recurring categories are employed which would be useful in comparing Hebrews with other literature.

The recurring categories in Hebrews point to a distinct set of metaphysical assumptions underlying the thought of the epistle. For example, the arguments of chapters one, seven, and eight are parallel; Christ (and the new covenant, 8:13) is superior to angels (chapter 1) and to levitical priests (chapter 7) because of his enthronement to the heavenly world. Angels and levitical priests are transitory, and therefore inferior. Similarly, the levitical cult of chapter 8 is ἐγγὺς ἀφανισμοῦ, and thus inferior to its heavenly counterpart. The Christian experience is identified with abiding, unshakable, and firm realities. The historical Israel is identified with tangible and transitory realities. There is, therefore, a constant metaphysical dualism underlying the author's value judgments.

This metaphysical dualism is closely connected to the categories of permanence and stability which are to be found throughout the book. The author has a special fondness for terms such as μένειν, βέβαιος, and ἀσάλευτος to describe the heavenly realities. Such categories emphasize the stability of the heavenly realities and point to metaphysical assumptions which have often been overlooked in analyses of the thought world of Hebrews.

The importance of metaphysics for an understanding of Hebrews has been recognized in previous research on Hebrews. E. Grässer and G. Theissen have seen the significance of the metaphysical dualism of Hebrews but have concluded that this is a Gnostic motif. U. Luz has argued that in the biblical

---

[48] Theissen, 13-32.

exegesis of Hebrews a typological interpretation is dominated by Hellenistic-Jewish ontological categories.[49] Herbert Braun has written, "Wer Metaphysik abhold ist, wird dem Inhalt der Gewissheit, wie sie im Hebräerbrief gefasst ist, zurückhaltend gegenüberstehen."[50]

Lala Kalyan Kumar Dey's book, *The Intermediary World and Patterns of Perfection in Hebrews*,[51] has pursued the question of the thought world of Hebrews in a very useful direction. While Dey is not primarily interested in the metaphysics of Hebrews, his work provides important suggestions for such a study, for he points to "an analogous frame of religious thought" in Hebrews and Philo. Dey argues that there is a consistent thought world in Philo which makes plausible the themes, comparisons, and transitions of Hebrews. In this framework

> angels, logos, heavenly man, Moses, Levi and Melchizedek in Hebrews belong to a single religious thought world. Here angels, logos, heavenly man, wisdom, etc. have to a large degree synonymous titles and interchangeable functions and they constitute the intermediary world between God and man. As intermediaries they are the agencies of creation and revelation. To this correspond two levels of religious existence. The intermediary world . . . mediates an inferior revelation and religious status of a secondary order. The higher level or *perfection* is characterized by unmediated and direct access to God and participation in the primary gifts.[52]

Dey argues that the readers of Hebrews were Christians who operated within a frame of religious thought comparable to that of Philo. In both writers the same "pattern of perfection" functioned as categories of religious experience. Philo, for instance, held that Moses was the example of perfection. It was he who left the body and went "outside the camp" of bodily things in order to approach God and to share in God's stability. Hebrews takes the same categories, but insists that only Jesus Christ has left the sphere of the flesh and entered into eternity. In addition, Philo and Hebrews share the same categories in describing the qualifications of a legitimate high priest. For Philo, the high priest shared in neither weakness nor sin; in Hebrews Jesus Christ is the high priest who is "holy, blameless, and higher than the heavens" (cf. Heb 7:26).

Dey's work is extraordinarily useful, as he has succeeded in taking Hebrews scholarship in a new direction. In his concern to illuminate the

---

[49] Luz, 331.
[50] "Gewissheit," 330.
[51] Missoula: Scholars Press, 1975.
[52] Dey, 7.

thought world of Hebrews, he has looked to the conceptual framework of Hebrews and Philo, not to the issue of literary dependence. In addition, his use of texts from the Middle Platonists and 4 Maccabees has broadened the discussion in a significant way.

Platonism, Apocalypticism, and Gnosticism

The investigation of the presuppositions of Hebrews must, if it is to contribute to an understanding of the epistle, be based on a more precise understanding of the background of the NT than previous literature has shown. Several works on Hebrews have, for instance, been based on such dichotomies as Platonic-eschatological or Philonic-apocalyptic. To assume that Hellenistic and Palestinian categories were separated into distinct units without influence on one another is to overlook the fluidity of first-century thought. Consequently, it is not necessary to attempt to reduce Hebrews either to one side of the dichotomy or the other. It is very possible that the author of Hebrews achieved his own combination of influences which came to him from several directions, as was commonly the case in synagogues of the diaspora.

A second area of concern is the present unclarity over the nature of Gnosticism in antiquity. Because the Nag Hammadi texts employ Platonic categories frequently, it is difficult to distinguish a Gnostic metaphysic from a Platonic metaphysic. Indeed, Gnosticism is discussed today by classical scholars as a category within the Platonic tradition.[53] Because Platonism itself was no unified movement, it is impossible to distinguish its world view from Gnostic views.

Previous research has been primarily limited to a comparison of Hebrews with Philo, Qumran, and other apocalyptic literature. Such research has consequently limited the alternatives too narrowly. If our concern is with the intellectual framework of the author of Hebrews, and not with his direct dependence on a single source, it is important to examine other literature of the period. L.K.K. Dey has correctly seen the importance of Middle Platonism for this task, inasmuch as Philo does not stand alone. Indeed, both Philo and Gnosticism are indebted to Middle Platonism in their respective world views. Thus it is important to compare the assumptions of Hebrews not only with Philo, but with the intellectual climate in which Philo lived.

The impact of Middle Platonism in late antiquity on Gnosticism, Philo, and the Christian Platonists in providing a coherent intellectual and meta-

---

[53] See John Dillon, *The Middle Platonists*; H. Krämer, *Der Ursprung der Geistmetaphysik*.

physical framework suggests that the metaphysical assumptions of Hebrews should be compared with this literature. Philosophical assumptions were appropriated in various ways by both Jewish and pagan writers. It is possible that the author of Hebrews, like Philo, Justin, and others, interpreted Scripture within a consistent and identifiable world view. This monograph is an attempt to account for the "strange new world" of Hebrews by examining the metaphysical assumptions of the author within a context that extends beyond Philo and Palestinian Judaism to the reflections of some Hellenistic philosophers.

CHAPTER II

HEBREWS 5:11-14 AND GREEK PAIDEIA

The relationship of Christianity to Greek *paideia* was the subject of much debate in the first four centuries of our era. As a community whose origins were Palestinian and Aramaic, but whose literature was written in Greek, early Christianity reacted in diverse ways to the Greek tradition of instruction.[1] There was, for example, the tradition which rejected Hellenistic *paideia* entirely, a view which is attested by Tatian and Tertullian.[2] Christians were encouraged to develop their own educational curricula, carefully avoiding the Greek educational models.[3] However, as W. Jaeger has observed, it was inevitable that early Christiantiy would accommodate its message to Greek models of instruction and demonstrate an appreciation for Greek education.[4] This response is to be seen in the apologists, in such Christian Platonists as Clement of Alexandria, and in the later Cappadocians. According to Jaeger, this positive response to Greek *paideia* was a crucial stage in the development of Christian theology.[5]

Although the impact of Greek philosophy on early Christianity became explicit only in the period of the apologists, this impact can be seen already in the NT.[6] Heb 5:11-14, for example, employs language that is greatly indebted to the tradition of Hellenistic *paideia* which was commonplace among philosophers of the Hellenistic period.[7] The motif of the two stages of

---

[1] See W. Jaeger, *Early Christianity and Greek Paideia*, 32-34.

[2] Cf. Robert Scholl, "Das Bildungsproblem in der alten Kirche," in H. T. Johann, ed., *Erziehung und Bildung in der heidnischen und christlichen Antike*, 507.

[3] T. Klausner, "Auswendiglernen," *RAC* I, 1034; Scholl, 511.

[4] W. Jaeger, "Paideia Christi," in Johann, *Erziehung*, 480. Jaeger describes a series of stages in the accommodation of Christianity to Greek philosophy and education: (1) the use of the Greek language; (2) the employment of concepts from the Greek environment (i.e., Acts 17; 1 Corinthians 12); (3) the direct appeal to the philosophers, as in the apologists; and (4) the creation of a Christian alternative to Greek philosophy in the formation of a Christian theology in the work of Clement of Alexandria and Origen.

[5] Jaeger, "Paideia Christi," 480.

[6] See E.A. Judge, "St. Paul and Classical Society," 19-36.

[7] James Moffatt, *The Epistle to the Hebrews*, 69. C. Spicq, *L'Épître aux Hébreux*, 1. 53, argues that the passage is evidence of literary dependence on Philo. Cf. R. Williamson's response in *Philo and the Epistle to the Hebrews*, 277-308. The debate is misplaced, as Philo

instruction, reflected in this passage, is unique in the NT but common in Hellenistic philosophy. The metaphors for instruction, including the "ABC's" and the milk and meat, were also common. The presence of this language raises the possibility that Hebrews represents an initial stage in the adoption of Hellenistic *paideia* and in the development of Christian theology as it was further expanded by Christian Platonists. The use of this language also suggests the possibility that the unusual set of categories of Hebrews is to be explained by the author's dependence on a structure of thought derived from Hellenistic philosophy.

Heb 5:11-14, with its unique language, is fundamentally important for illuminating the theological assumptions and intention of the author of Hebrews, for this passage stands as the author's introduction to a major section of the book (7:1-10:18). It provides one of the clearest insights into the author's own understanding of this work and of the categories with which he writes. This fact was recognized by Käsemann, who argued that 5:11-14 is a Gnostic topos introducing an esoteric *logos teleios*.[8] In Hebrews research, other conclusions have been drawn which reflect the various approaches to the book. E. Grässer suggested that the passage belongs conceptually to the categories of Greek philosophy,[9] while others have argued that the passage belongs only formally to the philosophic tradition.[10] Because of the importance of this passage in illuminating the author's categories and conceptual world, the purpose of this chapter is to analyze these categories within the framework of the epistle and of Hellenistic philosophy.

Ἐγκύκλιος Παιδεία and the Levels of Instruction

The concept of the two levels of instruction is well attested in the literature of antiquity. Prior to Plato, the Greeks had developed a basic curriculum for the youth which included grammar, rhetoric, dialectic, music, geometry, arithmetic, and astronomy. This curriculum was later designated by the terminus technicus ἐγκύκλιος παιδεία. In the Latin literature these subjects were known as the *liberales artes*.[11] In classical Greece, the purpose of an education in these subjects was to prepare the free citizen for his responsibilities in the polis.[12]

---

belongs to a larger circle of writers who used Platonic terminology. Hebrews must be seen within this larger context.

[8] E. Käsemann, *Gottesvolk*, 122-126. Cf. H. Windisch, *Der Hebräerbrief*, 46-47.

[9] E. Grässer, *Der Glaube im Hebräerbrief*, 137.

[10] Cf. A. Bonhöffer, *Epiktetus und das Neue Testament*, 62.

[11] H. Fuchs, "Enkyklios Paideia," *RAC* 5. 366. Cf. J. Christen, *Bildung und Gesellschaft*, 71.

[12] Fuchs, 366.

Plato, according to J. Moreau, was the first significant philosopher of education. It was in his writings, particularly in the Allegory of the Cave, that Plato developed his philosophy of education.[13] The goal of learning was, for Plato, to transcend the limited knowledge which exists in the darkness of the cave. Education, therefore, has the religious function of unveiling the real world of ideas, truth, light, and the Good. Learning involved the recollection of earlier experience (*Meno* 81c). The man who recalls what he once saw in God's proximity presses on to the world of ideas, thus reaching up to true being. Such a person is *teleios* (*Leg.* 2 653A), having attained insight and philosophical knowledge.

Within this system Plato refers several times to the common disciplines (*Theat.* 145; *Prot.* 318E; cf. *Rep.* 7. 531D, 534D) which exist as *propaideuma* for matters of ultimate importance (*Rep.* 7. 536E). Dialectic, for instance, prepares one to know the first principles. Astronomy prepares one to reach beyond the sensible world (*Rep.* 7 527B). Mathematics, according to Plato, is not valuable only for its normal functions in building and administration; it has the more important value of bringing the mind to a consciousness of higher ideals and values (*Rep.* 7 522A).[14] Thus for Plato education includes levels and sequential stages. The lower education has the primary purpose of leading in the search for the perfect good.[15]

Plato's reflections on the stages of education were the beginning of a development which was to become a significant feature of subsequent reflection. It was consistently argued by both Platonists and Stoics in the Hellenistic Age that the function of the *propaideia* was to lead to a higher truth. Seneca reports that Posidonius distinguished between the two stages of education. The liberal arts, according to Posidonius, are not useful for producing virtue; instead, they prepare the soul for the reception of virtue (Seneca, *Ep.* 88:20).[16]

> Just as the 'primary course' (*prima*), as the ancients called it, in grammar, which gave boys their elementary training, does not teach them the liberal arts, but prepares the ground for early acquisition of these arts, so the liberal arts do not prepare the soul for virtue, but merely set it going in the right direction.

[13] J. Moreau, "Platon als Erzieher," in Johann, *Erziehung*, 146. See also T. Ballauf, "Der Sinn der Paideia," in Johann, *Erziehung*, 132. T. Klausner, "Auswendiglernen," 1032. Cf. Plato, *Meno* 81a.

[14] S.R.C. Lilla, *Clement of Alexandria*, 170.

[15] *Ibid.*, 170.

[16] H. Chadwick, "Philo and the Beginnings of Christian Thought," in A. H. Armstrong, ed., *The Cambridge History of Later Greek and Early Mediaeval Philosophy* (Cambridge: University Press, 1970) 140.

According to Posidonius, philosophy served the religious function of educating the mind beyond the material realities. "The mind grows by contact with things heavenly, and draws into itself something from on high" (*Ep.* 88:23).

The Platonic view is represented also by Posidonius' student, Cicero, and by the rhetorician, Varro. Cicero argued that the essential function of the ἐγκύκλιος παιδεία is to sharpen the mind and enable it through freedom from the senses to handle ultimate questions.[17] Similarly, Varro agued that the ἐγκύκλιος παιδεία constitutes the preliminary instruction allowing the learner to ascend to the level of highest truth.[18]

The Middle Platonists of the first and second centuries A.D. exhibit a continuing interest in the Platonic distinction between the two stages of education, as is indicated by extensive discussions of the subject which are found in Plutarch, Maximus of Tyre, and Albinus. Even if the work, *de Liberis Educandis*, is not from Plutarch,[19] it offers an interesting perspective on the educational ideals of the period. The goal of education is to develop right actions, which are learned through the study of philosophy. Progress occurs when the mind is adequately exercised with good and useful thought. The exercise (ἄσκησις) is as important to the mind as gymnastics for the body, for practice develops the proper habits (ἔθος).[20] The point is illustrated by the image of agriculture. The teacher is like the farmer, nature is like the soil, and verbal precepts are like the seed. Thus the individual, like the plant, needs the right culture and exercise (γεγυμνασμένοις) in order to achieve the proper development.[21]

Both Albinus and Maximus of Tyre, the Middle Platonists of the second century, argue for the propaideutic value of the lower education. For Albinus, the general education is only a preliminary stage to philosophy, which is concerned with the knowledge of the Good.[22] For example, dialectic leads to the knowledge of the first principles and to the knowledge of divine things. Astronomy enables one to pass from the sensible to the intelligible world and to the knowledge of the Good. Similarly, geometry is concerned with those things which do not undergo change. It is through *askēsis* that one progresses from this lower education to the knowledge of the Good. This perspective suggests the strong impact of Plato's statements on his successors.

Maximus of Tyre's Thirty-seventh Discourse is devoted to the subject of

---

[17] *De Or.* 1. 17. 44. Cited in E. Fuchs, *RAC* 5. 387.

[18] Varro, *Disciplinae.* Cited in Fuchs, *RAC* 5. 387-388.

[19] See D.A. Russell, *Plutarch* (London: Duckworth, 1973) 18.

[20] *de lib. ed.* 2BC.

[21] *de lib. ed.* 2CE.

[22] Albinus, *Didaskalios* 162. 8-10, 17-18, 22-28, 30-32. Cited in Lilla, *Clement*, 171.

the ἐγκύκλια μαθήματα. Here he names geometry, music, poetry, logic, rhetoric, arithmetic, and gymnastics as the auxiliary disciplines. The goal of this education is to prepare the way for philosophy, which leads to God. Thus Maximus shares with the other Platonists the essentially religious understanding of education.

Epictetus shared the belief in the stages of training and in the function of philosophy as the goal of education. At the beginning stage, according to Epictetus, one is a νήπιος. Without a knowledge of the world which comes through philosophy, one remains a νήπιος. Progress and learning then follow exercise and practice in what has been learned. According to *Diss.* 1. 16. 3, "the philosophers exercise us first in the theory which later leads on to more difficult matters" (ἐπὶ τῆς θεωρίας γυμνάζουσιν ἡμᾶς οἱ φιλόσοφοι . . .). According to 2. 18, 27, the man who exercises himself (ὁ ἀσκητής) is the true athlete in training (γυμνάζων ἑαυτόν). Without such exercise, one remains a child, subject to the sense impressions and unable to acquire true knowledge.

This survey indicates the presence of a consistent pedagogical theory extending from Plato to the second century A.D., affirming the existence of two levels of education. The first level exists as a propaideutic to prepare the way for knowledge of ultimate reality. The highest stage of learning has the religious function of leading one beyond the material world to the intelligible world. According to both (pseudo-?) Plutarch and Epictetus, one proceeds from the one level to the other through exercise, for the discipline of learning is comparable to the training of an athlete.

Philo of Alexandria

The extensive Philonic corpus reflects Philo's interest in education from the lower to the higher disciplines, an interest which is evident in the wide variety of epistemological terms that are to be found in Philo. Philo's interest is not, however, in worldly educational striving.[23] Philo's interest in education is a constituent part of his belief in progress (προκοπή) toward perfection (τελείωσις), which is the human goal.[24] Philo's leading OT heroes were models of perfection insofar as they cut all ties to the world, drew near to God, and lived the virtuous life on earth as strangers.[25]

---

[23] W. Völker, *Fortschritt und Vollendung bei Philon von Alexandrien*, 167.

[24] Völker, *Fortschritt*, 167.

[25] Cf. L.K.K. Dey, *The Intermediary World*, 44-45. "Perfection in this pattern of thought means rising above the intermediary world . . . to the presence of God himself—immediate access . . . Perfection is associated with Sight—Israel, sinless, wholly cleansed minds, state of full knowledge . . . Imperfection, on the other hand, is defined in terms of inability to rise above the intermediary world, *need for instruction, teaching and exhortation, the guidance of Sophia, and Logos.*"

The way to perfection was, for Philo, knowledge. He refers to the ἐπιστήμη which filled his soul and to the desire for education which had led him since his youth.[26] On several occasions Philo explicitly describes this education as the way to perfection. Abraham, for example, inquired into the ἐγκύκλιος παιδεία when he was "not yet perfect" (*de Spec. Leg.* 3. 244). The advance to perfection is connected (*de Sac. A.C.* 7) with the progress from instruction to "the free unlabored knowledge" which comes in God's proximity. According to several Philonic texts (*de Fug.* 172; *de Mut. Nom.* 270; *de Praem. Poen.* 49), perfection comes through teaching.

Philo's comments on the problems posed by ignorance demonstrate his intense interest in learning as the way to perfection. Philo describes the initial learner as νήπιος and ἄπειρος (*de Mig. Ab.* 29; *de Ag.* 9; 160). Inexperience in the dogmas of the sophists could cause one to fall without firm footing (*Quod Det. Pot.* 41). Ignorance (ἄγνοια) is like the incapacity of the sense organs (*de Eb.* 80-82), for it leaves one unequipped to endure to the end.

This concern with the level of one's learning is associated with Philo's descriptions of the differing levels of advancement. According to *de Ag.* 159, there are three kinds of people: beginners (ἀρχόμενοι), those making progress (προκόπτοι), and those who have reached perfection (τελειώμενοι). The beginner is lacking in experience (ἄπειρος, 160) for a sustained struggle against the sophists. Thus one needs a period of advancement before one reaches the stability necessary for challenging the sophists in battle (162).

In a variety of texts, Philo indicates what is involved in this instruction. At this point his relationship to the philosophy of the period is evident, for he agrees with his contemporaries in positing successive stages of education. At the first stage are the ἐγκύκλια. These common subjects serve to sharpen the mind and equip the student for going on to higher studies. This level, sometimes called the μέση παιδεία (*de Congress.* 12, 14, 145; *de Cher.* 3, 6; *de Fug.* 183-188), is the presupposition for advancing to the second stage, philosophy (*de Eb.* 49), which includes virtue. The latter is the presupposition for advancing to the final stage, σοφία.[27] Thus the προκόπτων approaches the goal while he climbs to higher forms of knowledge.

The path of progress is illustrated by Philo in many tractates, but comes to the clearest expression in *de Congressu quaerendae Eruditionis gratis*. This tractate is based on the story of Hagar and Sarah and Sarah's request, "Go into my handmaid and beget children from her" (Gen 16:2). Philo

---

[26] *de Spec. Leg.* 3. 1; *de Congress.* 74-75.

[27] *de Congress.* 79; W. Bousset, *Jüdisch-christlicher Schulbetrieb*, 103. Cf. Völker, *Fortschritt*, 171.

argues that we are not to understand this story as an account of the jealousy of two women. The two women represent, instead, the two levels of learning: the ἐγκύκλιος παιδεία and philosophy. Before Abraham could study philosophy, it was necessary to investigate the ἐγκύκλιος παιδεία.[28] The same theme is developed elsewhere in the Philonic corpus. According to *de Gigantibus* 60, Abraham was a man of learning who·pursued the encyclia before he advanced beyond the material world (cf. *Leg. All.* 3. 244, cited above). Abraham was consistently described as the sojourner who arrived at perfection through advancement in knowledge.[29]

Philo's list of encyclia corresponds in *de Congress.* (15-18) to the usual lists among his contemporaries. The encyclia are described in *de Congress.* 19 as "the simple and milky foods of infancy" (πρὶν ἢ ταῖς ἀποικίλοις καὶ γαλακτώδεσιν ἐν ἡλικίᾳ τῇ βρεφώδει). This imagery of food for intellectual advancement is common in Philo. According to *de Sac. A.C.* 78, Philo says, "It is useful to feed the mind (ἐντρέφεσθαι) . . . first on human opinions, even if this education must finally be abolished in favor of higher teaching." According to *de Congress.* 167, "the soul . . . is fed by the lessons of instruction's doctrine."

The image of milk and solid food occurs elsewhere in the Philonic corpus. In *Quod Om. Prob. Lib.* 160, Philo describes the soul's advancement from the milk of the early instruction to the solid meat of philosophy. In *de Ag.* 9, milk is compared to the lower subjects which are suitable for childhood, for they lead to wisdom, temperance, and virtue.

While the reception of the enclyclia is important, such training is not an end in itself. Indeed, Philo is aware that many have become ensnared by the encyclia without going on to philosophy (*de Congress.* 77) and ultimately to wisdom. In *de Congress.* 79, wisdom is defined as the "knowledge of things divine and human and their causes."

The goal of learning is stated in similar terms in other Philonic texts. In *de Som.* 1. 126-129, for example, he says that the goal of learning is to prepare the soul for the ultimate vision. In *Quod Det. Pot.* 166, 171, he says that the ultimate goal is the purging of the soul through the vision of the good. According to *de Ebrietate* 33, one succeeds from the lower learning to the ὀρθὸς λόγος. In *de Sac. A.C.* 86, instruction leads one to a grasp of heavenly food, which is solid knowledge. These texts indicate the close relationship in Philo between knowledge and perfection. The goal of knowledge is the contemplation of the intelligible world and the grasp of things divine.

The imagery of food is often used by Philo in connection with the imagery of athletics. Indeed, it is striking how frequently Philo employs the

---

[28] This theme is similar to the account in Plutarch, *de lib. ed.*
[29] See *de Congress.* 22-23; *de Sac. A.C.* 44.

metaphor of athletic training in connection with the metaphor of food. Philo says in *de Sac. A.C.* 85:

> . . . if these things are to be our lasting possession we must continually exercise and discipline ourselves. . . . For contact . . . without abiding in it is as if we should taste food and drink, and then be barred from receiving its nourishment to the full.

In *Leg. All.* 1. 98, he speaks of the nourishment of the soul that is comparable to the nourishment of an athlete. The same analogy is used in *Quod Det. Pot.* 41, where Philo compares the nourishment and training necessary for the athlete to the training of the wise man.

A wide variety of Philonic texts indicates that it is not only learning which leads to perfection. Philo continues the athletic image by suggesting that practice leads to perfection. Thus Philo speaks frequently of those who are "perfect through practice" (cf. *de. Conf. Ling.* 181; *de Congress.* 35; *de Mut. Nom.* 85; *de Ab.* 53; *de Praem. Poen.* 36). In most instances Jacob is the model of perfection achieved through practice, as he is regularly called ὁ ἀσκητής (cf. *de Ag.* 42; *de Congress.* 35; *de Praem. Poen.* 36; *Quod Det. Pot.* 64; *de Mig. Ab.* 28; *de Eb.* 82). Indeed, he often distinguishes between Jacob, "the man of practice," and Abraham, the man of instruction (cf. *de Som.* 1. 170; *de Eb.* 80). Although Philo frequently describes his heroes as athletes, Jacob is the one who most frequently is described as the athlete in training.

Although Philo at times distinguishes between the man of instruction and the man of practice, he nevertheless insists that the man of instruction must "train himself."[30] According to *de Ab.* 53, teaching cannot be consummated without practice. In *de Sac. A.C.* 85-86, Philo says, "Continued exercise makes solid knowledge." In *de Mut. Nom.* 81, he describes those who are "drilled in the gymnastics of the soul" (τὰ τῆς ψυχῆς γυμνάσματα). According to *de Gig.* 60, "the mind . . . pursues the learning of the schools and the other arts, . . . which sharpens and whets itself, . . . and trains and drills itself (γυμνάζων καὶ συγκροτῶν ἐν τοῖς νοητοῖς αὐτόν), solid in the contemplation of what is intelligible by mind." The importance of "mental gymnastics" is further indicated in *Quod Det. Pot.* 41, γεγυμνασμένοι γὰρ περὶ τὰς τῶν λόγων ἰδέας οὐκέτ' ἀπειρίᾳ σοφιστικῶν παλαισμάτων ὀκλάσομεν. In all of these texts Philo assumes, with his contemporaries,

---

[30] See G. Stählin, Προκοπή, *TDNT* 6. 710, for the importance of ἀσκητής in Philo. Stählin observes the genitives which are often used with ἀσκητής: σοφίας (*de Eb.* 48; *de Virt.* 4); φρονήσεως (*Leg. All.* 1. 80; ἐπιστήμης (*Quod Det. Pot.* 69); φιλοσοφίας (*Quod Om. Prob. Lib.* 43); ἀληθείας (*Leg. All.* 3. 36).

that the instruction received must be "trained" and "practised" before one reaches perfection.

The image of agriculture is also frequently associated with Philo's description of intellectual advancement, an image which also appears in Plutarch. This imagery is the basis of the tractate, *de Agricultura*. In this tractate, which is based on the account of Noah's work as a husbandman in Gen 9:20-21, Philo gives an allegorical treatment of Noah's work. The mind, as the recipient of the seed, is the object of true husbandry. One progresses from νήπιος to τέλειος and from milk to solid food. Those who produce only weeds or who produce nothing at all are cut down (*de Ag.* 12, 17). Thus there is a special importance to the pursuit of soul-husbandry, as *de Agricultura* points out, for it determines the outcome of the indiviual who has reccived the good seed.

In several instances, the result of study and exercise is that one is enabled to find a stable resting place which will give one the capacity to endure to the end. The inexperienced one, according to *Quod Det. Pot.* 41, is likely to fall without a firm footing. It is the celestial food which provides sturdiness (*Quod Det. Pot.* 115). According to *de Sac. A.C.* 91, knowledge and exercise provide a stable resting place (cf. *de Congress.* 164). According to *de Praem. Poen.* 29, such contemplation enables one to soar beyond material things and to find his support and stay in the one who falters not (ἀκλινός).

Philo's suggestion that stability is found through knowledge must be seen in the context of his distinction between the instability of this creation and the stability of God's presence. According to *Leg. All.* 2. 83 and *de Post. Cain.* 23, God is steadfast, but the creation is unstable. Thus if stability is secured by mortals, it must be secured at the side of God. According to *de Gig.* 49, true stability is found at the side of God. According to *Quod Deus Immut.* 22-23, those who study philosophy "do not change with the circumstances, but with unbending steadfastness and firm constancy take in hand all that it behooves them to do." The privilege of the wise man, therefore, is to share in God's stability (cf. *de Conf. Ling.* 30, 31, 96).[31]

The goal of knowledge, according to *de Congressu quaerendae Eruditionis gratis*, is to acquire the steadfast heart which will enable one to endure in the "contest of life."

> Some faint ere the struggle has begun, and lose heart altogether, counting toil a formidable antagonist, and like weary athletes drop their hands in weakness and determine to speed back to Egypt and enjoy passion. But there are others who, facing the terrors and dangers of the

---

[31] See especially J. Pascher, *Der Königsweg*, 228-239.

wilderness with patience and stoutness of heart, carry through to its finish the contest of life, keeping it safe from defeat, and take a strong stand against the forces of nature (164).

Those who are fed by the lessons of instruction's doctrine (167) are able to endure.

This survey of the significant place of knowledge in Philo's thought indicates that the growth in knowledge cannot be separated from the frequent references to perfection. Knowledge includes, according to Philo, more than a scientific grasp of truth. Knowledge culminates in the vision of God which provides stability and endurance.[32] Without this knowledge one cannot progress to the goal of access to God.

Christian Platonism

It is not an easy task to assess the impact of Platonism on Christianity, as J. H. Waszink has observed, for the impact is diverse and often difficult to measure.[33] Nevertheless, Waszink's question, "What happens when a Platonist becomes a Christian?" is important for observing the developments in early Christianity. While early Christians responded in various ways, it is apparent that there was a growing appreciation of Hellenistic *paideia*, especially in the eastern half of the Mediterranean.

One response, even among the recipients of the classical education, was to disdain Greek *paideia* and to substitute Christian education as an alternative. Both Tatian and Athenagoras, for example, were critical of the normal education.[34] Tatian described the schoolmasters of his time as mere "babblers." Athenagoras contrasted true Christian education with the normal school education. This response is to be seen also in the early Christian academies and school curricula in which sections of the Bible were committed to memory.

The second response is to be seen in those who argued that Christianity was the absolute philosophy. This argument is to be seen in Justin.[35] However, it is in Clement of Alexandria and Origen that the impact of philosophy reaches a new development. Clement is heavily indebted to Philo. Consequently, his response to Greek *paideia* resembles that of Philo. Clement appreciates the ἐγκύκλιος παιδεία and makes it the first stage of Christian

---

[32] Völker, *Fortschritt*, 241.

[33] J. H. Waszink, "Bemerkungen," 137.

[34] Robert Scholl, "Das Bildungsproblem in der alten Kirche," in Johann, *Erziehung*, 507. See also W. Jaeger, *Early Christianity*, 32-34. See *1 Clem.* 21:6, 8-9 for references to the Christian *paideia*.

[35] Eusebius, *Hist. Eccl.* 4. 11. 8; Jaeger, *Early Christianity*, 29.

instruction.[36] He also argues that the philosophy of Plato is important for understanding God. The distinctively new element in Clement was the introduction of γνῶσις, a level of knowledge reserved only for the few. *Gnōsis* was a way of transcending *pistis*.[37] Through the use of "secret teachings" of Jesus and the allegorical method of interpretation, Clement intended to satisfy Gnostic appetites and arrive at the teaching which was more advanced than the catechism. Although this higher teaching employed philosophy, Clement maintained that the priority lay with the Christian faith as revealed in Scripture. The final goal of this philosophy was the goal shared by many Middle Platonists: union with God, an experience that was symbolized by the high priest's entry into the holy of holies or Moses' journey up Mount Sinai.[38]

Clement's development of a Christian theology employing Platonic categories and the allegorical method of interpreting Scripture served as the model for the work of Basil, Gregory Nazianzen, and Gregory of Nyssa. All of these leaders were the recipients of the classical education and indicated their appreciation of it. These writers employed the allegorical method of exegesis to find deeper truths and took up the Platonists' imagery of training for Christian education.[39] Christianity thus becomes for them what philosophy is to the philosopher. Platonic categories are employed in the service of Christian education.

Philo and Clement both served as models for the development of a Christian theology. This theology took over the functions of educating Christians in the same way that Plato had intended his philosophy to lead one to a vision of truth. Platonic categories were placed in the service of Christian teaching. The major difference between the two was the Christians' reliance on Scripture as the norm for wisdom.[40]

Hebrews 5:11-14

The Christian Platonists discussed above provide examples for determining "what happens when a Platonist becomes a Christian" and models for comparing Hebrews with these Christian Platonists. Such comparison should provide insights for assessing whether Hebrews is in any sense the work of a Christian Platonist.

---

[36] *Strom.* 1. 30. 1; 2. 60. 10-11; Lilla, *Clement*, 171.

[37] Lilla, *Clement*, 145; Jaeger, *Early Christianity*, 53.

[38] *Strom.* 5. 39-40; 6. 68; 2. 6; 5. 78; Chadwick, "Philo," 179. For the subject of "likeness to God" as the goal among Middle Platonists, see John Dillon, *The Middle Platonists*, 9.

[39] Jaeger, *Early Christianity*, 36-92. Cf. Jaeger, "Paideia Christi," in Johann, *Erziehung*, 499.

[40] Jaeger, "Paideia Christi," 499.

The relationship between Hebrews and the educational ideals of Hellenistic philosophy can be seen when we observe the function of the *paideia* language in the epistle. Heb 5:11-14 is the beginning section of a lengthy parenesis which extends through 6:12. The subject of the parenesis, as νωθροί in 5:11 and 6:12 indicate, is the presumed, or possible, "sluggishness" of the readers.[41]

This reference to the spiritual malaise of the readers links this parenesis to the other pareneses in this "word of exhortation" which also describe the spiritual condition of the readers. From these pareneses, which normally serve as transitions to new themes, we are able to learn more about the spiritual lethargy of readers who are in danger of "drifting away" (2:1) and "throwing away" (10:35) their confidence (παρρησία). The frequent exhortations, in a style characteristic of ancient homilies, employ the exegetical themes in the service of practical needs.[42] The author attempts to encourage his readers to "hold on" to their confidence and to "run the race."

Although the parenesis in 5:11-6:12 has similarities to the other pareneses in the book, it is indisputable that it holds a unique place in its structure.[43] Unlike other pareneses, this one does not serve as the transition to a new theme. It stands as the interruption of the theme of the high priesthood of Christ, which extends from 4:14 to 10:18.[44] Apparently this major theme was intended to inculcate παρρησία in the readers, as the presence of the term in the parallel exhortations in 4:16 and 10:19 indicates. Thus the author, having begun to develop the theme which was to provide "confidence" in the readers, interrupts his thought at 5:11 and does not resume it until 7:1. Apparently, therefore, the purpose of 5:11-6:12 was to provide the basis for a complicated theme intended to develop the confidence of the readers. The development of this "main point" (8:1) requires the preparation which is given in 5:11-6:12.[45]

It is likely that features in the immediate context, 5:1-10, prompted the interruption of this major theme. The author has given a christological interpretation of Pss 2:7 and 110:4, interpreting them as references to the

---

[41] The use of this language for parenetic purposes corresponds with the fact that Hebrews is a "word of exhortation" (13:22) or sermon. In the apologists, whose work was primarily intended to defend the faith, philosophical language was used to demonstrate that Christianity was the true philosophy. For the genre of Hebrews, see H. Thyen, *Der Stil der jüdisch-hellenistischen Homilie.* For the function of philosophy among the apologists, see H. B. Timothy, *The Early Christian Apologists and Greek Philosophy.*

[42] Käsemann, *Gottesvolk,* 156.

[43] *Ibid.,* 119. Cf. P. Andreissen, "La communauté des 'Hébreux,'" 1056.

[44] E. Käsemann, *Gottesvolk,* 119.

[45] *Ibid.,* 119.

"perfecting" and "installation" of Christ to a new status. Such references prompted the author, in Kuss' words, to "catch his breath."[46] Περὶ οὖ in 5:11, therefore, is a reference to the words about the status of Christ as the one "perfected" and "designated" (προσαγορευθείς) with the status of exalted high priest.

Accusation

The section of the parenesis in 5:11-14 is divided into two parts. Verses 11-12 are primarily an indictment of the readers, while vv 13-14 give the author's pedagogical theory. The indictment is given in the expression, ἐπεὶ νωθροὶ γεγόνατε ταῖς ἀκοαῖς, and the parallel expressions, χρείαν ἔχετε τοῦ διδάσκειν ὑμᾶς τινὰ τὰ στοιχεῖα τῆς ἀρχῆς τῶν λογίων τοῦ θεοῦ and χρείαν ἔχοντες γάλακτος in 12. The indictment stands alone among the pareneses of Hebrews.[47] Other pareneses attempt to warn the readers from drifting away (cf. 2:1). This parenesis proceeds with a direct accusation (5:11-12), followed by warnings (6:4-6) and words of encouragement (6:7-20).

The unique feature of this parenesis is also to be seen in the content of the indictment. The accusation is not directed toward lethargy in general, but against mental and intellectual lethargy. Indeed, 5:11-12 is filled with expressions which were commonplace in philosophical discussion.[48] Νωθροί . . . ταῖς ἀκοαῖς was a common expression for mental obtuseness.[49] The expression is in direct contrast to γεγυμνασμένα in 5:14, indicating intellectual inertia.[50] The problem of the readers, therefore, is not inertia in general. Intellectual inertia has accompanied the general weariness of spirit.

---

[46] O. Kuss, *Der Brief an die Hebräer*, 76.

[47] H. Windisch (*Hebräerbrief*, 47) suggests that 12:4 ("You have not yet resisted to the point of shedding your blood") is also an indictment. The text, however, is to be read as an account of the relationship between the church and public authorities. While some have endured imprisonment and the plundering of their property, no one has yet died a martyr's death. P. Andriessen denies that 5:11-12 is an indictment, inasmuch as the parallel passage in 6:12 implies that the readers are not already νωθροί. Ἐπεί in 5:11 would thus have the meaning, "otherwise." Andriessen, "Communauté," 1057. Cf. also P. Andriessen and A. Lenglet, "Quelques passages difficiles," 212-214. While Andriessen's view has the obvious advantage of harmonizing 5:11 with the rest of Hebrews, it ignores the parallel expressions in 5:12, χρείαν ἔχετε . . . χρείαν ἔχοντες, which indicate the author's dissatisfaction with his readers.

[48] On πολύς (ἐστι) ὁ λόγος for "there is much to say," cf. Dion. Hal. *ad Amm.* 1. 3; Philo, *Quis Rer. Div.* 133, 221.

[49] Νωθρός, a common Greek term for "sluggish," occurs only here and at 6:12 in the NT. It occurs also in the LXX of Prov 22:29 (cf. Sir 4:29; 11:12) with the meaning of "backward" or "slack." Moffatt, *Hebrews*, 69. With ἀκοή it denotes dullness. Cf. Heliodorus 5. 10; Plutarch, *De Def. Or.* 20; Philo, *Quis Rer. Div.* 12; Plato, *Theat.* 144b. Cf. H. Preisker, Νωθρός, *TDNT* 4. 126.

[50] C. Spicq, *L'Épître aux Hébreux*, 2. 142.

While literary parallels to the form of this indictment are not obvious, the assumption behind it is one which the author shares with his contemporaries. Progress consists in intellectual growth. Philo shares the disdain for ignorance, for those whose minds forever wander over numberless subjects (*Quis Rer. Div.* 12), and for those who remain in ignorance and inexperience. The author of Hebrews shares this conviction. Thus the accusation of 5:11 emphasizes the maturity of the readers with respect to their growth in knowledge.[51] The readers are condemned specifically for their intellectual lethargy.

Although this condemnation employs imagery that is known elsewhere in the NT, there is an emphasis here which is unique to Hebrews. The imagery of milk and meat and the accusation form are similar to 1 Cor 3:1-3 (cf. 1 Pet 2:2). The distinctive feature of Hebrews is that the imagery suggests levels of instruction. Γάλα here refers specifically to a beginning stage of instruction. Its meaning in v 12b is to be seen in the parallel to 12a. Χρείαν ἔχοντες γάλακτοςis parallel to χρείαν ἔχετε τοῦ διδάσκειν ὑμᾶς τινὰ τὰ στοιχεῖα τῆς ἀρχῆς τῶν λογίων τοῦ θεοῦ. In 6:1, the author uses the parallel expressions, ὁ τῆς ἀρχῆς τοῦ χριστοῦ λόγος and θεμέλιος. In each instance, the author envisions a lower level of instruction which is taught and from which one passes to a higher level of instruction. The lower level of instruction is described as "milk," "ABC's" (στοιχείον), and as a "foundation" (θεμέλιος). All of these terms were used for the beginning of philosophical study.[52] There is implicit in the rebuke an insistence on intellectual development. The mental obtuseness referred to here is a component of the general lethargy of the readers.

The use of these categories suggests an acquaintance with the language of Greek *paideia*. Nevertheless, the author has substituted for the ἐγκύκλιος παιδεία an alternative version. There is no explicit evidence in Hebrews that the author employed Greek education as the first stage of Christian training. The "foundation" consists in the catechetical material of 6:2. However, as A. Seeberg has argued, the list in 6:2 is not inclusive.[53] The "word" mentioned in 5:12, 6:1 cannot be separated from the frequent references to God's word throughout the epistle. It is a "word" which God has "spoken" in Jesus

---

[51] E. Käsemann (*Gottesvolk*, 126) has argued that 5:11-14 belongs to the usual form which introduces esoteric teaching. However, his parallels lack the strong quality of accusation which Hebrews shares with 1 Cor 3:1-3. It is also to be noticed that Hebrews lacks the esoteric quality of Gnostic texts.

[52] On γάλα, cf. Philo, *de Ag.* 9; *de Congress.* 15-18; Epictetus, *Diss.* 2. 16. 39; 3. 24. 9. On στοιχεῖα, cf. Philo, *de Congress.* 149-150; cf. Seneca, *Ep.* 88:20; on θεμέλιος, cf. Epictetus, *Diss.* 2. 15. 18.

[53] A. Seeberg, *Der Katechismus der Urchristenheit*, 248-249.

Christ (1:2) and which now addresses the community, confronting it with a decision (cf. 2:1-3; 4:2; 12:25) to accept salvation. It includes words spoken "by the Lord" (2:3) and communicated in the past through teachers (13:7). The "beginning word" includes, therefore, the Christian proclamation which the community first heard. Probably it includes also the original confession of faith in Jesus as God's exalted high priest.[54] Such "milk" was the foundation which replaced the ἐγκύκλιος παιδεία.

The second stage of instruction, in contrast to the "beginning word," is the λόγος δυσερμήνευτος, which is equivalent to the "solid food." There is no insistence on the esoteric character of the word, for it is a word for the whole community (ἡμῖν). Nevertheless, it is a word beyond the grasp of the obtuse. The term δυσερμήνευτος was used in antiquity for a sublime message.[55] Philo uses it in *de Som*. 1. 188 for the contrast between the knowledge of the material world and that knowledge "which no words can tell or express." Origen uses the term λόγος δυσερμήνευτος, particularly against Celsus' criticism of Christian belief, to describe the sublimity of the Christian message.[56]

In Hebrews, the λόγος δυσερμήνευτος is apparently the cultic section of 7:1-10:18. It consists in the expansion of the themes of purification and the high priesthood, which are mentioned in the original confession.[57] These themes are developed through an exposition of the OT which is not yet known to the readers. The cultic traditions of Leviticus 16 and elsewhere are interpreted as a "parable" of this age (9:9) and of the inadequacy of the old cultus (9:9-10). Indeed, the author develops this theme of the "parabolic" character of OT institutions only "in part" (9:5). His purpose is to show that the institutions of the OT are only inferior copies of the vastly superior work

---

[54] Cf. G. Bornkamm, "Das Bekenntnis im Hebräerbrief," *Studien zu Antike und Christentum*, 201. The confession in Heb 1:3 has such a rhetorical and theological significance that it is the "confession" which other sections, especially 7:1-10:18, expand.

[55] See Artemidorus, *Onerocrit*. 4. 66; τοῦτον οὖν τὸν τρόπον καὶ οἱ ὄνειροι μεμιγμένων τῶν ἐν αὐτοῖς σημαινομένων εἰκότως εἰσι ποικίλοι καὶ τοῖς πολλοῖς δυσερμήνευτοι. The expression in Hebrews is similar to Dionysius Halicarnassus, *De Comp*. 8. 46: περὶ ὧν καὶ πολύς ὁ λόγος καὶ βαθεῖα ἡ θεωρία. Philo (*de Post. Cain*. 18) has an interesting parallel, when he describes the wise man who journeys toward ἐπιστήμη and σοφία. One makes a preliminary stay in contact with divine words, after which he recognizes that he is engaged in a chase of a quarry that is "hard to capture" (ἐξαναχωροῦντος).

[56] See P. Andriessen, "La communauté," 1058. Cf. Origen's Commentary on John 1:21 (87): "The theory of the soul is vast and difficult" (ὁ περὶ ψυχῆς λόγος πολὺς καὶ δυσερμήνευτος ὤν). The same explanation is given of the doctrine of the resurrection (πολὺν ὄντα καὶ δυσερμήνευτον) and of the Sabbath rest of God (πολύς ἂν εἴη . . . δυσερμήνευτος λόγος).

[57] On the confession, cf. 3:1; 4:14; 10:23. It appears that the original confession, part of which is given in 1:3, referred to the high priesthood of Christ. Thus the confession is the "foundation," while the λόγος δυσερμήνευτος is an expansion of the confession.

of Christ (9:6-14) in the heavenly sanctuary. The λόγος δυσερμήνευτος thus concerns this work of Christ. It is developed by the author's unique method of exegesis, according to which the OT is read with dualistic assumptions in order to demonstrate the metaphysical superiority of the work of Christ.[58]

This higher knowledge has analogies to Philo and the Middle Platonists, both of whom distinguished the knowledge of the lower studies and the knowledge of the divine world. According to *de Som.* 1. 59, Abraham is an example of one who progressed from the knowledge of the senses to the highest knowledge. According to *de Eb.* 33, our two parents are the lower learning (μέση . . . παιδεία) and the ὀρθὸς λόγος which leads one to the vision of God. In *Quod Om. Lib.* 160, the stronger meat is philosophy, which leads us to the goal. This goal, according to *de Praem. Poen.* 29, is to "gaze and soar beyond the material things" and to contemplate the immaterial world. The soul, according to Philo, requires 'celestial nourishment, manna (*Quod. Det. Pot.* 85; *de Sac.A.C.* 85). Progress, for both Philo and Hebrews, consists in advancement to a knowledge of heavenly realities.

The parenesis which follows the λόγος δυσερμήνευτος indicates the significance of this "solid food" for the readers. This parenesis is parallel to the earlier one in 4:14-16, which served as the transition to the λόγος δυσερμήνευτος. The earlier one encouraged the readers, προσερχώμεθα οὖν μετὰ παρρησίας τῷ θρόνῳ τῆς χάριτος, while the latter addresses a community, ἔχοντες οὖν, ἀδελφοί, παρρησίαν εἰς τὴν εἴσοδον τῶν ἁγίων ἐν τῷ αἵματι Ἰησοῦ . . .προσερχώμεθα. . . . The community which has heard the λόγος δυσερμήνευτος now has the παρρησία for approaching God. This παρρησία is the basis for the threefold hortatory subjunctive, προσερχώμεθα . . . κατέχωμεν . . . κατανοῶμεν. . . .

Παρρησία, an important word for Hebrews, has "a particularly objective character."[59] It is the right of access to God based on the high priestly work of Christ.[60] It presupposes the work of Christ in purifying the conscience and in giving the Christian the confidence to stand in God's presence. It is closely identified with perfection in Hebrews, for both perfection and confidence (παρρησία) presuppose the heavenly work of Christ in granting access to God's sanctuary (cf. 9:9; 10:1, 14). This παρρησία is an objective reality which must now be preserved (3:6), even if the community is tempted to throw it away (10:35). Παρρησία is, therefore, a certainty which has been granted by the heavenly work of Christ and a privilege for those who now have access to God.

---

[58] See Chapter VI of this study.
[59] H. Schlier, Παρρησία, *TDNT* 6. 884.
[60] E. Grässer, *Glaube*, 36-37.

Philo shares with the author of Hebrews the close identification between παρρησία and a pure conscience. According to *Quis Rer. Div.* 6, only the one who is pure from sin and the judgments of his conscience has the παρρησία to stand before God. According to the same tractate (21), Moses was among the "wise" who could stand before God with παρρησία. Παρρησία is the certainty of those who become disfranchised from the world, but rely solely on God to be their franchise (ἐπιτιμία). Παρρησία is thus the right of approaching God with a clean conscience and free speech.[61]

The emphasis on certainty, which is implied in the word παρρησία, is a dominant motif in the remainder of the parenesis, as the threefold "let us" clauses indicate. The παρρησία is the presupposition for the exhortation, προσερχώμεθα μετὰ ἀληθινῆς καρδίας ἐν πληροφορίᾳ πίστεως. To "draw near" is now a possibility because the high priest has opened up the access to God (10:19-20). The "true heart" is the equivalent of the heart that has been "sprinkled from an evil conscience" (cf. 9:11-14), a theme that has been developed in 9:1-10:18. Those who approach God in this way have the privilege of coming ἐν πληροφορίᾳ πίστεως. Πληροφορία, which is used also in 6:11, is the word for "certainty."[62] Apparently, the full assurance of faith in 10:22 is parallel to the "full assurance of hope" in 6:11. Both expressions describe the certainty and stability of the believer, a certainty that is created by the work of Christ and enables the reader to endure "until the end" (6:11).

The second appeal, κατέχωμεν τὴν ὁμολογίαν τῆς ἐλπίδος ἀκλινῆ, is also based on the high priestly work of Christ. At the beginning of the readers' Christian experience, they had accepted the confession (cf. 3:1; 4:14). The author has expressed his concern already over whether the readers will "hold on" (κατέχω) to their "confidence" (3:6, παρρησία) or "substance" (ὑπόστασις), rather than drift away (2:1). To "hold on" to the "confession" in 10:23 is equivalent to holding on to the confidence or substance in 3:6, 14. Κατέχω, "hold fast," is a significant image for remaining stable.[63] It is reinforced here by ἀκλινῆ, a NT *hapax*, which means "unchangeable." The λόγος δυσερμήνευτος enables the readers to hold fast without changing. Those who are unchangeable will not "drift away" (2:1).

The author's use of ἀκλινῆ is similar to Philo's use of the same word.[64] Philo used the word frequently for the immutability which belongs to God

---

[61] See Völker, *Fortschritt*, 254-255. In *Quis Rer. Div.* 5-21, Philo uses as examples of παρρησία the occasions where Moses intercedes for the people (Exod 32:32; Num 11:13, 22).

[62] BAG, 676.

[63] The word has the meaning, "hold fast." Cf. Luke 8:15; 1 Cor 11:2; Bauer, 424.

[64] R. Williamson, *Philo*, 33-35, shows that ἀκλινής is an important Philonic word which was used for God and for friends of God. He denies that Hebrews is closely analogous.

alone. Thus Philo, in *Leg. All.* 2. 83 and *de Post. Cain.* 23, compares the stable (ἀκλινής) character of God with the creation, which is forever unstable (cf. *de Conf. Ling.* 96; *de Mut Nom.* 176; *de Som.* 2. 219-220). Consequently, only one who stands by God's side can be ἀκλινής (*de Gig.* 49). Philo says in *de Praem. Poen.* 30 that only he who can soar above the material things and take God as his sole support with an unswerving faith will be blessed. According to *Quod Deus Immut.* 22-23, those who study philosophy acquire this unswerving quality.

The third appeal, κατανοῶμεν ἀλλήλους . . ., is a summons for the continued mutual exhortation that will allow the church to endure. Κατανοῶμεν is supplemented by the participial phrases, μὴ ἐγκαταλείποντες τὴν ἐπισυναγωγὴν ἑαυτῶν and ἀλλὰ παρακαλοῦντες. The possibility of apostasy has led the author already to call for this mutual exhortation. That the community needs endurance is indicated in 10:36 and 10:39. The exhortation in 10:24-25 is a call to endurance, based on the παρρησία granted by the work of Christ.

The exhortation of 10:19-25 now allows us to see the important role which the λόγος δυσερμήνευτος has in Hebrews. The exhortation, based on the reminder of what Christians have (ἔχοντες), is a call to weary Christians to maintain steadfastness, constancy, and the stability enabling them to endure (cf. 10:36). Indeed, the dominant point is summarized in the final words, where ὑποστολή is contrasted to πίστις. Ὑποστολή, "shrinking back," is not the proper stance of the Christian. Πίστις, involving endurance (10:36) and constancy, has become the possibility of the Christian through Jesus Christ. The λόγος δυσερμήνευτος, with its complicated exegesis and dualistic framework, provides the Christian with a basis for standing firm by demonstrating the metaphysical dignity of the high priest.

This function of the words that are "hard to explain" is similar to the role which philosophy plays for Philo in providing stability. A major theme in Philo is the distinction between the world of change and the stable world of God. Thus the goal for the sage is to share in God's stability by giving up his ties to the unstable creation. For Hebrews, stability is acquired by being granted access to God through Christ.

The goal of sharing God's stability is particularly associated in Philo with the higher studies (see above, p. 22). Such studies are associated with the acquiring of stability, perfection, and purified consciences, and the capacity to finish the "strenuous toil in the arena" (*de Som.* 1. 166-167; *de Cher.* 80-81). For both Philo and Hebrews, the higher training produces steadfastness. Both writers, recognizing that faith involves maintaining one's distance from the values and opinions of the culture, saw the need for a resource for maintaining one's steadfastness. For Philo, it is philosophy; for Hebrews, it is the λόγος δυσερμήνευτος.

A Theory of Education

In vv 13-14 the author turns from the direct accusation of his readers to a general observation indicating his theory of education. The reference to milk in verse 12 now leads the author to distinguish between the νήπιος, who is nourished by milk, and the τέλειος, who is nourished by solid food. This terminology is not unique to Hebrews. Immature Christians who are still nourished by milk are described as νήπιοι in 1 Cor 3:1 (cf. 1 Cor 13:11-12). The "perfect man," the goal of the Christian development, is contrasted to the prior status of νήπιοι in Eph 4:13-14. What is apparently unique to Hebrews in the NT is the use of these categories to apply to distinctive levels of Christian education.

Νήπιος, "child," was commonly used with reference to child-like naïveté, as when Lucian satirizes the Christian's self-designation as παῖδες by calling them νήπιοι.[65] That Hebrews uses the term especially for intellectual naïveté is indicated by the phrase, ἄπειρος λόγου δικαιοσύνης. Ἄπειρος commonly used by Philo to mean "inexperienced." In *Quod Det. Pot.* 41 Philo argues that the person who is inexperienced in difficult arguments would fall without firm footing. He describes progress as consisting in development from inexperience (ἄπειρος) to perfection in *de Ag.* 158. Since for both Philo and Hebrews education is the goal of the believer, ignorance and inexperience must be overcome if one is to endure.

The λόγος δικαιοσύνης is the equivalent of the λόγος δυσερμήνευτος of 5:11 and the "solid food" of 5:12, 14. It consists in the exposition of 7:1-10:18. To be ἄπειρος λόγου δικαιοσύνης is to lack the capacity for endurance, for endurance involves knowing the truth which provides steadfastness.

The goal of the believer, according to 5:14, is to progress from νήπιος to τέλειος.[66] This reference to perfection in Hebrews must be placed within the context of the author's frequent references to perfection. For Hebrews, Christ is the exemplar of perfection in the completion of the salvation event (cf. 2:10; 5:9; 12:2). This perfection involved both his sufferings and the exaltation (2:10; 5:9; 7:28). As the ἀρχηγός he provides perfection also for those who follow him. This perfection involves, for both Hebrews and Philo, the purified conscience and access to God (cf. Heb 9:9; 10:1, 14).[67] Perfec-

---

[65] *Pereg. Mort.* 11. Cf. the terminology in Epictetus, *Diss.* 3. 24. 53; Philo, *de Mig. Ab.* 29. See G. Braumann, "Kind," *Theologisches Begriffslexikon zum Neuen Testament* 2. 776.

[66] H.P. Owen, "The 'Stages of Ascent,'" 250, argues that Hebrews posits three levels of development: νήπιος, τέλειος, and reception of solid food. Against this view, one must observe the parallels νήπιος-γάλα and τέλειος-στερεά τροφή, which indicate only two levels of development.

[67] See Dey, *Intermediary World*, 203.

tion, therefore, is closely related to παρρησία in 10:19, as both terms are used for the access to God with a purified conscience.

For the author of Hebrews, there is apparently a dialectical understanding of perfection, for he can describe it as both a present (10:14) and a potential reality. In 5:14; 6:1, the author assumes that perfection is only potential. Inasmuch as τελείων δέ ἐστιν ἡ στερεὰ τροφή, the challenge of 6:1, ἐπὶ τὴν τελειότητα φερώμεθα, is a summons for the community to progress from the milk to solid food in the present. Perfection is the quality of those who grasp the λόγος δυσερμήνευτος and stand on solid ground.

The nature of Christian progress is stated in the phrase τῶν διὰ τὴν ἕξιν τὰ αἰσθητήρια γεγυμνασμένα ἐχόντων πρὸς διάκρισιν καλοῦ τε καὶ κακοῦ, which stands in apposition to τελείων. The imagery, drawn from athletics, appears frequently among the philosophers, for whom it was a common assumption that one "practised" or trained oneself in lower learning before progressing to perfection. The terms ἕξις, αἰσθητήριον, and γυμνάζω are all terms which are used for physical conditioning. Ἕξις, a *hapax legomenon* in the NT, refers to the "state of the body" or "conditioning" of the soul which comes through practice. The word appears in both Philo and Albinus to contrast the one who has achieved a "fixed state" with the one who is still learning. Philo uses the term in his contrast of the child and the wise man. Only the latter has reached the fixed state (ἕξις, *Leg. All.* 3. 210). Albinus uses ἕξις in describing the characteristic of one who has so developed his skills as no longer to be potentially a grammarian or flute player. The one who has acquired some of these characteristics (ἕξεων) will be able to act on the basis of that characteristic (ἕξεων) which he has acquired (*Didask.* 26).[68] Αἰσθητήριον, "sense perception," was used in the derivative sense for intellectual understanding and spiritual discernment.[69] Both words appear frequently in connection with γυμνάζω in discussions of intellectual progress.[70]

Philo offers a particularly significant parallel to the pedagogical theory of Heb 5:14, for training holds an important place in Philo's view, as the

[68] See the discussion in Mark Kiley, "A Note on Hebrews 5:14," *CBQ* 42 (1980) 501-502. See also John Dillon, *The Middle Platonists*, 298. On ἕξις, see also LSJ, 595. Cf. Plato, *Phil.* 11d, ἕξις ψυχῆς; Philo, *Leg. All.* 3. 210, οὐκ ἀπολογικῆς ἕξεως; Aristotle, *Ethnic.* 2. 4. p. 1106a 14-15, ἡ τοῦ ἀνθρώπου ἀρετὴ εἴη ἂν ἕξις ἀφ' ἧς ἀγαθὸς ἄνθρωπος γίνεται. . . .

[69] G. Delling, Αἰσθητήριον, *TDNT* 1. 187.

[70] Γυμνάζω, "exercise naked" (Josephus, *Ant.* 6. 185; 2 Macc 10:15), was often used in the figurative sense. Cf. Epictetus, *Diss.* 1. 26. 3, πρῶτον οὖν ἐπὶ τῆς θεωρίας γυμνάζουσιν ἡμᾶς οἱ φιλόσοφοι; Philo, *de Virt.* 18, γυμνάσαι ψυχήν.

For γυμνάζη with either ἕξις or αἰσθητήριον, see Aristotle, *Rep.* 7 (6). 4. 7, τὰς πρὸς τὰ πολεμικὰ πράξεις μάλισθ' οὗτοι γεγυμνασμένοι τὰς ἕξεις; Galen, *de Diagnosc. puls.* 3. 2. p. 144. 72, ὃς μὲν γὰρ ἂν εὐαισθητότατον φύσιν τε καὶ τὸ αἰσθητήριον ἔχῃ γεγυμνασμένον ἱκανῶς . . .

frequency of γυμνάζω/γυμνασία and ἄσκησις in his works indicates. We have seen above (p. 24) that Philo also taught that perfection involves "gymnastics" in the intelligible things. According to *de Ag.* 159, those who reach the goal of perfection arrive through constant practice. Philo's consistent references to Jacob as the trained athlete (*de Sob.* 65) indicate the role of athletic training for him.

Philo does not limit the imagery of athletic training to descriptions of the educational process. The imagery of athletics is also used for the discipline and conditioning which must characterize the sage who pursues his faith until the end. According to *de Cher.* 80-81, we should receive blows like an athlete, not like a slave. The man of faith is involved in the "contest of life" (*de Congress.* 164). Random strikes of misfortune provide training for the believer (*de Jos.* 26). Jacob's exercise included suffering (223). According to *de Mut. Nom.* 81-83, the sage is one who is able to finish the contest and carry off the prize to victory, having been trained in the gymnastics of the soul. Philo's heroes are all athletes.[71] Their training involves not only the practice in instruction, but the practice of adversity as well.

The athletic image of Hebrews 5:14 does not stand alone in the epistle, for other references point to a training through adversity. According to 10:32, the readers have already endured "the contest" (ἄθλησις) with much suffering. In 12:1, the readers are invited to "run the race." According to 12:11, the readers' sufferings are actually the training which provides *paideia*.[72] The readers, needing endurance in the midst of suffering, are therefore provided with an image from athletics in order to enable them to remain steadfast. Their sufferings involve the discipline which will allow them to win the prize in the contest.

For both Philo and Hebrews, training involves both suffering and instruction. The two accompany each other. The final goal for both is perfection.

The Agricultural Image

Near the conclusion of the parenesis (6:7-8), the image is changed from the education of a child to the care given to a plant. This image follows the stern warning of 6:4-6, and provides a fitting summary of the parenesis. In the typical parenetic style of the author, exhortation and warning are brought together.[73] The earlier part of this parenesis in 5:11-14 leads to the

---

[71] Cf. *Quod Om. Prob. Lib.* 110-111; *Leg. All.* 1. 98; 3. 14. 70, 72, 201; *de Mig. Ab.* 27; *de Ab.* 256; *de Vit. Mos.* 1. 106. Jacob, Moses, and Abraham are all compared to athletes.

[72] The imagery of athletic training for suffering is found elsewhere in the literature of Hellenistic Judaism. Cf. 4 Macc 17:11-16.

[73] Cf. 2:1-4; 3:16-4:1; 12:25-29.

exhortation, ἐπὶ τὴν τελειότητα φερώμεθα. The warning reminds the readers of the consequences of failure to submit to the necessary training. Thus the parenetic material of 5:11-6:6 has described the two possibilities that remain open to the community.

These two possibilities are suggested in the agricultural image, which employs language that is reminiscent of the early chapters of Genesis.[74] The individual is compared to land which produces either good or bad vegetation. The result can be either that the land μεταλαμβάνει εὐλογίας or τὸ τέλος εἰς καῦσιν.[75] The land which is blessed by God is not only the recipient of nature's gifts; it is also "cultivated" (γεωργεῖται) by individuals.

This agricultural image was commonly used in Philo for the educational task. Indeed, the image of "cultivating" is parallel to the imagery of athletic training, for in some Philonic texts the emphasis is on "cultivating" one's knowledge rather than "training" it. This emphasis, in fact, is the major point of the Philonic tractate, *de Agricultura*. This tractate develops the theme that Noah was a γεωργὸς γῆς (Gen 9:20). For Philo, the work of a γεωργός is the nourishment of the soul (9), leading it from the milk appropriate to babes to the strong food appropriate for mature men. The work of the γεωργός is thus to develop the education which produces character and to eliminate the destructive vices (10-11). The result of good husbandry will be the production of "beneficial fruits, namely fair and praiseworthy conduct."

This husbandry involves both the cultivation of the lower and the higher learning. Without soul-husbandry, the vices of folly, licentiousness and cowardice would take control (cf. 17-18).

The agricultural image for education, which was an important feature of Philo's pedagogy, was probably well known in Hellenistic times, for it is attested also in (Pseudo-)Plutarch.[76] Hebrews employs the image in order to emphasize the significance of "cultivating" the knowledge of God's revelation. Γεωργεῖται in 6:7 is the parallel of γεγυμνασμένα in 5:14 as a word for the means of Christian progress.

Many of the images of Heb 5:11-6:8 are to be found elsewhere in the NT. Indeed, the Pauline literature contains the imagery of milk-solid food (1 Cor 3:1-3), the imagery of the athletic contest (1 Cor 9:24-27), and the imagery of agriculture (1 Cor 3:6-9). What is distinctive to Hebrews among NT documents is the use of these images to describe an intellectual progress in the Christian faith as a constituent part of the author's understanding of

---

[74] Gen 1:11; 3:17-18.
[75] C. Spicq, *Hébreux*, 2. 155.
[76] *de lib. ed.* 2EF.

perfection. The reception of the "full knowledge of the truth" (10:26) was important for remaining steadfast.

This examination permits an evaluation of whether the author is deeply indebted to Greek *paideia* or whether he may be described as a Christian Platonist. The question permits no easy answer, especially when one considers that Platonism went in diverse directions in the Hellenistic Age. There was, for example, the esoteric direction of Clement of Alexandria and of the Gnostics who employed Platonic terminology in their systems.[77] It is significant that Heb 5:11-14 betrays none of the esoteric tendencies of such Christian Platonists as Clement and Origen.[78]

We may also notice that Hebrews indicates no interest in the general liberal arts education and in the study of philosophy as states of education. In this respect, one can find Philo's heir not in Hebrews, but in Clement, Origen, and the Cappadocians. All of these writers were indebted to Greek education, and found a place for it in the development of their theology, while Scripture remained for them the norm of truth.

No early Christian writer before Clement showed the kind of indebtedness to Greek *paideia* that Philo had shown. Thus Hebrews does not exhibit the thorough indebtedness to Greek educational models that later became common among Christian writers. Nevertheless, there is a connection between Hebrews and Greek *paideia* that is to be seen in the structure of the thought of the author of Hebrews. While the author does not speak of the ἐγκύκλιος παιδεία and φιλοσοφία as stages of growth, he shares the conviction of his contemporaries that one advances from lower to higher studies through training. His higher studies are concerned with "heavenly realities"—the heavenly high priesthood of Christ—which are deduced from his method of interpreting Scripture. This knowledge enables the community to stand before God with παρρησία.

Later Christian Platonists employed the allegorical method in order to demonstrate that Christianity was the true philosophy. It is significant that Clement of Alexandria found the truths for his Christian philosophy in the OT narratives concerning the high priest's work in the tabernacle.[79] Philo had previously used the allegorical method to demonstrate the deeper truth of the cultic narratives of the OT.[80] Hebrews' use of these narratives as a "parable" (9:9) may indicate that the author was aware of other non-literal

---

[77] J. Dillon, *Middle Platonists*, 384-402, describes the various Gnostic sects as a "Platonic underworld," as they frequently adapted Platonic terminology for their own purposes.

[78] H. P. Owen ("Stages," 250) rightly says that Hebrews avoids such common terms as θεωρία, ἐπιστήμη, γνῶσις, and σοφία. Ἐπίγνωσις is, however, used in 10:26.

[79] See above, p. 42. Clement's interpretation is greatly indebted to Philo, *de Vit. Mos.* 2.

[80] Cf. *de Som.* 2. 231-235.

treatments of these passages. For the author, as for Philo and the later Christian Platonists, Scripture is the source of knowledge. The knowledge of this material served the same function for the author which philosophy served for his contemporaries.

If one can judge from Heb 5:11-14 and 6:7-8, the author is not a "Christian Platonist" in the same way that Clement of Alexandria was. Nor does he have the same indebtedness to Greek *paideia* which is found in Philo. Nevertheless, his understanding of progress has much in common with Philo and the Christian Platonists. Platonism provided the structure of his thought, which was then filled with content from the biblical revelation.[81]

Origen's evaluation of Hebrews is significant at this point, as W. Bousset observed.[82] Origen claimed that the thought of Hebrews belongs to Paul, but that the style and presentation have the character of lecture notes which a student wrote down after a lecture. What Origen said about the authorship is not important, but it is significant that Origen, with his extensive Greek education, saw Hebrews as a σχόλια, or lecture.

---

[81] See W. Jaeger, *Early Christianity and Greek Paideia*, 98. Jaeger says that Greek philosophical education provided a complete analogy to Christian theology in the work of Gregory of Nyssa. The basic categories of Greek philosophy provided the framework to be filled with Christian content.

[82] Boussett, 313.

CHAPTER III

THE ESCHATOLOGY OF HEBREWS: A STUDY OF 12:18-29*

The eschatology of the Epistle to the Hebrews has been a central issue for debate in discussion of the intellectual world of the author. This debate appears to result from the fact that Hebrews contains both passages which assume the spatial dualism of Plato (i.e., 8:5) and statements which assume the apocalyptic, temporal dualism of the two ages (i.e., 1:2; 6:4). This apparent ambiguity has led to a variety of solutions to the question of the eschatology of Hebrews. James Moffatt regarded the problem as an example of the author's own inconsistency.[1] Most studies of the eschatology of Hebrews have resolved the problem by choosing either the Platonic (or Philonic)-sounding passages or the apocalyptic passages as the decisive ones for understanding the author's intellectual framework. The title of J. Cambier's monograph, *Eschatologie ou Hellénisme dans l'Épître aux Hébreux*,[2] reflects the common assumption that Hebrews must be regarded either as apocalyptic or Hellenistic. This choice between alternatives has led Cambier and others to treat Hebrews as either apocalyptic or Hellenistic and to ignore passages which did not fit the chosen alternative or to minimize their significance.[3]

It is impossible to deny the presence in Hebrews of an eschatological

---

*Adapted from *JBL* 94 (1975) 580-587.

[1]   James Moffatt, *The Epistle to the Hebrews*, liv

[2]   J. Cambier, *Eschatologie ou Hellénisme dans l'Épître aux Hébreux*.

[3]   R. Williamson, in *Philo and the Epistle to the Hebrews*, 142-150, argues consistently that the futurity of the eschatological gift distinguishes Hebrews from Philo. O. Hofius (*Katapausis*) interprets the eschatology of Hebrews totally within the framework of rabbinic and apocalyptic Judaism. Philo is only briefly considered in the *Nachtrag* of the second edition (pp. 248-259), where Hofius denies any substantial parallels between Hebrews and Philo. O. Michel (*Der Brief an die Hebräer*) concedes the presence of metaphysical language but consistently argues that it is only a means for giving clarity to the eschatological element (cf. 78-79). A similar position is taken by C. K. Barrett, "The Eschatology of the Epistle to the Hebrews," in W.D. Davies and D. Daube, *The Background of the New Testament and its Eschatology*. Barrett argues that "the eschatological is the determining element" (366). The opposite tendency is to be seen in J. Cambier (cited above, note 2) and J. Héring, "Eschatologie biblique et idéalisme platonicien," in Davies and Daube, *Background*, 450-453, both of whom suggest that a transcendent perspective takes precedence over the futurity of the eschatological gift.

hope.[4] This eschatological hope is not the Hellenized view of the immortality of the soul which appears in 4 Maccabees,[5] Philo,[6] and other Jewish documents that reflect the encounter between the Jewish tradition and Greek thought. It has been observed that Hebrews shares with other NT writings the tension between the "already" and the "not yet." According to Hebrews, the "last days" (1:2) and "coming age" (6:5) have already begun. The church now waits for the consummation, or final "day" (10:25; cf. 9:28; 10:36-39). The traditional apocalyptic distinction between the two ages is assumed in several texts (cf. 2:8; 3:13; 9:9,11; 10:1). In addition, there is a consistent future orientation that is to be seen in the frequent references to God's promise (4:1; 6:12,15,17; 7:6; 8:6; 9:15; 10:36; 11:9,13,17,39: 12:26) and to the Christian hope (3:6; 6:11, 18; 7:19; 10:23). There is, therefore, a "not yet" to Christian existence (cf. 2:8) and a waiting for the end which distinguish the eschatological hope in Hebrews from that of Philo and 4 Maccabees.

A difficulty in giving a thorough analysis of the eschatology of Hebrews is that the author does not give a detailed view of the endtime comparable to the descriptions which are found in the Synoptic Gospels, Paul, or the Jewish apocalypses. Furthermore, isolated references to a future hope in Hebrews neither establish the epistle as an apocalyptic document nor exclude the presence of Hellenistic influence. A study of both Jewish and Gnostic apocalypses demonstrates the variety of ways in which eschatological hopes were formulated. Some apocalypses reflect the influence of Hellenistic metaphysical thought, while others do not.[7] Thus the presence of an eschatological hope in Hebrews, which is not to be denied, does not indicate that Hebrews shares the assumptions about the end with any particular apocalypse. Previous research has often lacked precision in comparing the eschatology of Hebrews with other literature.

The most detailed description of the eschaton in Hebrews is provided in

---

[4] Cf. E. Käsemann, *Gottesvolk*, 11. The function of "promise" in Hebrews "bedeutet, dass die göttliche Offenbarung hier konstitutiv und grundsäztlich den Charakter der Verheissung trägt, also rein eschatologischer Art ist."

[5] Cf. the terms ἀθανασία (14:5; 16:13), ἀθάνατος (7:3; 14:6; 18:23), and ἀφθαρσία (9:22; 17:12) in 4 Maccabees. These terms suggest a relationship to Platonic and Pythagorean thought. See U. Breitenstein, *Beobachtungen*, 158-175.

[6] *de Plant.* 37; Williamson, *Philo*, 144.

[7] I have shown in my unpublished dissertation, *"That Which Abides": Some Metaphysical Assumptions in the Epistle to the Hebrews* (Vanderbilt University, 1974), that there was considerable variety in the way apocalypses described the end-time. There is evidence of Hellenistic influence on the Jewish apocalypse *2 Enoch* which is not apparent in *4 Ezra* or *2 Baruch*. Gnostic apocalypses discovered at Nag Hammadi combine traditional apocalyptic traditions wih Greek metaphysical categories. In the *Tractate Without Title* and the *Apocalypse of Adam*, the eschatological catastrophe is followed by the disappearance of the material world and the abiding of the heavenly *typos* (cf. *TWT* 173:33-175:2).

12:27-28, where the author contrasts the *metathesis* of the created order with the stable and abiding character of "that which cannot be shaken." This understanding of reality becomes the basis for the parenetic comment in 12:28 which calls on the church to "have grace" in view of the fact that it is the recipient of the "unshakable kingdom." These comments form the conclusion to a section in which the author has contrasted the earthly voice at Sinai with the heavenly voice at the eschatological Mount Zion, and are to be understood in the context of the carefully structured section, 12:18-29.

It is commonly recognized that Heb 12:27-28 is of great importance for understanding the eschatology of Hebrews, as the eschatological promise (cf. 12:26), which is often mentioned in Hebrews, is described in some detail. Käsemann describes the passage as an "ausserordentlich wichtige Stück"[8] in the framework of the epistle. Michel recognizes this pericope as a more detailed description of the eschatological drama than is given in earlier references in the epistle[9] and evidence that Hebrews views the end within the context of Israelite prophecy. O. Hofius refers to this pericope as evidence that the eschatology of Hebrews is characterized both by a living, imminent expectation of the end and by the same framework that is found in 4 Ezra.[10] Because this passage describes in some detail the hope which is referred to elsewhere in Hebrews, an exegesis of it is a useful way of examining the eschatology of Hebrews.

The pericope 12:18-29 is closely connected to the exhortation in 12:12-17, as the γάρ in 12:18 indicates. The community has been encouraged to make its path straight (12:12) and not to repeat the apostasy of Esau (12:15-17). The church, which is on its way to the heavenly κατάπαυσις (3:7-4:13) or πόλις (13:14), has become weary in its pilgrimage.[11] The exhortation in 12:12-17 which comes as encouragement and as threat, conforms to the author's usual manner of exhortation.[12] Christian existence is pilgrimage to the heavenly κληρονομία (9:15; 11:8; cf. 6:17; 11:7; 1:14; 6:12). Esau, who threw away his inheritance for the sake of food, is the prototype of all who throw away the heavenly reality for the sake of the earthly one.[13] Against this

---

8 Käsemann, *Gottesvolk*, 18.

9 Michel, *Hebräer*, 121.

10 Hofius, *Katapausis*, 141-142, 148-150, 258.

11 Cf. 3:12; 4:1; 5:11; 10:25, 36. The readers belong to the second generation (2:1-4) and have lost the enthusiasm which they had formerly experienced (10:32). Cf. Chapter II of this study for the analysis of the readers' situation.

12 Cf. 10:29-30, where promise and threat are combined in one parenesis. Cf. also 6:4-20; 3:7-4:13. In each case the author combines severe warning with the encouragement to accept the heavenly blessing.

13 Esau is here, as in much of Jewish literature, the example of the worldly man who, for the sake of the momentary reality, gave his birthright away, thus indicating that he was "pro-

background, γάρ provides the transition to 12:18-29, and suggests that the following material is intended to provide grounding for the exhortation and warning in 12:12-17. The church is not to be "worldly" like Esau, who threw away the heavenly gift for the earthly gain.

It has long been suggested that the author is working with a tradition which he has taken over and adapted.[14] The basic structure, with the comparison of the earthly Sinai and the heavenly Zion, is contained in Gal 4:25-26 and *Jub.* 4:26. The comparison of Sinai and Zion is present also in *Midrash Tanchuma B*,[15] which claims that all of the signs which God did in the wilderness he will do in the messianic age. Two of these signs are the hearing of the voice (Exod 20:18) and the shaking of the earth, features which are important in Heb 12:18-29. It is also significant that Hag 2:6, cited in Heb 12:26, was frequently used in apocalyptic texts to describe the coming eschatological earthquake.[16] These parallels suggest that the author has taken over an eschatological tradition which compares the events relating to Sinai with the events of the eschatological Zion. The author has supplied his own interpretation to his tradition. To understand this pericope is, therefore, to understand the author's redaction of his tradition.

Although it is not possible to reconstruct every detail of the author's tradition with certainty, some aspects of the tradition and redaction can be established with confidence. The basic structure—the comparison of Sinai and Zion—comes from the tradition (12:18, 22, 26). In addition, the carefully balanced features which describe Sinai (12:18-21) and Zion (12:22-23) probably come from the author's tradition, as the presence of motifs which are of interest to the author nowhere else seems to suggest.[17] The tradition, therefore, seems to have contained a comparison between the events of Sinai and the events of Zion, in which the two events were described by the careful rhetorical balancing of terms. The author's redaction of his tradition is especially evident in those places where recurring themes appear as evaluative and interpretive comments in the pericope. By the careful observation of these redactional comments, one can understand how the author uses his tradition.

---

fane." Esau is frequently described as the representative of this aeon, as a man who chose this world as his part, because he wanted to enjoy his life here and now (*Gen. R.* 63, 65; *Targ. Jer. 1* Gen 25:32, 34). Cited in R. Völkl, *Christ und die Welt*, 352.

[14] E. Käsemann, *Gottesvolk*, 27-29; Michel, *Hebräer*, 469.

[15] Cited in Str-B 3. 750.

[16] *Jub.* 1:29; *1 Enoch* 45:1; *4 Ezra* 10:25, 28; cf. also *Sib. Or.* 3. 675; *4 Ezra* 6:11, 17; *2 Baruch* 59:3.

[17] The references to "myriads of angels," to the heavenly archives where names were written, and to departed "spirits" is common in apocalyptic literature (cf. *1 Enoch* 40:1; Rev 3:5; *3 Enoch* 43:1), but are mentioned nowhere else in Hebrews.

The contrasting οὐ προσεληλύθατε . . . ἀλλὰ προσεληλύθατε added by the author to the tradition,[18] governs the structure of 12:18-24 and points to the contrast which the author intends to draw between Sinai and Zion and between Israel and the church. The way in which the author develops this contrast is shown by his addition of the word ψηλαφημένος as a descriptive term for the Sinai event. The description of Sinai as ψηλαφημένος is probably a reflection of Exod 19:12-13, which promises death to anyone who touches the mountain (cf. Heb 12:20). Such a reference to the danger of touching the mountain in the original narrative served to indicate the awesome nature of the Sinai experience. The inference which the author draws from the story is that Sinai was tangible. The Christian community, unlike the old people of God, has not come to "what may be touched."

Although the author uses no terms suggesting intangibility for the Christian experience at Zion, it is evident that such a contrast between the tangible Sinai and the intangible Zion is in view. The contrasting οὐ προσεληλύθατε . . . ἀλλὰ προσεληλύθατε, in which ψηλαφημένος is an interpretive word for the Sinai event but not for Zion, indicates that such a contrast is in view. That which is "heavenly" (ἐπουράνιος) is set over against that which is ψηλαφημένος. This contrast indicates that ψηλαφημένος is used by the author as a code-word for "earthly" in a metaphysical sense. The Sinai event is evaluated and interpreted with the assumptions which indicate the author's metaphysical dualism.

It is apparent, from the contrast between ψηλαφημένος and the heavenly Zion, that ψηλαφημένος has the primary meaning of "earthly" or "sense-perceptible."[19] Such a view corresponds to that perspective that is found in the Platonic tradition, where the sense-perceptible world was distinguished from the intelligible world. For Plato that which is touchable belongs to the sphere of sense-perception (*Phaedo* 99e; *Tim.* 28b, 31b).[20] God is described in other Hellenistic literature as αψηλάφητος.[21] Hebrews'

---

[18] Προσέρχεσθαι, which is a cultic term in the OT for the high priest who comes before God to sacrifice (Lev 9:5-7), is an important word for the author. It is used regularly in Hebrews, not for the priestly approach to God, but for the assembly (cf. 4:16; 7:25; 10:22) of the whole congregation in worship.

[19] H. Windisch (*Der Hebräerbrief*, 112) has correctly noted that ψηλαφημένος "bezeichnet gut die ganze Sinnlichkeit, in der sich die atliche Gottesoffenbarung bewegt."

[20] See E. Norden *Agnostos Theos*, 14-16. Cf. Philo, *de Cher.* 57, 73; *de Post. Cain.* 20; *Leg. Gaium* 6.

[21] A Jewish or Christian magical prayer (Codex Parisinus Graec 2316) invokes God ἄφραντε, ἄφθαρτε, ἀμίαντε, ἀψηλάφητε, ἀχειροποίητε. Cited in Reitzenstein, *Poimandres* (Leipzig: Teubner, 1904) 186. Cf. Ignatius, *Pol.* 3:2, where God is described as τὸν ἄχρονον, τὸν ἀόρατον, τὸν ἀψηλάφητον, τὸν ἀπαθῆ.

use of ψηλαφημένος can be understood by a comparison of similar terms in the epistle which are used in the context of a two-sphere world view. Ψηλαφημένος is to be compared with βλεπόμενον (11:1), χειροποίητος (9:11, 24), and ταύτης τῆς κτίσεως (9:11). These terms always appear in texts where the sense-perceptible world is contrasted with the heavenly world. The author regularly identifies the experience of Israel with the created order, which is to be contrasted with the "true" (8:2) or heavenly world to which the church has access as a result of the exaltation of Christ. Thus by the use of ψηλαφημένος, the author indicates that he does not think merely in typological terms of old event and new event, as his tradition probably did. His intention is not to point to the correspondence between Sinai and Zion; rather Sinai becomes merely an event in the created order. This reinterpretation of the tradition is made in the context of a cosmological dualism.

Although ψηλαφημένῳ implies that ὄρει is to be the noun, ψηλαφημένῳ serves in a much wider way to describe the entire Sinai theophany. The list of phenomena is cited from Deut 4:11 and Exod 19:12-13.[22] It is probable that the author is working with a tradition which enumerates the Sinai phenomena and which had the intent of indicating the awesome character of the Sinai theophany. Rabbinic literature shared the OT's positive evaluation of the theophany as a vehicle of God's revelation. This rabbinic appreciation of a theophany as an event that is perceptible to the senses is reflected in Rabbi Simeon ben Laqish's statement:

> A proselyte is more precious to God than that multitude which stood at Mount Sinai. If that multitude had not seen the thunder, flames, lightning, quaking mountains, and sound of the trumpet, they would not have taken the kingdom of God upon themselves.[23]

The positive evaluation of the theophany was one way in which the exodus story was interpreted in the Hellenistic Age and was, therefore, a tradition which the author of Hebrews could easily have appropriated. The references to thunder, fire, flames, lightning, and earthquakes could be used to emphasize the awesomeness of the Sinai event.

The term ψηλαφημένος, by which the author characterizes the entire Sinai event, gives a negative interpretation to the theophany. The fire of Deut 4:11 is no longer the vehicle of theophany; it is not, as with Philo, πῦρ οὐράνιον (*de Dec.* 44). It is earthly fire of the world of sense perception. The fire is interpreted from a metaphysical standpoint, according to which mate-

---

[22] One may compare Heb 12:18-20 with Deut 4:11 (LXX): καὶ προσήλθετε καὶ ἔστητε ὑπὸ τὸ ὄρος, καὶ τὸ ὄρος ἐκαίετο πυρὶ ἕως τοῦ οὐρανοῦ σκότος, γνόφος, θύελλα, φωνὴ μεγάλη. The reference to σάλπιγξ comes from Exod 19:13, 19.

[23] *Tanch.* לך לך 17a. Cited in Str-B 2. 586.

rial objects can only be inferior agents for the expression of the nature of God. The thunder, lightning, earthquake, trumpet and voice have become "natural phenomena."[24]

This negative evaluation of the Sinai event, which distinguishes the author from rabbinic interpretations, has its closest analogies in the Alexandrian tradition which is represented by Philo and his Alexandrian Jewish predecessor, Aristobulos.[25] The loyalty of both writers to the Jewish tradition would have prevented them from giving an interpretation of the Sinai theophany that is as negative as the interpretation in Hebrews. Nevertheless, the philosophical loyalties of both writers are to be seen in their handling of the Sinai theophany. Both Aristobulos and Philo saw a conflict between the account in Exodus 24 and their convictions about the transcendence of God.[26] Aristobulos was troubled by accounts of God's descent to a specific place, a concern which is shared by Philo.[27] Philo argues that the fire at Sinai was not real (*Q. Ex.* II. 47 on Exod 24:17). Both Philo (*de Dec.* 33) and Aristobulos (Eusebius, *PE* 13. 12. 3) are troubled by the idea of the audibility of God's voice to human ears. Philo speaks, consequently, of the "invisible voice" at Sinai (*de Dec.* 33). The theophany described by Philo (*Q. Ex.* II. 47) belongs to the experience of the crowd.

> (This is said) because, as has been said before, the glory of God is the power through which he now appears; the form of this power is like a flame or rather, it is not but appears (to be so) to the spectators. And so, (Scripture) adds, 'before the sons of the seeing one,' indicating most clearly that there was an appearance of flame, not a veritable flame.

Philo and the author of Hebrews obviously derived differing conclusions from the Sinai theophany because of their respective loyalties. Philo is concerned about the "sense perceptible" character of the event, as he wishes to minimize the material nature of the theophany. Hebrews, by contrast, emphasizes the material nature of the theophany in order to contrast it with the Christian experience at Mount Zion. Nevertheless, both writers share essentially the same categories. Hebrews' characterization of the Sinai event as ψηλαφημένος indicates the author's use of categories that were employed among Alexandrian Jews with philosophical training.

---

[24] F.J. Schierse, *Verheissung und Heilsvollendung,* 176.

[25] N. Walter, *Der Thoraausleger Aristobulos,* 63-65.

[26] Walter, *Aristobulos,* 64. On Philo's view of theophany, see H. Hegermann, *Die Vorstellung vom Schöpfungsmittler im hellenistischen Judentum.*

[27] Walter (*Aristobulos,* 64) has shown that Aristobulos represents a less developed stage of philosophical reflection than Philo, who is more thoroughgoing in his concept of the transcendence of God.

It is probable that the author's tradition contained the contrast between Sinai and the heavenly Zion, as in *Tanch. B*. This eschatological coloring of Zion is supplemented with references to the heavenly πόλις and the heavenly Jerusalem in 12:22. These terms were frequently used interchangeably in apocalyptic texts in a variety of ways for the salvation in the end-time. In Rev 3:12; 21:2, the heavenly Jerusalem and πόλις are brought together; they are to be equated with the heavenly Zion in Rev 14:1.[28] Thus Hebrews is using well established traditions. Yet the author's interpretation of his tradition shows his distance from them. His understanding of these added references is still governed by the contrast between οὐράνιος and ψηλαφημένος (12:18, 22), which shows that the heavenly Zion of the author is not the physical Zion of the apocalyptic literature. It has become the heavenly world of Hebrews, which does not belong to the world of sense perception. It is to be identified with the heavenly world οὐ χειροποίητος (9:24) of the exaltation, the world ἥν ἔπηξεν ὁ κύριος, οὐκ ἄνθρωπος(8:2). The author's understanding of the πόλις is comparable to Philo's interpretation of the πόλις in terms of the κόσμος νοητός.[29]

The author's interpretation of his tradition becomes apparent again in 12:27, where he takes up and comments on the apocalyptic expectation of the eschatological shaking of the cosmos. Indeed, Hag 2:6, quoted by the author in 12:26, was frequently cited in apocalyptic texts which refer to this eschatological shaking (*2 Bar.* 59:3; *4 Ezra* 6:11-17; 10:25-28). In the apocalyptic texts there was the expectation of the abiding new heavens and new earth which were to come into being after the eschatological shaking. But in Hebrews there is no new heaven and new earth.[30] For Hebrews there is a new turn in the argument: τὸ δὲ ἔτι ἅπαξ δηλοῖ τὴν τῶν σαλευομένων μετάθεσις ὡς πεποιημένων.

Μετάθεσις can mean either "removal" or "transformation."[31] If one understands the term to mean "transformation," Hebrews would stand in the

---

[28] In apocalyptic, the heavenly city is described in *2 Bar.* 4:1-6; 32:2; *4 Ezra* 7:26; *1 Enoch* 90:28-32. There is no fixed understanding of the heavenly city in apocalyptic. According to Rev 21:2, the heavenly city comes down to earth. In *1 Enoch* 90:28-30, the new Jerusalem will be built on the same site as the old Jerusalem. See especially, K.L. Schmidt, "Jerusalem als Urbild und Abbild."

[29] Philo speaks of a heavenly *polis* in terms that are derived from Platonism. The κόσμος νοητός, the "intelligible world," is the metropolis of the sage. Cf. *de Som.* 1. 46. Cf. also Chapter IV of this study.

[30] E. Grässer (*Der Glaube*, 173) has observed that there is in Hebrews a changed attitude toward the future, and that Hebrews alters a traditional apocalyptical imagery. M. Peel ("Gnostic Eschatology and the New Testament," *NovT* 12 [1970] 158) has shown that in Gnosticism there is a similar attitude toward the future. There is the expectation of a world conflagration, but no materialistic conception of the new heavens and new earth (cf. *Adv.H.* 1. 23, 2; 1. 7).

[31] BAG, 512.

tradition of the apocalyptic expectation of the transformation of the created order (cf. *Jub.* 1:29; *1 Enoch* 45:1; Rom 8:21-24). But the ἵνα clause which follows implies that τὰ μὴ σαλευόμενα will remain. Therefore, the μετάθεσις of heaven and earth must be understood as "removal." Thus the author reads his text of Hag 2:6 in such a way as to find the annihilation of the created order and the abiding of a sphere which is unaffected by the final catastrophe. Such a reading of the texts reflects assumptions not found in such Jewish apocalyptic texts as *4 Ezra* and *2 Baruch*, for in the Jewish apocalyptic literature the world conflagration is normally followed by a world transformation (cf. *4 Ezra* 7:75; 10:27; *1 Enoch* 45:4).

A careful analysis of the language of 12:27 indicates the nature of the author's assumptions. The author changes the σείσω of Hag 2:6 to σαλευόμενα in 12:27. In apposition to τῶν σαλευομένων stands τῶν πεποιημένων. Πεποιημένα is to be understood as "what is merely made," and reflects the author's dualistic world view.[32] The term is to be compared especially to χειροποίητος (9:11, 24), ταύτης τῆς κτίσεως (9:11) and ψηλαφημένος (12:18), terms which regularly reflect the author's cosmological dualism. Πεποιημένα is the equivalent of γένεσις/τὰ γενόμενα in the Platonic literature for that which is made. Whereas Plato (*Tim.*37D) distinguishes the eternal from that which he describes as γένεσις, Hebrews distinguishes that which abides from that which is "made." The same distinction occurs in Philo (*de Opif. Mund.* 12; cf. also 16, 19, 31), who distinguishes between the earthly sphere of change and the eternity of the world of forms. For our author σαλευόμενα and πεποιημένα are parallel terms, inasmuch as both terms are descriptive of the earthly sphere. One may compare Philo's understanding of the world, in which σαλεύειν was regularly used of that which belongs to the earthly sphere.[33] In Philo's cosmology, only God and the intelligible world remain unshakable and immutable.

It is apparent that the author reads σείσω of Hag 2:6 with certain

---

[32] Hebrews does not deny that God is creator (cf. 1:2-3; 11:3). Nevertheless, the author moves in a dualistic direction by his radical distinction between the world that is χειροποίητος/ πεποιημένος and the heavenly world that is "not of this creation" (9:1). Hebrews' view comes very close to Philo's understanding of the creation. God's ποιεῖν of θεῖα is to be distinguished from his πλάσσειν of θνητά (*Leg. All.* 1. 21). Matter (οὐσία), as μηδὲν ἔχουσα καλόν, is affixed by God to the good (*de Op. Mund.* 12), but it does not derive from him. Although Hebrews does not use the same vocabulary as Philo in describing the created order, there is a remarkable similarity in the world view of Philo and the author of Hebrews. See H. Braun, Ποιέω, *TDNT* 6. 461-463.

[33] *de Post. Cain.* 19-29; cf. also *de Mut. Nom.* 54; *Leg. All.* 2. 89; 3. 97-100; *de Dec.* 58. These texts demonstrate Philo's view of the mutability of the created order. Philo's argument is regularly made in the context of the dualistic distinction between the immutable and mutable spheres, a distinction derived from Plato (*Tim.* 37D).

metaphysical assumptions. For him, that which is shakable belongs to the world of sense perception; and that which is perceptible to the senses is by nature transitory. He is not interested in the nearness of the end; nor is his interest primarily in the end-time catastrophe, as it was understood in the apocalyptic texts. The author's interpretation of the tradition in 12:27 shows his distance from the traditional apocalyptic ideas of the end-time catastrophe, and the fact that his interpretation is influenced by Greek metaphysics. As G. Theissen has observed,

> Zu dem urchristlichen Bild von der Äonenwende treten neue gedankliche Kategorien; der Gegensatz zwischen Himmlischem und Irdischem, der auch als Gegensatz von Urbild und Abbild (10:1), Erschütterbarem und Unerschütterlichem begegnet. Hier meldet sich ein metaphysisches Denken, dass nicht mehr vom faktischen Vergehen der Welt, sondern von ihrer prinzipiellen Vergänglichkeit spricht.[34]

The clause in 12:27b illuminates further the author's understanding of the *metathesis*: ἵνα μείνῃ τὰ μὴ σαλευόμενα. The author does not speak of the new heavens and new earth which follow the eschatological shaking, nor the appearance of the unshakable world. Instead, he knows two worlds already possessing full reality, one of which is material, and therefore shakable; the other is not material, and is unshakable. When the material world disappears, only the world that is presently unseen (11:1) and untouchable (12:18) remains. Τὰ μὴ σαλευόμενα refers, therefore, to the "axiologically" heavenly world of Christ's exaltation, the world that is οὐ χειροποίητος (9:24).[35] The author knows a world that is unaffected by the end-time catastrophe. This world, because it is not πεποιημένον, remains. Such a conception of the end-time is unknown in the Jewish apocalyptic texts which speak of the final catastrophe.

What assumptions about the world have informed the clause in 12:27? The distance which separates the author's view from the materialistic conceptions of the apocalyptic texts which speak of the "new heavens and new earth" is striking. The closest analogies to the author's reference to τὰ μὴ σαλευόμενα come from the realm of Greek metaphysics, as seen in the Platonic literature, in Philo, and in Gnosticism.[36] Stability is, in Philo,[37] in

---

[34] *Untersuchungen*, 108.

[35] A. Cody (*Heavenly Sanctuary and Heavenly Liturgy*, 85) has distinguished between the "cosmologically" and "axiologically" heavenly in Hebrews. The "cosmological" heaven is referred to in 12:26.

[36] On the relationship between Gnosticism and Platonism, cf. H. Krämer, *Der Ursprung der Geistmetaphysik*, 223-263.

[37] *de Post. Cain.* 23; *de Som.* 2. 221, 237.

the Hermetica,[38] and in Plotinus[39] the characteristic of the intelligible world. The Platonic literature abounds in terms used for the stability of the non-material sphere; words such as ἀκίνητος (Plato, *Tim.* 38A), στάσις and ἑστώς (Philo, *de Som.* 2. 221; Plotinus, *En.* 3. 7, 3, 5, 8, 23, 25), all signifying stability, occur with special frequency among Platonists in references to the intelligible world. Τὰ μὴ σαλευόμενα is parallel to these terms as a description of what is not "made."

There exists also a close connection between τὰ μὴ σαλευόμενα and the use of ἀσάλευτος in the Gnostic literature. Ἀσάλευτος and its Coptic equivalent, *atkim,* occur frequently in the Gnostic literature in references to the stability of the heavenly world.[40] In the *Naassene Sermon,*[41] in the *Sophia Jesus Christ,*[42] and in the *Apocryphon of John,*[43] ἀσάλευτος appears along-side terms taken from Platonic metaphysics as a cosmological term used for the intelligible world. Both in Hebrews and in the Gnostic texts, the "unshakable" refers to that which has no contact with sense perception. The author of Hebrews thus comes to his text with metaphysical assumptions which show many affinities with Platonism and Gnosticism.

Μένειν is used here, as in 1:11 (διαμένειν) and in 7:3, 23-24, exclusively for the non-material world. This use of μένειν is unique to Hebrews among NT writings. It is also to be distinguished from the apocalyptic view of "abiding." Whereas μένειν is used in the LXX of Isa 66:22 for a rebuilt Jerusalem, in Hebrews it is used for that which is non-material. This use of μένειν for the abiding of the supercelestial reality appears frequently in the Platonic literature. In *Timaeus* 37D, as in Plotinus' tractate, *On Time and Eternity,* μένειν is used for the intelligible world. Similarly, Philo uses μένειν for the intelligible world and for the sphere of ideas. E. Grässer has rightly said that μένειν in Hebrews is used not only as a "Zeitbegriff," which "auf die Dauer einer Sache bzw. ihre Zukünftigkeit (abhebt), sondern als Qualitäts-begriff," which accents "das Wesen einer Sache, hier ihre Stabilität."[44] This understanding of stability is set in dualistic terms which must be understood in the light of the Platonic understanding of the stability characteristic of the intelligible world.

The metaphysical statement in 12:27 is the basis for the encouragement in 12:28, as διό indicates (cf. 12:12 for this use of διό). The church receives

---

[38] *CH* 11. 2, 4.
[39] *Enneads* 3. 7. 6. 6; 7. 3. 35.
[40] Cf. S. Giversen, *Apocryphon Johannis,* 158.
[41] Hippolytus, 5. 7. 6.
[42] *Sophia Jesus Christ,* 88:9.
[43] *Apocryphon of John* (BG) 65:2; 73:5; 88:3-5.
[44] *Der Glaube,* 174.

the unshakable kingdom (βασιλείαν ἀσάλευτον παραλαμβάνοντες). Βασιλείαν λαμβάνοντες is a traditional formula, used commonly for "receiving a
kingship."[45] What is of interest to the author is that the kingdom is ἀσάλευτος. Ἀσάλευτος does not refer to unlimited duration (cf. Dan 7:14). Rather,
it refers to the stability of the heavenly world. This view is remarkably
similar to the reference in the Gnostic texts to those who "receive an immortal kingdom" (*Tractate Without Title* 175:1-5; *Apoc. Adam* 76:17). The
"immortal kingdom" of these texts is the sphere which does not pass away in
the eschatological catastrophe. This sphere belongs to the heavenly world of
incorruption. The church, unlike Israel (12:18), receives a kingdom that is
non-material and thus non-transitory. It is this fact, grounded in the metaphysical argument in 12:27, which provides the stability and certainty for the
community. Because the church has access to a stable reality (12:27-28),
it can now maintain its faithfulness that is urged in 12:12-17. This stability, grounded in a Platonic metaphysic, thus serves the author's parenetic interest.

Attention to the way in which the author of Hebrews has appropriated
an eschatological tradition that was common in Jewish apocalyptic literature
demonstrates that, while there is a definite eschatology in Hebrews, it has
been reshaped with metaphysical interests. This fact is of decisive importance for understanding the eschatology of Hebrews.

[45] BAG, 625.

CHAPTER IV

FAITH IN HEBREWS

The emphasis on faith which is apparent in Hebrews 11 appears to indicate the incompatibility between Hebrews and the philosophy of the Hellenistic Age. A catalog of heroes of πίστις, introduced as patterns of imitation, is unthinkable in any Greek tradition.[1] It is well known that the critique of Christianity which was offered by Platonist philosophers was directed largely at the Christians' insistence on πίστις. Πίστις was the state of mind of the uneducated, who believe things on hearsay without being able to give reasons for their belief.[2] In fact, what astonished pagan observers was the very behavior which is praised in Hebrews: the willingness to suffer for the undemonstrable.[3]

G. Ebeling has written that faith is not a category that is fundamental to religious experience, but rather belongs exclusively to the Christian language tradition.[4] Thus the Christian emphasis on faith was often rejected by ancient philosophers. Celsus is the first recorded example of the philosophical attack on faith.[5] His contemporary, Galen, treated Christianity as a defective philosophy and equated the Christians' insistence on faith with superstition.

If I had in mind people who taught their pupils in the same way as the followers of Moses and Christ teach theirs—for they order them to accept everything on faith—I should not have given you a definition.[6]

For Galen, Christians are like quacks who warn men against the doctor, "Take care that none of you touches science (ἐπιστήμη); science is a bad thing, knowledge (γνῶσις) makes men decline from the health of the soul."[7] The same charge against Christians is to be found in Porphyry[8] and Julian.

[1] R. Walzer, *Galen on Jews and Christians*, 49.

[2] E.R. Dodds, *Pagan and Christian*, 120.

[3] Dodds, *Pagan and Christian*, 120.

[4] G. Ebeling, *Was heisst Glauben?* Cited in D. Lührmann, "Pistis in Judentum," 19.

[5] Origen, *Con. Cels.* 1. 9, 6, 11; 6. 11.

[6] R. Walzer, *Galen*, 14-15. The passage survives only in the Arabic translation of Galen's work against Aristotle's theology, entitled Εἰς τὸ πρῶτον κινοῦν ἀκίνητον.

[7] Walzer, *Galen*, 53.

[8] Porphyry, *Against the Christians*; cf. A. Von Harnack, *Theologische Untersuchungen* 37. 4 (1911). Walzer, *Galen*, 54.

As Julian exclaims, "There is nothing in your philosophy beyond the one word, 'Believe.'"[9]

The elevation of knowledge over faith reflects the view of Plato, for whom πίστις was not a major category.[10] When Plato refers to πίστις, he indicates that it holds a position in relation to truth which is inferior to ἐπιστήμη. Πίστις is a lower kind of cognition which is appropriate to objects of the senses. In *Rep.* 6. 511de, for example, νόησις, διανοία, πίστις, and εἰκασία are enumerated as levels of one's relation to truth. In *Rep.*7. 533e-534a, the sequence is ἐπιστήμη, διανοία, πίστις, and εἰκασία The latter two are described with the term δόξα, while the former two are categorized under νόησις. For Plato, νόησις stands in the same relation to δόξα as ἐπιστήμη to πίστις. In *Tim.*29c, πίστις is contrasted with ἀλήθεια. In this text Plato says, "As reality is to becoming, so is truth to belief" (ὅτιπερ πρὸς γένεσιν οὐσία, τοῦτο πρὸς πίστιν ἀλήθεια). The distinction between ἐπιστήμη and πίστις appears also in *Rep.* 10. 601e. Thus πίστις holds only a secondary relation to truth for Plato.

Plato's positive appreciation of faith is to be seen in *Rep.* 6. 505e, where he refers to πίστις μόνιμος, "steadfast faith," and in *Tim.*37c, where he speaks of δόξαι and πίστεις, which are βέβαιοι and ἀληθεῖς, but still to be distinguished from νοῦς and ἐπιστήμη. Thus there is a role for faith in Plato, but one which is strictly secondary to knowledge. True beliefs can be held without knowledge and may be sufficient for action, but they are insecure unless they are based on rational knowledge.[11]

Despite the Platonists' frequent criticisms of the Christians' reliance on faith, Plato's successors increasingly found an important place for *pistis* in their systems, for faith became the "bridge to the divine."[12] The significant place which was given to faith was especially developed in debates with the Sceptics in the Hellenistic Age, becoming a philosophical commonplace.[13]

Plutarch, who was both a priest at Delphi and a Platonic philosopher, attempted to find a middle ground between the extremes of atheism and superstition. In *de Supers.* 165b, the position of the atheist is described as ἀπιστία τοῦ θεοῦ or ἀπιστία in the one who could help him (165c; 167e). Atheism is thus a falsified reason which prevents one from "seeing the gods" (167d). In *de Iside et Os.* 360 τιμή and πίστις are mentioned as the common possession of all mankind, while ἀπιστία is an aberration introduced by the

---

[9] Greg. Naz., *Or.* 4 (Contra Julianum), cap. 102 (Migne, Vol. 35, col. 636). Dodds, *Pagan and Christian*, 122.

[10] R. Bultmann, Πίστις, *TDNT* 6. 177.

[11] R. Walzer, *Galen*, 51. W. Völker, *Fortschritt und Vollendung*, 239.

[12] W. Theiler, *Die Vorbereitung des Neuplatonismus*, 143.

[13] O. Michel, "Glaube," *Theologisches Begriffslexikon* 1. 566.

atheists. In *Pyth. Or.* 402e (18), the πίστις of the fathers is praised as specifically connected with a belief in providence and prophetic gifts. It is the work
of philosophy to seek explanations which will take away obstacles to faith.
Thus for Plutarch πίστις was primarily belief in the existence of the gods, a
belief which also included their πρόνοια.

A similar understanding of πίστις remains a consistent feature in the
philosophy of late antiquity. Faith is primarily the belief in the existence of
the gods. Seneca, who does not use *fides* in relation to the gods, employs the
verb *credō*. In *Ep.* 95:50 Seneca says that one's duty is to "believe in the
gods" (*primus est deorum cultus deos credere*). In Sextus Empiricus, the
essential issue is to believe in the existence of the divine.[14] In Lucian also,
πιστεύειν is used for the existence of the gods (*Pseudolog.* 10). While in
ancient Greek νομίζειν was used for the belief in the existence of the gods,
πιστεύειν was used in the later period.[15]

In Middle Platonism and Neoplatonism, πίστις was more closely connected with knowledge. The Aristotelian theme of the absolute and trust-
worthy principles which require no demonstration was accepted in Middle
Platonism.[16] These principles were accepted by faith. According to Antiochus of Ascalon, *pistis* (*fides*) is identified with συγκατάθεσις, a Stoic term
for principles which are evident both to sensation and to mind.[17] This view
was also accepted by Cicero,[18] and later by Clement of Alexandria.[19] Thus in
Middle Platonism, the dichotomy between πίστις and ἐπιστήμη was not as
pronounced as in Plato himself. Πίστις was connected with those things
which require no demonstration.

In the Hermetica, philosophical language is employed for the description of faith. Here faith is explicitly connected with knowledge: τὸ γὰρ
νοῆσαι ἐστι τὸ πιστεῦσαι, ἀπιστεῦσαι δὲ τὸ μὴ νοῆσαι (9:10). This passage
occurs in a context where the writer is describing the nature of God, using
Platonic categories (9:9).[20] The facts concerning God's nature outside of time
(9:9) are *pista*, but to the ignorant they are *apista* (9:10). When the *nous* of
man is led to the truth, according to 9:10, it rests in faith (καὶ τῇ καλῇ πίστει

---

[14] Sext. Emp., *Adv. Math.* 9. 61.

[15] Bultmann, 179.

[16] S. Lilla, *Clement of Alexandria*, 123.

[17] Lilla, *Clement*, 127; Cicero, *De Fin.* 4. 9; *Ac. Pr.* 2. 37, 38, 39.

[18] Cf. *De Fin.* 4. 9. Lilla, *Clement*, 128.

[19] Cf. Clement, *Strom.* 2. 54, 55 for Clement's understanding of συγκατάθεσις. In other
texts, Clement connects πίστις with πρόληψις, "preconception." *Strom.* 2. 16. 3. This preconception is then supplemented by knowledge. Lilla, *Clement*, 130.

[20] The Platonic distinction between time and eternity (*Tim.* 37B) is employed here in the
description of God.

ἐπανεπαύσατο). Thus *pistis* here is combined with the reception of truth. Whereas in Plato *pistis* functioned only at the level of opinion, in the Hermetica it is connected with the knowledge of the divine.

The relationship between Hermetic epistemology, Plato, and the NT is also indicated in 7:3-4, where the writer speaks of the tragedy of *agnōsia* concerning the divine things. This knowledge of the divine things demands a special apprehension of divine reality. The divine is, in the characteristic Platonic categories, perceived οὐ γὰρ ἐστιν ἀκουστός, οὐδὲ λεκτός, οὐδὲ ὁρατὸς ὀφθαλμοῖς, ἀλλὰ νῷ καὶ καρδίᾳ (7:2). This apprehension of the higher reality by the *nous* is set wihtin a context of Platonic dualism, and is equivalent to *pistis* in 9:10.

Pistis became a basic requirement of pagan philosophy. Porphyry chided the Christians for their insistence on *pistis*, but at the same time made *pistis* the first condition of the soul's approach to God. Porphyry listed four *stoicheia* in one's relation to God: πίστις, ἀλήθεια, ἔρως, and ἐλπίς.[21] Indeed, Porphyry connects faith and knowledge, as in the phrase in *Ad. Marc.* 288. 5, διὰ γνώσεως καὶ τῆς βεβαίας πίστεως. There are some who neither believe in the gods nor in providence (οἱ μήτε εἶναι θεοὺς πιστεύσαντες μήτε προνοίᾳ θεοῦ διοικεῖσθαι τὰ ὅλα), but Porphyry argues that πιστεύσαι γὰρ δεῖ ὅτι μόνη σωτηρία ἡ πρὸς τὸν θεὸν ἐπιστροφή.[22] This faith then leads to knowledge and hope in God. Thus *pistis* in Porphyry is necessary in the approach to God. *Pistis* is the belief that the divine exists and that providence is effective in the world.

There was, as the work of Plutarch and Porphyry suggests, a growing tendency to give to faith an indispensable role in one's relation to the divine. This emphasis, obviously directed against the sceptics, was focused on both the existence and the providence of the divine. Within this tradition, the distinction between πίστις and γνῶσις was increasingly removed. Thus πίστις was at times described with the categories which were, in Plato's work, limited to ἐπιστήμη.[23]

Philo of Alexandria

For anyone who approaches Philo from the background of Greek philosophy, there is a remarkable new element in the place which πίστις holds in his thought.[24] Philo described πίστις as the queen (*de Ab.* 270) and the

---

[21] Porphyry, *Ad Marc.* 288. 17-18. Theiler, *Vorbereitung*, 149.

[22] *Ad Marc.* 288. 15.

[23] Cf. Theiler, *Vorbereitung*, 149-151. Plotinus, Simplicius, Jamblichus, and Proclus give a significant place to πίστις as the "bridge to God."

[24] Völker, *Fortschritt*, 239; Lührmann, "Pistis," 31.

highest (*Quis Rer.* 91) of all virtues, and the necessary presupposition for drawing near to God (*de Ab.* 269-70). Indeed, Philo uses πίστις in connection with other important concepts, such as εὐσέβεια, παρρησία, and συνείδησις, all of which were important in the religious life.[25] In Philo's description of such heroes as Abraham and Moses, faith is given a significance beyond that accorded it in the OT.[26]

Philo's achievement was that he took the concept of faith from the OT and explained it in the Greek language and with Greek concepts, thus giving it a meaning and presuppositions different from the OT.[27] One fundamental presupposition in Philo's view of faith, for example, was his dualistic distinction between this creation and God. Thus Philo took the LXX statements about God's character as πιστός and gave them an entirely new orientation. He frequently refers to this creation as ἄπιστος (*Quis Rer.* 93), or as full of ἀπιστία (*de Conf. Ling.* 57). Thus the world is not worthy of one's trust, for it is by nature unstable. Indeed, Philo raises the question in *Leg. All.* 2. 89, "How should one come to believe in God?" He answers, ἐὰν μάθη, ὅτι πάντα τὰ ἄλλὰ τρέπεται, μόνος δὲ αὐτὸς ἄτρεπτός ἐστι.

In contrast with the instability of the world, only God is πιστός. His words are oaths which are worthy of one's absolute trust; his promises are reliable (*Leg. All.* 3. 204). His πιστός character is connected with his immutability. He alone stands unmoved, while the whole creation is in movement (*de Post. Cain.* 23). Thus πιστός is equivalent to such words as ἀκλινής (*Leg. All.* 2. 83), ἀμετάβλητος (*de Cher.* 90), ἄτρεπτος (*Leg. All.* 2. 33), and ἑστώς (*de Post. Cain.* 23), all of which are used to describe God.[28] In this way Philo connected the LXX word πιστός with the negtive theology which he inherited from Greek philosophy. For Philo, God's faithfulness is a motif which is understandable only against the background of this dualism.

Although only God is πιστός in Philo's view, there is a level at which his people can share in πίστις, for it is a common assumption in Philo's view that access to a stable reality also provides stability. Consequently, πίστις is connected with detachment from the world and reliance on God, a common Philonic theme exemplified by both Abraham and Moses. Indeed, Philo cites frequently those texts which refer either to the faith of Abraham or of Moses.

The connection between the faithfulness of God and the faith of the individual can be seen in Philo's treatment of the story of Abraham which

[25] Völker, *Fortschritt*, 254.
[26] Lührmann, "Pistis," 31.
[27] *Ibid.*
[28] M. Peisker, *Der Glaubensbegriff bei Philon*, 8.

appears in several tractates. *De Ab.* 262-272, for example, is based on Gen 15:6, "Abraham trusted in God." In this text Philo says that Abraham trusted God because he recognized that such things as fame, power, and wealth were inherently unreliable. Therefore Abraham recognized that faith was the queen of the virtues and "fulfillment of bright hopes," inasmuch as it is "firmly stayed on him who is the cause of all things" (*de Ab.* 269). Thus belief in these transitory things is disbelief in God, and disbelief in them is belief in God (269). Such πίστις is rewarded by the πίστις of God, which was confirmed by his oath and promise (273).

Quis Rerum Div. 90-101 is also derived from Gen 15:6. In this passage Abraham's faith is described as "the most perfect of virtues" (ἡ τελειοτάτη ἀρετή). As in *de Ab.* 262-266, πίστις is contrasted here with trust in repute, riches, office, health, and many other things (92). Trust in God, according to this passage, is equivalent to distrust in created being, which is untrustworthy (ἀπιστῆσαι γενέσει τῇ πάντα ἐξ ἑαυτῆς ἀπίστῳ), for only God is πιστός (93). Faith involves "celestial understanding" (μεγάλης καὶ ὀλυμπίου ἔργον διανοίας ἐστί), and thus has an intellectual component. It involves resting on the Existent only, "firmly and without wavering" (βεβαίως καὶ ἀκλινῆς, 95). Πίστις is, therefore, a stability that rests on the immutable reliability of God.

Similar arguments are presented in *Leg. All.* 3. 203-233, which are based on Gen 22:16-17 and Num 12:7. In a discussion of the propriety of God's swearing (Gen 22:16), Philo says that an oath is intended to assist faith. Then he adds, "Only God and one who is God's friend is faithful" (*pistos*), citing Num 12:7, "Moses was faithful in all God's house." In 3. 228, both Gen 15:6 and Num 12:7 are cited to show that both Abraham and Moses were "faithful." Such faithfulness, which was based on the reliability of God, obviously excludes vain human reasonings and calculations (3. 226-233). Faith, therefore, involves a reliance on God and a distrust of the creation.

In the Philonic passages which describe πίστις, the positive content of faith is described in various ways. It includes, as we have noticed, a reliance on God's promises. The role of God's promise is also indicated in *de Mig. Ab.* 43-44. In other texts, faith is a conviction that God is the creator. According to *de Conf. Ling.* 141, Abraham was the first believer, for he was the first with a solid, unshakable notion that the most high was the unique cause. According to *de Conf. Ling.* 31, πίστις is "the most stable quality" (βεβαιοτάτη διάθεσις). According to *de Mut. Nom.* 155 and *Praem. Poen.* 30, faith sees in God the final cause, a fact which allows one to turn from self to God (cf. *Quis Rer.* 92; *Sac. A. C.* 70; *Q. Gen.* 3.2). In all of these texts it is more than a subjective conclusion. It is a firm conviction and stance in life in which one turns from the world to God. It is to be seen both in Abraham's pilgrimage and in Moses' ascent to God, both of which involved a renunciation of this world.

The world-renunciation which is common in Philo is often pictured as a pilgrimage. The man of faith is, therefore, a stranger and a sojourner on earth whose real country is heaven. Abraham is thus not only the exemplar of faith; he is also the exemplar of the pilgrim whose country is in heaven. According to *Quis Rer.* 26-27, Abraham describes himself as a wanderer (μετανάστης) and outcast (ἀπελήλαμαι), and an alien (ἠλλοτρίωμαι) from his father's house. His fatherland (πατρίς) is God. Abraham's experience teaches us, according to *Quis Rer.* 267, that our life in the body is that of a sojourner in a foreign land (παροικεῖν ὡς ἐν ἀλλοδαπῇ). This theme is treated at considerable length in the tractate *de Abrahamo*. Abraham obeyed the voice to begin the journey from his native land, despite the attractions offered by Chaldea. He made the journey because he was capable of seeing beyond the truths of the Chaldeans, who observed only visible existence (ὁρατὴν οὐσίαν) instead of the invisible and intelligible world (69). Abraham then followed the pure beam and was established by the sight of the intelligible world (70-71). Abraham was thus able to see the invisible (74-79). His wandering was a life of insecurity in the desert (85). Such a story, according to *de Ab.* 262-276, is a great example of faith. Faith consists in a pilgrimage which is made possible by a belief that the pilgrimage leads one on a path which is safe and unshaken (269).

Abraham's departure is perceived in *de Mig. Ab.* 9 as an exodus from the body, "this foul prison house." It is also described as a departure from sense perception (αἴσθησις). Its destination is the abode in the father's land, the inheritance where labor is no longer necessary (28-30). A similar view is given in *Leg. All.* 3. 83: Abraham lived as a stranger on earth.

In *de Conf. Ling.* 75-82, Philo employs Gen 11:2 as the basis for his comments on the importance of pilgrimage for the man of faith. The wicked of Gen 11:2 lived on the plain "as though it were their fatherland" (ὡς ἐν πατρίδι). They did not sojourn there as on a foreign soil (οὐχ ὡς ἐπὶ ξένης παρῴκησαν), but decided instead on a permanent stay. By contrast, the wise are appropriately called sojourners (παροικοῦντες). Their life in the body is temporary. The heavenly region, the place of their citizenship (ἐν ᾧ πολιτεύονται), is their native land (πατρίς); the earthly region is a foreign country in which they live as sojourners (78). Thus Abraham, Isaac, Jacob, and Moses are described as sojourners (76-82). One's task is to leave the world of the body and of the senses, as the great heroes of faith have demonstrated.

V. Nikiprowetzky has suggested that the center of Philo's thought was the notion of the migration from flesh to spirit, from the material world to the intelligible world.[29] Consequently, Philo finds references regularly in Scripture to the idea of the life on earth as that of a stranger. One sojourns here as in a foreign city. In this city he does but sojourn until he has exhausted his appointed span of life (*de Cher.* 120-121). In *Q.Gen.* 4. 74, Philo asks, "But does not every wise soul live like an immigrant and sojourner in this mortal body, having (for its real) dwelling place and country the most pure substance of heaven, from which (our) nature migrated to this place by a law of necessity?" According to *de Som.* 1. 181, the soul exists in the body as in a strange land. According to *de Congress.* 84-87, our task is to recognize our duty to hate the habits and customs of the lands in which we live, which are symbolized by Egypt and Canaan.

This situation of being in a strange land is closely connected with the references to the better city or country. Thus Jacob's temporary residence with Laban is symbolic of the soul's expectation of a city (*de Som.* 1. 46). According to *de Som.* 2. 250, the city is called Jerusalem. According to *de Som.* 1. 181, the destiny of the soul is not to remain forever in its prison; God will free the soul and bring it back to its native city.

In the present existence, one is aware of the fatherland through the gift of a special perception. We have noticed that Abraham surpassed the Chaldeans because he could see what was invisible to them (*Quis Rer.* 98). According to *de Plant.* 17, man, in contrast with the animals, is especially equipped to see the heavenly world. Although for Philo the true reality is invisible, he argues on numerous occasions that the wise man is especially gifted to "see the invisible" (cf. *Quod Deus Immut.* 3; *de Post. Cain.* 15), a view which was apparently derived from Plato. According to *Praem. Poen.* 27, "belief in God" is the perpetual vision of the existent."[30] In *de Abr.* 57, Philo says that "the sight of the mind, the dominant element in the soul, surpasses all the other faculties of the mind." In *Q.Gen.* 4. 96, Philo gives an allegorical explanation of Gen 27:1, "Isaac was old and could no longer see." He explains the blindness of the patriarch as the result of a voluntary procedure. Isaac fixed his eyes on intelligible realities, allowing him to see beyond the material world. Thus the pilgrim, who experiences all of the frustration of being a stranger, is especially gifted to see his homeland, the invisible world.

Because of Philo's emphasis on faith and his strong emphasis on the life of the stranger, the question of Philo's philosophical loyalties has been raised. Lührmann has correctly shown that Philo's view of faith differs greatly from that of the OT.[31] On the other hand, it has also been shown that

---

[29] V. Nikiprowetzky, *Le Commentaire de l'Écriture chez Philon d'Alexandrie*, 239.

[30] R. Williamson, *Philo and the Epistle to the Hebrews*, 364.

[31] Lührmann, "Pistis," 31.

the use of πίστις as a central category distinguishes Philo from most of his philosophical contemporaries. It is likely, therefore, that Philo's view reflects a unique combination of OT and philosophical categories. The way for this transformation was already prepared by the increasing interest in faith among the Platonists of the period. Faith is largely intellectualized, having for Philo a function similar to ἐπιστήμη in Plato. Philo's view of faith as the renunciation of earthly things would be coherent with elements of both Stoicism and Platonism. His view of pilgrimage, with its idea of living as a stranger and its notion of belonging to another world, reflects Platonic elements also, for it presupposes the Platonic view of the intelligible world as one's place of origin.[32] Thus Philo has taken an OT theme and interpreted it with the categories of the philosophy of the period. Faith is the bridge between the "stranger" and the country to which he belongs.

The wise man, according to Philo, can endure the insecurity of being a stranger, because he has found his security elsewhere. Faith, which is directed toward God's reliable oath and promise, is identified with stability. According to de Virt. 216, πίστις is the most sure and certain of all virtues (ἡ τῶν ἀρετῶν βεβαιοτάτην). Βέβαιος is frequently Philo's descriptive word for faith (de Plant. 70, 82; de Virt. 216; de Conf. Ling. 31). Thus the man of faith finds his security not in the perceptible world, but in the intelligible world. Although the Platonists did not frequently connect πίστις with this concept,[33] the notion of finding one's stability in the intelligible world is of Platonic origin.

Pistis in Heb 10:32-39

The meaning of faith in Hebrews 11 is to be seen within the author's general parenetic purpose, including especially the exhortation of 10:19-39. Before this section, πίστις has been referred to as the necessary response to God's promises (4:2; 6:12), while ἀπιστία is mentioned as both the immediate danger to the church (3:12) and the cause of Israel's failure (3:19). Immediately before chapter 11, the author's concern with the πίστις of the community is reflected in the parenetic comments in 10:22, 38. These references indicate that chapter 11, with its historical retrospective and descrip-

---

[32] The origins of Philo's concept of faith are much disputed. Völker (Fortschritt, 258) argues that Philo is chiefly indebted to Judaism for his understanding of faith. E. Brehier sees the background in the Stoic's indifference to material things. E. Brehier, Les Idées Philosophiques et Religieuses de Philon d'Alexandria, 222. Philo's view of living as a stranger is certainly compatible with the "Stoicizing Platonism" of his day. Plato's Apology (41A) and Phaedo (61-67) both describe this existence as a temporary residence away from home. Cf. note 109.

[33] Cf. however, CH 9. 10.

tion (11:1) of faith, serves the parenetic purpose of the author. Thus the parenesis provides the context for undersanding Hebrews' view of faith.[34]

The parenesis, which is a transition in the structure of Hebrews, is divided into two sections. In 10:19-31 the author appeals to his community both by exhortation (10:19-25) and severe warning (10:26-31). The community appears to be faced with two alternatives: to "draw near" to the heavenly world through the blood of Christ, thus "holding on to the confession without wavering" (10:23), or to "sin deliberately," thus profaning the blood of Christ. The church, as a recipient of the heavenly calling, is thus faced with a real choice between drawing near to the heavenly world in worship or committing apostasy. The basis of the appeal is the soteriological significance of the blood of Christ, which means for the community either access to God (10:20) or a thing to be profaned (10:29).

Against this alternative, 10:32-39 presents a turn in the argument. The call for faith in 10:39 is based on the memory of former days (10:32-34). The dominant word here is ὑπομένω/ὑπομονή (10:32-34, 36), which is closely related to παρρησία (10:35) and πίστις (10:39). This part of the parenesis provides the transition between the exhortations of 10:19-31 and the chapter on faith. The concrete situation of the church is considered, as the author appeals to the church to endure and thus not to "sin deliberately."

The appeal in 10:32 begins with a retrospective on the church's past. Such an exhortation is not unusual in Hebrews, as the author elsewhere refers to the community's past (cf. 6:10). Indeed ἀναμιμνῄσκεσθε, which is parallel to the exhortations of 10:19, 22, 23,[35] is reminiscent of the appeal to memory in 6:10; 13:7. Φωτισθέντες is apparently a reference to the original conversion (6:4). What is especially significant about the community's past is stated in the phrase, πολλὴν ἄθλησιν ὑπομείνατε παθήματων, which introduces the specific references to suffering in 10:33-34. The community's sufferings, which are also mentioned in 12:4-11, indicate that the readers shared the precarious existence in relation to the society which is mentioned in other NT literature (cf. 1 Thess 2:14-16). Παθήματα were, from the beginning, a constituent part of Christian existence,[36] even if no one here has suffered a martyr's fate (12:4).

The author's interpretation of these sufferings is indicated by πολλὴν ἄθλησιν ὑπομείνατε. At the moment when the community needs ὑπομονή

---

[34] G. Dautzenberg, "Der Glaube im Hebräerbrief," 162. Cf. O. Michel, Hebräerbrief, 59.

[35] C. Spicq, *Hébreux*, 2. 327.

[36] In the Pauline literature the accent falls on Paul's suffering as an apostle (cf. 2 Cor 1:5-7; Phil 3:10; cf. Col 1:24), although the suffering of the church is also mentioned (Rom 5:1-4; 8:18). 1 Peter, obviously written during a time of persecution, attempts to provide a theology of suffering (1 Pet 1:11; 4:13; 5:1; 9).

(10:36), the author refers back to their past endurance. Ὑπομονή is an ideal for the author, for he refers also to Jesus as the one who "endured" (12:2-3) as the basis of his appeal for the community to continue its contest δι' ὑπομονῆς in 12:1-3.

Ὑπομένω/ὑπομονή is an ideal in the NT in general, where the category is frequently connected with eschatological sufferings.[37] Ὑπομένω, "to endure,"[38] is also an ideal in the OT, Greek philosophy, and in Philo. In the OT it has the primary meaning of "wait on," with God as the object.[39] In philosophy it was commonly used as a subdivision of ἀνδρεῖα, with the assumption that endurance of hard things is sometimes necessary καλοῦ ἕνεκα.[40] In Hebrews ὑπομονή is obviously closely related to πίστις. Both in 10:32-39 and in 12:1-2 the two terms are related. The "faith" and "endurance" of Jesus are both mentioned in 12:1-3. Faith, therefore, is closely associated with endurance in Hebrews.

Hebrews' use of ὑπομένω with ἄθλησιν indicates the close affinity between the author and the literature of Hellenistic Judaism. Both in 10:32 and 12:1-2 ὑπομονή is connected with the image of the contest (cf. 5:14; 12:11). Ἄθλησις is used only in Hebrews in the NT. The imagery of the contest is especially known in 4 Maccabees, where the martyrs are exemplars of endurance in the contest. Those who experienced torture were engaged in a contest which was divine, for on that day they were tested for their ὑπομονή (17:11-12). The noble martyrs were athletes (17:16), while the world was the crowd of spectators (17:15-16). Ὑπομένω/ὑπομονή appears consistently in 4 Maccabees in the context of the metaphor of the contest in order to describe the endurance of the exemplars of faith.[41]

Philo also consistently uses the athletic imagery. In some instances he uses it to describe the training in philosophy characteristic of the sage.[42] In other instances, the metaphor is used in connection with endurance and suffering. In *Quod Deus Immut.*13, he speaks of the one who "with endurance and courage perseveres to the finish in the contest" (τοὺς ... διὰ ἀνδρείας καὶ ὑπομονῆς ἐπὶ κτήσει τοῦ ἀρίστου διάθλουσαν ἄθλους). In *de Cher.* 80-81, Philo recognizes that suffering is a necessary part of the faithful

---

[37] Matt 10:22; 24:13; Rom 8:24; 12:12; cf. 1 Pet 2:20; 2 Cor 1:6.

[38] BAG, 853.

[39] F. Hauck, Ὑπομένω, *TDNT* 5. 583. Cf. Ps 32:20; Isa 64:3; Hab 2:3.

[40] Aristotle, *Eth. Nic.* 3. 10, p. 115b, 17-23; cf. Philo, *Quod Deus Immut.* 13; *de Cher.* 78; *de Mut. Nom.* 197; Hauck, Ὑπομένω, *TDNT*, 5. 582.

[41] 4 Macc 1:11; 7:9; 9:8, 30; 15:30; 17:4, 12, 17, 23. Cf. ὑπομένειν in 4 Macc 5:23-6:9; 7:22; 9:6, 22; 13:12; 15:31, 32; 16:1, 8, 17, 19, 21.

[42] Cf. *Leg. All.* 1. 98; 3. 72. Moses (*de Mig. Ab. 27*; *Leg. All.* 3. 14), Jacob (*de Sob.* 65); and Joseph (*de Jos.* 26) are described as athletes. Cf. chapter 2 of this study.

life. Consequently, he says, "We should receive blows like an athlete," not like a slave. According to *Leg. All.* 3. 201, one meets adversity like an athlete. The same imagery is employed in *de Congress.* 164, where Philo compares those who faint early in the contest with those who carry through the contest of life to its finish. According to *de Jos.* 26, both Joseph and Jacob were drilled through suffering.

The image of the contest for the physical suffering, which later was used for Christian martyrs, was especially appropriate for both Philo and 4 Maccabees in a way that was not appropriate to their non-Jewish contemporaries. Both Philo and 4 Maccabees belong to a minority culture which was subject to persecution and acts of violence. Because they identified with this minority culture, the image of the contest was a useful way of giving a positive interpretation of the fate of their people. Indeed, both Philo's *In Flaccum* and 4 Maccabees give vivid descriptions of the public abuse which the Jews encountered. This complex of imagery, which appears to be well known in Hellenistic Judaism, is shared by the author of Hebrews. The writer, along with Philo and the author of 4 Maccabees, holds the conviction that suffering is the fate of the believer, and that it is comparable with the athletic contest.

The contrasting μέν . . . δέ statements of 10:33-34 give the details of the παθήματα of 10:32. Ὀνειδισμοῖς τε καὶ θλίψεσιν θεατριζόμενοι indicates the public nature of the sufferings. Θεατρίζω, used only here in the NT, means "hold up to shame"[43] or "expose publicly."[44] The term is reminiscent of 1 Cor 4:9, θέατρον ἐγενήθημεν. The imagery is also reminiscent of 4 Macc 17:14, "the world and the human race were the spectators," and of Hebrews 12:1, where Christians are described as the athletes in the contest. One may compare Philo's *In Flaccum,* where the Jews are put on public display in the theater and subjected to abuse.[45] Ὀνειδισμός, "reproach,"[46] also suggests public shame. The reference to ὀνειδισμός in 10:33 anticipates 11:26 and 13:13. In both texts, ὀνειδισμός is used for the shame of Christ which is shared by believers (cf. Ps 69:10; Rom 15:3). Θλίψις is a word regularly used in the NT for the eschatological sufferings.[47]

The δέ clause emphasizes another aspect of the suffering in 10:33-34.

---

[43] LSJ, 787.

[44] BAG, 354.

[45] *In Flac.* 72, 74, 84-85, 95, 173. Cf. Josephus, *C. Apion* 1. 43: ἐν θεατροῖς ὑπομένοντες (θάνατον τρόπους). In Stoic literature there is the idea of the man fighting misfortune as a spectacle to gods and men. Both Hebrews and Philo, by contrast, use the image in a negative sense to describe public abuse. Cf. G. Kittel, Θέατρον, *TDNT* 3. 43.

[46] BAG, 573.

[47] Cf. Mark 13:19 par; 13:24; Rom 5:3; 2 Cor 1:4; 4:17; 6:4.

The author's strong doctrine of the community (cf. 3:12-13; 10:25) is emphasized, inasmuch as the accent is on the sympathy of the members for each other. Κοινωνοὶ τῶν οὕτως ἀναστρεφομένων and συνεπαθήσατε emphasize their care for one another, both in suffering and in bonds (cf. 13:3).[48] The community thus shared its alienation together (cf. 12:12-15).[49]

In 10:34 the historical retrospect reaches its crucial point in the final reference to the experience of persecution and the community's resource for enduring: τὴν ἁρπαγὴν τῶν ὑπαρχόντων ὑμῶν [50] μετὰ χαρᾶς προσδέξασθε γινώσκοντες ἔχειν ἑαυτοὺς κρείττονα ὕπαρξιν καὶ μένουσαν. Just as Christ could accept his humiliation with "joy" (12:2), the church also has accepted its alienation "with joy." The reason for the community's endurance is to be seen in the play on words ὑπάρχοντα . . . ὕπαρξις. Ὕπαρξις, which means "substance" or "existence,"[51] is contrasted with ὑπάρχοντα, "property." Ὕπαρξις is used regularly in Philo for "the existent," i.e., God (de Op. Mund. 170; de Som. 1. 231; de Dec. 83), and is connected especially with God's eternity. In Hebrews it obviously refers to the heavenly reality, of which the readers have become partakers (cf. 3:1). Κρείττων is regularly used in contexts which describe the metaphysical superiority of the Christian possession.[52] Μένουσα also is regularly used in Hebrews for the metaphysical superiority and stability characteristic of the heavenly world.[53] The "abiding possession" is equivalent, therefore, to the "abiding city" of 13:14 and to the "city" which the exemplars of faith have sought (cf. 11:11, 16; 12:22). Γινώσκοντες ἔχειν . . . ὕπαρξιν expresses the church's relationship to the better possession. Ἔχειν is regularly used for the Christian possession of access to God in the heavenly world (cf. 4:14; 10:19; 13:14). Γινώσκεντες, expressing the church's relationship to the stable possession, is equivalent to "seeing" in 11:13, 26, 27. Philo uses the term on several occasions with ὕπαρξις (cf. de Post. Cain. 168; de Som. 1. 231; de Spec. Leg. 35) to describe

---

[48] Similar solidarity in persecution is reported by Philo, In Flac. 72.

[49] In 10:33 the author uses terminology in describing Christian solidarity similar to the language of Christ's solidarity with his people. Cf. συνεπαθήσατε in 10:34 and συμπαθῆσαι in 4:15. Cf. κοινωνοὶ in 10:33 and κεκοινώνεκεν . . . μετέσχεν in 2:14. The people of God maintain the same solidarity with each other as they have been granted by Christ.

Several important witnesses have δεσμοῖς μου (κ D² K). However, only δεσμοῖς fits the context, which concerns the sufferings of the readers, while the alternate reading is found in Paul (Phil 1:7, 13, 14, 17).

[50] Cf. Polybius 4. 17. 4, ἁρπαγὰς τῶν ὑπαρχόντων; 4 Macc 4:10, ἡ τῶν χρημάτων ἁρπαγή. Michel, Hebräer, 359.

[51] BAG, 845; LSJ, 1853.

[52] See 1:4; 6:9; 9:23; 11:16; 12:24. See Chapter VIII of this study.

[53] See Heb 7:3, 23; 12:27; 13:14. Cf. Chapter III of this study.

one's relationship to the existent.[54] This relationship to the stable possession, according to 10:34, provided the church's basis for enduring.

It is striking to observe the extent to which 10:32-35 anticipates the essay on faith in its content. Indeed, the readers are themselves the exemplars of the stance which the author wants to inculcate in chapter 11. They have exhibited a remarkable endurance in their Christian lives analogous to that stance which is described in chapter 11. Their enduring of ὀνειδισμός is similar to the experience described in 11:26. Both in chapter 11 and in 10:32-34, the capacity to endure presupposes a relationship to the unseen world.

Undoubtedly a call for endurance that is based on hope is common in all of the literature which concerns persecution. In 4 Maccabees, the author says on more than one occasion that the faithful mortals were driven on by the hope of immortality.[55] Philo shares with Hebrews the conviction that access to a stable reality gives one steadfastness.[56] He also shares the indifference toward material things which would allow one to accept the loss of material things "with joy."[57]

The imperative of 10:35 is parallel to the historical description of 10:32-34, as it encourages the readers to exhibit the same behavior in the present as they had exhibited in the past. Μὴ ἀποβάλητε οὖν τὴν παρρησίαν is closely related to ὑπεμείνατε (10:32), as failure to endure is equivalent to throwing away one's confidence. Παρρησία, like ὑπομονή, suggests certainty and steadfastness. In Hebrews it is specifically regarded as a gift granted through the work of Christ (10:19; 4:14-16). Ἀποβάλητε is a strong word, suggesting the "throwing away" of a precious gift (cf. 3:6; 4:14).[58] Just as in the past the "abiding possession" provided steadfastness, in 10:35 the Christian expects the μισθαποδοσία. This word, which is used only in Hebrews (2:2; 11:26; cf. 11:6, μισθαποδοσία), is employed both in 11:6, 26 in descriptions of the nature of faith. Thus the imperative of 10:35 calls for the same stance which is mentioned in 11:6, 26. Παρρησία is thus closely identified with πίστις, inasmuch as both are oriented toward the "reward." Thus according to

---

[54] Philo can describe one's relationship to the "existent" both in terms of "knowing" and "seeing" (*de Virt.* 215; *de Praem. Poen.* 45-46).

[55] 4 Macc 16:25; 17:12, 18.

[56] Cf. especially *de Som.* 2. 223-237; *de Post. Cain.* 23; *de Gig.* 49-54.

[57] The goal of faith, according to Philo, is detachment from the world, which is to be seen in one's indifference to all earthly things, including fame, honor, wealth, beauty, and health. Compared to the eternal, all earthly things are only transitory goods (*de Sac. A.C.* 129; *Quod Det. Pot.* 136, 157; *de Congress.* 25). Philo praises the Therapeutae for their indifference to the worldly possessions (*de Vit. Contemp.* 19f.). See Völker, *Fortschritt*, 138-141. E. Brehier, *Idées*, 221.

[58] C. Spicq, *Hébreux*, 2. 330. Cf. Dio Chrysostom, *Or.* 34 (17). 39, δέδοικα μὴ τελέως ἀποβάλητε τὴν παρρησίαν. Windisch, *Hebräerbrief*, 97.

10:35, the church in the present is called on to imitate both its past behavior (10:32-34) and the stance of past believers.

It is in the language of reward that Hebrews is most distinguishable from the philosophical reflection of the period. While Plato shared with Hebrews the positive appreciation of endurance for the sake of the good, the former rejected the notion of moral striving for the sake of reward.[59] Philo speaks frequently of a reward, but in most instances this reward was experienced primarily in the present life.[60] Nevertheless, no document from the Jewish tradition could completely exclude the idea of recompense, which has a significant place in the OT. Thus both Philo and 4 Maccabees are certain that a recompense follows death.[61]

The imperative of 10:35 is followed by a continuing reference to the readers' situation in 10:36. Once more ὑπομονή stands in a close relationship with παρρησία in 10:35. Κομίσησθε τὴν ἐπαγγελίαν, which is equivalent to receiving the reward in 10:35, also occurs in 11:13, 19, 39 as the goal of πίστις (cf. 6:12). In Hebrews ἐπαγγελία does not refer, as it does in the Pauline literature, to the promise which has already been fulfilled in Christ. For Hebrews, the faithful "did not receive the promise"[62] Thus the promise of entering his "rest" still remains open (4:1). Indeed, it is the confidence in the reliability of God as ὁ ἐπαγγειλάμενος (10:23) which gives the church stability in the present (cf. 6:17-19). The ἐπαγγελία of Hebrews is, therefore, the equivalent of κατάπαυσις (chs. 3-4) and the heavenly city of chapter 11. It is the goal of the people of God to "go out" on their pilgrimage.

In view of the fact that ἐπαγγελία is an important category in the NT, it is striking that the term is seldom used in the LXX. The term was developed in a later period, and in the apocalyptic literature it came to be used for the eschatological hope.[63] Hebrews stands closer to that tradition than to Paul, for ἐπαγγελία is used here for the final goal of the people of God. Nevertheless, Hebrews is not fully in the tradition found in 2 Baruch and 4 Ezra, for the author lacks the "materialism" that is characteristic of the apocalyptic

---

[59] E. Würthwein, Μισθός, TDNT 5. 704. Plato, Rep. 2. 367d; 10. 612b.

[60] de Som. 2. 34; de Plant. 134, 136. Cf. especially the tractate de Praem. Poen., where Philo indicates the various rewards which were given to the sages (1-56).

[61] On 4 Maccabees, cf. above, note 55. On Philo, see Leg. All. 1. 80, "There is a reward" (Gen 30:18). In Quis Rer. Div. 26, Philo speaks of "something better than a reward." On Philo's belief in immortality, cf. de Ab. 204; Q.Gen. 4. 11; Quis Rer. Div. 249-263; 313-315; Leg. All. 3. 40-44, 203; de Virt. 207, 216; de Som. 2. 244. See. S. Sandmel, "Virtue and Reward in Philo," 217.

[62] 11:13, 39; cf. however, 6:12.

[63] Cf. 4 Ezra 4:27; 5:40; 7:119; 2 Baruch 51:3. J. Schniewind and G. Friedrich, Ἐπαγγελία, TDNT 2. 580.

literature.⁶⁴ He anticipates the coming of the stable, unshakable city, promised (12:26) in the future.

The quotation of Hab 2:4, cited with the author's own theological interests in evidence, is intended to buttress the appeal of 10:35-36, as ἔτι γάρ indicates. The passage is frequently cited by Paul and by contemporary Judaism, with each writer actualizing it for his own needs.⁶⁵ For Paul the text of Habakkuk conveyed the doctrine of justification by faith in Christ.⁶⁶ In Qumran, the passage is a reference to the community's need for faithfulness to the law in a time of struggle.⁶⁷ The author's reshaping of the LXX text allows him to see in the passage the contrast between two modes of behavior in a time of struggle: πίστις and ὑποστολή. Ὁ ἐρχόμενος is a reference to the Messiah's return.⁶⁸ Πίστις is no longer, as in the LXX, a reference to God's faithfulness;⁶⁹ it is a reference to the stance of the believer. The community, which holds to the belief in the promise of the end-time (cf. 9:27; 12:25-27), lives by πίστις.

The meaning of faith in Hebrews becomes apparent in the contrast between πίστις and ὑποστολή in 10:39. Ὑποστολή, which is used only here in the NT (cf. ὑποστέλλω in v. 38; Acts 20:20, 27; Gal 2:12), means "hold back."⁷⁰ Its equivalent in Hebrews can be seen in the reference to apostasy (3:12) and to "deliberate sin" in 10:26. Against this background πίστις means steadfastness. It is thus closely related to ὑπομονή and παρρησία, signifying the steadfastness of the one who, despite suffering and disappointment, maintains his orientation toward God.

E. Grässer correctly says that this understanding of faith is far removed from the Pauline view, and that Hebrews stands closer to the prophetic idea of the righteous one whose steadfastness allows him to remain firm in wait-

---

⁶⁴ See chapter 3 for the author's reshaping of apocalyptic assumptions.

⁶⁵ Cf. 1QpHab on Hab 2:4. On the exegesis of Hab 2:4 in Judaism, see Michel, *Hebräer*, 364-365. See also D. Lührmann, "Pistis in Judentum," 35. Discussions of faith in Judaism were normally given in connection with Deut 9:23; 2 Kgs 17:14, and Hab 2:4. Non-Greek-speaking Judaism demonstrated a strong emphasis on faith analogous to that which is found in Philo, 4 Maccabees, and Wisdom. Lührmann, "Pistis in Judentum," 36.

⁶⁶ Lührmann, "Pistis in Judentum," 37. E. Grässer, *Der Glaube*, 44. Dautzenberg, "Glaube," 171.

⁶⁷ Lührmann, "Pistis in Judentum," 35.

⁶⁸ Cf. Matt 3:11; 11:3; 21:9. The addition of the article ὁ to the LXX text allows the author to give a messianic interpretation to the text. E. Grässer, *Glaube*, 43.

⁶⁹ In Hebrews, μου is removed from πίστεως to δίκαιος, thus connecting faith with the response of the people. Although this reading is not found in many manuscripts, the reading ὁ δὲ δίκαιός μου ἐν πίστεως is supported by p⁴⁶, and is to be preferred. Alternative readings in D p¹³ probably resulted either from a scribe's knowledge of the LXX or from a knowledge of Paul's citation, Rom 1:17; Gal 3:10.

⁷⁰ W. Bauer, *Lexicon*, 855.

ing on God.[71] However, πίστις cannot be explained only against the background of the OT. The view represented in Hebrews is similar in some respects to 4 Maccabees, where the martyrs, who believed in the future, were exemplars of both ὑπομονή and πίστις (4 Macc 15:24; 16:22; 17:2). Philo also held that πίστις is oriented toward a stable reality, allowing one to find security not in this creation, but in the one who is stable (see p. 61). Hebrews and Philo both identified πίστις and παρρησία,[72] and both connected πίστις with the steadfastness of the one who is oriented to the unseen and abiding world. Such a stance gives one an indifference to this world, allowing the believer to accept the confiscation of property "with joy" (10:34). The author's reflections on πίστις in 10:32-39 anticipate the further treatment of the subject in chapter 11.

Pistis in Hebrews 11

The reference to πίστις in 10:39 is the transition to the major development of the theme in chapter 11, a chapter so distinctive in its rhetorical style that its relationship to the rest of Hebrews has been questioned.[73] Although the rhetorical style has analogies to the Jewish literature of the period, there is an obvious relationship between this chapter and the rest of the epistle. This relationship is to be seen in the fact that the theme of both 10:32-39 and 12:1-11 is the idea of ὑπομονή in suffering. This ὑπομονή is connected in both sections with πίστις. The purpose of chapter 11, with its introductory ἔστιν δέ and its repeated πίστει, is to provide the foundation for this appeal to the church to endure through suffering. This foundation instructs the community in the nature of the πίστις called for in 10:39 by giving both a general statement about πίστις (11:1, 3) and by describing the exemplars whose lives were "witnesses" (cf. 11:2) to the nature of faith.[74]

---

[71] E. Grässer, *Glaube*, 44. Grässer is incorrect, however, in arguing that πίστις in Hebrews is not used in a christological connection (cf. 146-147). Πίστις and ἐλπίς both presuppose the christology of Hebrews, according to which "unwavering faith" is based on the work of Christ in opening (10:19-20) the way to the heavenly world.

[72] Völker, *Fortschritt*, 254.

[73] On the rhetorical form of chapter 11, see H. Windisch, *Hebräerbrief*, 98. Windisch suggests the existence of a Jewish *Vorlage*. Cf. C. Spicq, *L'Épître aux Hébreux*, 1. 76. While Jewish models for Hebrews 11 are certainly to be found in such texts as 4 Macc 16:16-23; Sir 44-50; Philo, *de Virt.* 198-205, the content of chapter 11 suggests that the work is the author's composition.

[74] The author has not collected his list of "witnesses" from OT texts which speak of faith. Indeed, he cites only one text which has the word πίστις. This reading is, of course, dictated by the author's interests. D. Lührmann ("Pistis," 19-38) has shown that πιστεύω/אמן became a major category for describing man's relationship to God only in the Hellenistic Age. In Greek-speaking Judaism, according to Lührmann, "ist Philo . . . der erste und einzige, der ent-

Ἔστιν δὲ πίστις in 11:1 obviously refers back to 10:39, where πίστις was the equivalent of ὑπομονή. While the phrase appears to introduce a definition, 11:1 does not provide a complete definition of πίστις, for there are elements of the subject which are not brought within the scope of πίστις in 11:1.[75] Nevertheless, 11:1 is a foundational statement for the rest of chapter 11, as 11:2 indicates. The men of the past gave their witness ἐν ταύτῃ; i.e., within the scope of faith given in 11:1.

In 11:1 πίστις is described in a way which makes apparent the author's philosophical training. Πίστις is described with the parallel phrases, ἐλπιζομένων ὑπόστασις, πραγμάτων ἔλεγχος οὐ βλεπομένων. Πίστις "is," therefore, both ὑπόστασις and ἔλεγχος. Its object is "things hoped for" and "things not seen." Such a statement, with its use of words from a philosophical background,[76] is far removed from the descriptions of faith in Paul or other early Christian literature. In fact, while the terminology is strongly influenced by Greek philosophy, it is scarcely connected with πίστις in Greek literature. The author's relationship to both biblical and classical sources can be determined only by an examination of the language of 11:1.

The parallelism of ὑπόστασις and ἔλεγχος indicates that the two terms must be interpreted in light of each other. Ἔλεγχος has the basic meaning, "proof," "means of proof," "refutation," or "conviction." The term does not refer to a subjective belief, but to the "proof" of a matter.[77] In Philo, the term often has the meaning "proof" or "means of refutation." The phrase, πραγμάτων ἔλεγχος οὐ βλεπόμενων, is "the most Greek of all Greek concepts," according to E. Grässer.[78] The combination with πράγμα is analogous to the usage in Greek literature, where it was used for "the proof of the matter."[79] Thus ἔλεγχος suggests that faith is "proof."

Faith is also characterized as ὑπόστασις, a term which has been very problematic for interpreters. The term is derived from the verb ὑφίστημι, which means "support," "set under" (as a support), or "settle" (as with a sediment).[80] Consequently, the basic meaning of the noun is *hypo-stasis*, "to

schlossen *pistis* als Begriff aufnimmt zur Bezeichnung dessen, was das Spezifikum des Judentums ist" (32).

[75] Spicq (*L'Épître aux Hébreux* 1. 76) describes 1:1 as a definition analogous to statements in Philo where ἐστι comes at the beginning of an explication of a theme. Such a parallel is of limited value for suggesting a relationship between the two writers, as the function of such statements is very different. Williamson, *Philo*, 309–310.

[76] Windisch, *Hebräerbrief*, 99.

[77] F. Büchsel, Ἔλεγχος, *TDNT* 2. 476.

[78] E. Grässer, *Der Glaube*, 126.

[79] Epictetus, *Diss.* 3. 10, 11.

[80] LSJ, 1895. H. Köster, Ὑπόστασις, *TDNT* 8. 572.

stand under."⁸¹ The word thus was used in a metaphorical sense for reality. In Hebrews its meaning must be ascertained from its usage elsewhere in the epistle (1:3; 3:14), from common Greek usage, and from the parallel to ἔλεγχος.⁸² The parallel to ἔλεγχος suggests the translation "reality," which is common in Greek literature. The same meaning is also appropriate for 1:3, where Christ is the χαρακτήρ of the "reality" of the transcendent God. According to 3:14 this "reality" is a fact to which the community must hold. This ὑπόστασις is, according to 11:1 (cf. 1:3), invisible and transcendent. "Reality" is not found in those things which are present and visible, but in those things which are "hoped for" and "invisible." Ὑπόστασις, meaning "reality," is parallel to ὕπαρξις in 10:34. The two terms both can be rendered "reality." In Hebrews the terms describe a reality that is transcendent.⁸³

To interpret ὑπόστασις as "invisible, transcendent reality" is not only consistent with Hebrews in general; this interpretation is consistent also with Philo and Middle Platonism. Although Philo uses the term ὑπόστασις only three times, his perspective is evident also in his use of the verb ὑφίστημι, which denotes real existing as distinguished from mere appearance.⁸⁴ Thus the verb is used only of the soul and of God.⁸⁵ Thus he says in *Quod Det. Pot.* 160, ἐπεὶ καὶ ὁ θεὸς μόνος ἐν τῷ εἶναι ὑφέστηκεν. In *Quod Deus Immut.* 177, he contrasts ὑποστῆναι and purely shadowy existence. In *de Som.* 1. 88, Philo contrasts the shadowy existence in this world with the world of intelligible reality (νοητῆς ὑποστάσεως). Similarly, in Albinus the term is used for the reality of the intelligible world.⁸⁶

The faith of Hebrews 11:1 is thus "reality" and "proof," not subjective experience. H. Köster argues that the terms ὑπόστασις and ἔλεγχος say nothing about the nature of faith itself, but rather about the reality of the transcendent things.⁸⁷ Thus, according to Köster, ὑπόστασις is reality and not realization. Such a view is obviously plausible on the basis of the grammar of 11:1. However, one must consider that 11:1 is a rhetorical statement that is intended to summarize the nature of faith, as it is further described in

---

⁸¹ E. Grässer, *Glaube*, 48.
⁸² Köster, Ὑπόστασις, 585.
⁸³ For ὕπαρξις in Philo, see above, p. 65.
⁸⁴ Williamson (*Philo*, 343) argues that ὑπόστασις occurs only three times in Philo, and that the category bears no relationship to Hebrews, as there is no great verbal similarity in the use of ὑπόστασις. However, the important issue here is the view of reality shared by the two writers. Both understand reality as invisible.
⁸⁵ Köster, *TDNT* 8. 583.
⁸⁶ *Didask.* 25. 1. Köster, *TDNT* 8. 577.
⁸⁷ Köster, *TDNT* 8. 587. "Hence one should not ask how far faith is ὑπόστασις, but what ὑπόστασις has to say about the things hoped for."

10:32-39 and 11:3-40. Comparison with these passages indicates an emphasis on the believer's experience. Indeed, an instructive parallel to 11:1 is offered in 10:34, where the πίστις/ὑπομονή of the community is the issue. The church has survived the struggle of faith in the same way as the heroes of chapter 11, γινώσκοντες ἔχειν ἑαυτοὺς κρείττονα ὕπαρξιν καὶ μένουσαν. The "better possession" is obviously the transcendent heavenly world. Ὕπαρξις is parallel to ὑπόστασις in 11:1. Thus in 10:34 the church lives by its knowledge (γινώσκοντες) of the better possession.

The emphasis on "knowing" (11:3), "remembering" (11:22), and "seeing" (cf. 11:13, 26) in chapter 11 indicates further that πίστις is a "realization" of the transcendent reality. Πίστις, therefore, is not only "reality" and "proof." It is also a "knowledge" and perception of the unseen world. Thus the repeated πίστει means "in the recognition of what constitutes true reality."

The translation of ὑπόστασις as "realization" is compatible not only with the epistemological words of chapter 11. It is also compatible with the view of πίστις in other texts in Hebrews. The term in 10:39 is the equivalent of ὑπομονή. Ἀπιστία is the equivalent of ἀποστασία (3:12, 19). Thus πίστις obviously contains an element of "steadfastness" in relation to the stable possession of the heavenly world.

The parallelism of ἐλπιζομένων and οὐ βλεπομένων is a typical example of the author's combination of categories from both the Hebrew and Hellenistic traditions. That faith is connected with hope or promise is a common assumption outside the biblical tradition and among Greek philosophers.[88] For Philo, πίστις is the "fulfillment of bright hopes."[89] The connection between πίστις and ἐλπίς in Hebrews has already been indicated in such parallel passages as 6:11 (πληροφορία τῆς ἐλπίδος) and 10:22 (πληροφορία πίστεως). This identification of faith and hope is also to be found in both Philo and the OT.[90] In 3:6 (cf. 3:14); 6:18; 10:23, the term is indistinguishable from πίστις, for it concerns the unwavering stability of God's people which has been made possible by Christ's exaltation (6:18-19). The Christian lives in the awareness of a promise of entering God's rest which still remains open (4:1, 3, 9, 11).

The importance of ἐλπίς is demonstrated in the remainder of chapter 11, where the author employs a variety of terms to demonstrate that faith

---

[88] Faith was regularly connected with God's providence. Cf. Plutarch, *Pyth. Or.* 18; on faith and promise, cf. Seneca, *Ep.* 71. 17.

[89] *de Ab.* 268.

[90] In the OT, faith frequently can be used in the sense of "waiting on God." Cf. Hab 2:4. Cf. also G. Dautzenberg, "Der Glaube," 163.

involves ἐλπίς. Noah, for example, built the ark after being warned περὶ τῶν μηδέπω βλεπομένων. Sarah's faith was based on the fact that πιστὸν ἡγήσατο τὸν ἐπαγγειλάμενον (11:11). Similarly, Abraham offered Isaac, ὁ τὰς ἐπαγγελίας ἀναδεξάμενος (11:17). Isaac blessed Jacob, having looked to "the things to come" (περὶ μελλόντων). According to 11:26, Moses looked toward the reward (μισθαποδοσίαν, cf. 11:6). Thus πίστις in Hebrews is forward-looking, for πίστις is closely identified with hope.

The reference in 11:1 to faith as ἐλπίς does not, by itself, distinguish Hebrews from Philo, who also connected πίστις with promise and hope. Nevertheless, ἐλπίς in Hebrews presupposes a view of the future which would have been unacceptable to Philo, for Hebrews has not denied the early Christian expectation of the return of Christ (9:27; 10:25; 10:36-39). Thus ἐλπιζομένων in 11:1 points to the expectation of a final eschatological event.[91]

It is significant that ἐλπιζομένων is parallel to οὐ βλεπομένων, for the parallelism indicates the connection between the author's temporal and spatial dualism. The contrast between the visible and the invisible realities was fundamental to Platonic dualism. According to *Phaedo* 79A, δύο εἴδη τῶν ὄντων, τὸ μὲν ὁρατόν, τὸ δὲ ἀειδές.[92] The same distinction appears regularly in Philo.[93] This distinction between the visible and the invisible is also to be seen in the phrase ἀόρατον ὡς ὁρῶν in 11:27. It is not correct to reduce οὐ βλεπόμενα to τὰ μηδέπω βλεπόμενα, as Williamson has done.[94] The author has a distinctive spatial dualism by which he distinguishes between the material and heavenly world. Οὐ βλεπομένων is equivalent to such terms as οὐ ψηλαφημένος (12:18), ἀσάλευτος (12:28), and οὐ χειροποίητος (9:11), all of which use the negative to indicate the distinction between the two spheres of reality. The world that is "unseen" is the abiding and stable reality (12:27-28). For Hebrews 11:1, faith is not only the recognition of the future reality. It is also the "proof" and realization of the metaphysically superior and stable reality. Just as believers in 12:28 "receive an unshakable kingdom," here they have the proof of the unseen reality (cf. 10:34).

The superior reality is further described in chapter 11 with the imagery drawn from the political sphere. Over against this *kosmos* (11:7, 38), which

[91] For Hebrews' combination of Platonic metaphysics and eschatological hope, see Chapter III of this study. Such a combination is not uncommon, as it is attested in texts which were influenced by both Platonism and the OT, particularly in Gnosticism. The Gnostic apocalypses commonly combine eschatological expectation with the Platonic words for transcendence.

[92] Cf. Plato, *Rep.* 6. 509d; 7. 524c. Ὁρατός is the opposite of νοητός. Cf. *Rep.* 7. 524c.

[93] Philo adopts and extends the view and terminology of Plato. Ἀόρατος and ὁρατός are regularly contrasted with each other. See W. Michaelis, *TDNT* 5. 368.

[94] R. Williamson, *Philo*, 340.

is never the home of the believer, one is called to seek another πατρίς (11:14) and πόλις (11:10, 16). These terms are equivalent to οὐ βλεπομένων in 11:1. The use of these terms to describe the unseen world is a familiar theme in Philo's writings. In Philo's description of our existence as strangers in a strange land, he refers to our real home with the terms πατρίς and πόλις (see above, p. 59). Although for Philo the πόλις is invisible, it is perceptible to the believer through his special capacity to see the invisible (*de Plant.* 17; *de Praem. Poen.* 27). Philo and Hebrews, despite basic differences in their views,[95] share a common view of faith as the stranger's belief in a transcendent city. Despite differences between Philo and Hebrews in their descriptions of the πόλις, Hebrews stands closer to Philo in his use of common terminology than to any other known writer of the period.[96]

The description of faith, which is similar but not identical to Philo's view, is supplemented by the further explanation in 11:3. Faith involves knowing that the world was created by the word of God, an affirmation that was assumed in Judaism. The affirmation logically follows 11:1, for it is not concerned with the first in the list of witnesses, but with the nature of faith itself. Indeed, πίστει νοοῦμεν is implied in 11:1, where πίστις is "realization." The point of the statement is in 11:3b, which continues the description of 11:1: εἰς τὸ μὴ ἐκ φαινομένων τὸ βλεπόμενον γεγονέναι. Thus 11:3a, which transfers the OT view of creation into the terms of Greek ontology, provides the presupposition for the articular infinitive of 3b. E. Grässer correctly observes that 11:3 presents a remarkable combination of faith and religious knowledge. "Es geht um die Erkenntnis, dass die sichtbare Welt nicht den Grund-Satz von den alleinigen Realität des unsichtbare Welt aufhebt, weil sie selber ihren Ursprung aus dem Unsichtbaren hat."[97]

---

[95] See Williamson, *Philo* 327. Cf. H. Braun, "Das himmlische Vaterland," 323. Both writers point to Philo's belief in the heavenly origin of the soul as a major difference between the two writers' view of the *polis*. There is also, as Braun shows (323), an asceticism and negative view of the body in Philo's statements which are not found in Hebrews. There is also a difference in the two writers' view of time (Braun, 323), as the *polis* of Hebrews is also a future city.

[96] Braun, "Vaterland," 320. "Dass die zwischen Philo und dem Hebräerbrief analoge Terminologie von 'himmlischen Vaterland' und 'Stadt Gottes' nicht auf einem Zufall beruht, geht daraus hervor, dass auch weitere mit diesen Begriffen verbundene Vorstellungsreihen sich auf beiden Seiten finden." Braun refers to the whole complex of concepts, including the idea of sojourning and the dualism of heaven and earth. "Beiderseits, bei Philo und im Hebräerbrief, wird der Dualismus von Himmel und Erde, von einheimischer Existenz und Fremdlingsdasein alttestamentlichen Texten entnommen, die in ihrem Wortsinn mit diesem Dualismus nichts zu tun haben. Um diesen Dualismus gleichwohl aus den Zitaten zu gewinnen, muss der zitierte Text modifiziert werden." Both Philo (*de Conf. Ling.* 76, 79) and Hebrews (11:9, 10) use OT texts with the same dualistic assumptions.

[97] Grässer, *Glaube,* 130. The combination of "faith" and "knowing" is a theme which the author of Hebrews shares with later Platonists. Cf. *CH* 9. 10. W. Theiler (*Vorbereitung,* 149-

The statement in 11:3 expresses the fundamental distinction between the two spheres of reality. The doctrine of creation implies for the author the dualism of the two spheres of reality. Τὸ βλεπόμενον[98] (cf. οὐ βλεπομένων in 11:1) is the material world, φαινόμενα. Φαινόμενα, which appears nowhere else in the NT, has a long history in Greek philosophy. The word is used for the world of appearance, in contrast to the invisible world.[99] Because the real world is the unseen (11:1), faith is not directed toward an unstable reality. Thus the heroes of 11:4-39 "knew" that the reality of the heavenly world (cf. 10:34) was qualitatively superior to the earthly existence. In the same way, Philonic faith presupposed a knowledge of the first cause of all things (de Conf. Ling. 141; de Mut. Nom. 155).

Having called the readers to faith and ὑπομονή in 10:36-39, the author describes πίστις in 11:1, 3 with categories drawn from Platonic dualism and the OT. The author demonstrates that faith is a recognition that reality is not to be found in the phenomenal world. It is a certainty of the transcendent and future world. It involves both ἐλπίς and ὑπομονή.[100] While the author does not deny the traditional eschatological categories, his interest is heavily influenced by Platonic dualism. What is said about knowledge in Plato is here said about faith.

The people of God have already demonstrated this faith, according to 10:34, in their recognition of the abiding reality. According to 11:2, the πρεσβύτεροι were witnesses to the same stance in life. Thus 11:2 is the transition to the recital of witnesses in 11:4-40. The author intends for the list to serve as an elaboration of 11:1-3. The names listed here are not connected with πίστις in the OT. Yet for the author they are witnesses of the description of 11:1-3, 6.

Faith, Sojourning, and Dualism

It is the knowledge that essential reality is not in the phenomenal world which allows the man of faith to be a stranger to this world.[101] Thus, because

---

151) has shown that the tendency in the later period was to elevate the role of faith to a position similar to knowledge.

[98] Τὰ βλεπόμενα is attested by several manuscripts (D² lat syr), and fits logically in 11:3. Τὸ βλεπόμενον is to be preferred, as it has superior attestation (κ p¹³), and is the more difficult reading. Cf. Windisch, Hebräer, 100.

[99] Cf. Philo, de Op. Mund. 16; de Conf. Ling. 172; CH 5. 1. God, the creator, is ἀφανής and the source of all things φανερά. Τὸ φαινομένων is equivalent to γεννητόν, the Platonic word for the material world.

[100] E. Käsemann, Gottesvolk, 22.

[101] Ibid., 24. "So wird Glaube zur getrosten Wanderschaft; weil Vergangenheit der Diatheke und Zukunft der Vollendung für ihn festliegen, findet er die Kraft zur Überwindung der irdischen Gegenwart."

the πρεσβύτεροι sought another homeland (11:10, 14, 16), they were indifferent to their own land. Indeed, there are two passages in chapter 11
where κόσμος is used in a decidedly negative way. According to 11:7 Noah,
by his act of faith, κατέκρινεν τὸν κόσμον. The summary statement of 11:38
expresses this anti-worldliness in even stronger terms. The description of the
men of faith is followed by the statement, ὧν οὐκ ἄξιος ὁ κόσμος. One may
compare the dualistic use of κοσμικός in 9:1. In Hebrews κόσμος/κοσμικός
refers specifically to the earthly sphere in contrast to the heavenly world in the
same way as κτίσις in 9:11. Thus the man of faith, by recognizing that true
reality is the unseen world, condemned (κατέκρινεν, 11:7) this world, which
was not worthy of him. Such a usage of κόσμος implies a strong dualistic
orientation. As with Philo, πίστις involves a distrust of this creation
(ἀπιστία τῇ γενέσει).[102]

This distance from the creation is developed under the category of the
sojourner or stranger. Because the man of faith has a better possession
(10:34), his earthly existence is a sojourn. Abraham παρῴκησεν εἰς γῆν τῆς
ἐπαγγελίας ὡς ἀλλοτρίαν ἐν σκηναῖς κατοικήσας (11:9). In the summary of
11:13-16, the men of faith are characterized as ξένοι καὶ παρεπίδημοι ἐπὶ
τῆς γῆς. According to 11:38, those of whom the world was not worthy lived
ἐπὶ ἐρημίαις πλανώμενοι καὶ ὄρεσιν καὶ σπηλαίοις καὶ ταῖς ὀπαῖς τῆς γῆς.
Faith, therefore, involves living as a stranger and alien to this world.

Hebrews' references to sojourning in chapter 11 must be placed within
the larger context of the epistle. The image corresponds to the author's
imagery of pilgrimage, which appears throughout the book. The imagery is
associated with Christ's work as ἀρχηγός (2:10; 12:2) and πρόδρομος
(6:20).[103] The people of God are on the way to the heavenly κατάπαυσις
(chaps. 3-4), which is comparable to the entry before God in 10:19-20. In
other instances the author uses the image of the voyage (2:1; 6:19). Thus they
are encouraged to "go out" (13:13) and to "enter in" (4:11) as they follow the
pioneer. Indeed, chapter 11 employs ἐξελθεῖν (11:8; cf. 11:15, 22) for the life
of the believer.[104] The goal in each instance is the invisible πόλις or
κατάπαυσις.

The imagery of pilgrimage is used in other NT texts besides Hebrews.
However, although Hebrews differs from Philo at significant points, [105] its use
of terms for pilgrimage to describe alienation from this world is closer to

---

[102] On Philo, see above, p. 56-57. The dualistic use of *kosmos* in Hebrews 11 makes
Williamson's denial of dualism in Hebrews nothing less than astonishing. Cf. Williamson,
Philo, 328, 366.

[103] Käsemann, *Gottesvolk*, 24.

[104] Käsemann, *Gottesvolk*, 24.

[105] See *de Mut. Nom.* 209; *Leg. All.* 1. 108; *Quis Rer. Div.* 267.

Philo than to other NT texts. "Alienation" (11:9) in Hebrews is the fate of those whose home is in the invisible world and who "condemn" (11:7) this world. Although Hebrews does not connect this motif with the dualism of body and soul, as does Philo, the two writers share a complex of ideas: the concept of life as exodus,[106] of a present relationship to the heavenly reality, and the alienation from this world. The latter allows the believer to be indifferent to earthly possessions (cf. 10:34).[107] While the idea of living as a stranger is shared with other writers of the period,[108] Hebrews and Philo place it within a similar dualistic context which is influenced by Platonic thought.[109,110]

Faith as the Endurance of Suffering

The acceptance of the role of stranger implies that one will also suffer the indignities of the alien. Already, the recipients of Hebrews have suffered for their commitment (10:32-34). At the conclusion of the recitation of the exemplars of faith, chapter 12 resumes the exhortation to accept suffering (12:4-11), for suffering is the fate of the pilgrim (12:12). Thus in chapter 11 and 12:1-3, a major characteristic of those who were on their pilgrimage was the acceptance of suffering. Perhaps this assumption lies behind the reference to the death of Abel (11:4). Certainly Moses was a model of suffering, μᾶλλον ἑλόμενος συγκακουχεῖσθαι τῷ λαῷ τοῦ θεοῦ ἢ πρόσκαιρον ἔχειν ἁμαρτίας ἀπόλαυσιν (11:25). Indeed, in a startling anachronism, the author says that he shared τὸν ὀνειδισμὸν τοῦ χριστοῦ (11:26).

This concept of faith as the acceptance of suffering is the major feature of the recitation in 11:32-37, where the heroes acted διὰ πίστεως. Here heroism in war, martyrdom, and suffering stand together as examples of

---

[106] Cf. Philo, de Spec. Leg. 1. 43; Leg. All. 3. 29, 39, 48, 71; de Fug. 80, 94; de Ab. 86; de Sac. A.C. 70-71. Cf. Spicq, Hébreux, 1. 81.

[107] On Philo's indifference to worldly possessions, see especially de Vit. Contemp. 19-21. See above, p. 58.

[108] Cf. Eph 2:12-18; Jas 1:1; 1 Pet 1:1; 2:11; Diogn.; Ps. Phoc.

[109] See above, pp. 59-61. Cf. Plato, Phaedo 61e, περὶ τῆς ἀποδημίας ἐκεῖ; Phaedo 67b; Ap. 41a. Porphyry spoke of this life as an exile from heaven (ad Marc. 5).

[110] While the pilgrimage language of Hebrews is obviously drawn from the LXX (Gen 12:1-2; 23:4; 35:7), the motif of human existence as a journey is well-known in Greek literature. Especially under the influence of the theocentric interest of Middle Platonism, the goal of life was understood as a "flight" to God. Albinus (Didask. 81, 19) says that the end of human life is ἐνθένδε ἐκεῖσε φεύγειν ὅτι τάχιστα. See R. E. Witt, Albinus and the History of Middle Platonism, 123. The imagery of the voyage, which is employed in Heb 6:20, is also important for describing human existence in Philo (de Post. Cain. 142, 163), 4 Macc (7:3), Plato (Leg. 803a), and later in the work of Gregory Nazianzen. See B. Lorenz, "Zur Seefahrt des Lebens in den Gedichten des Gregorius von Nazianzen," VC 33 (1979) 234-245.

faith.[110a]The passage is strongly reminiscent of 4 Maccabees, in which the heroism of the martyrs was also an example of faith.

The public shame (ὀνειδισμός), which the readers have experienced (10:33), belongs to the very nature of faith (11:26; 13:13). "Dass die Glaubenswanderschaft zu allen Zeiten Durchzug durch ein Kampf- und Todeszone sein muss, war schon ausgeführt und wird am Beispiel Jesu noch einmal deutlich aufgewiesen" (12:1-3).[111] But the knowledge of the invisible reality meant that death is not the ultimate fact. The suffering of Moses was made possible by his "seeing the invisible" (11:26-27). The martyrs of 11:35 anticipated the resurrection. Even in death the blood of Abel continues to speak (11:4). The death of Jesus, which was also a model of faith, was the prelude to his exaltation to God's right hand (12:1-2).

R. Völkl correctly suggests that in Hebrews there is no suggestion of a flight from the world in an ascetic sense.[112] With 4 Maccabees, the author identifies πίστις with ὑπομονή in suffering. This endurance is the result of a definite world view in which one already belongs to another world.

A comparison of Philo's view is instructive at this point. Philo does not reflect on the subject of suffering with the intensity of the Epistle to the Hebrews, perhaps because of the different social situation in which he lived. Nevertheless, there are suggestions of Philo's view of suffering. The tractate *In Flaccum* describes the situation of Jews who were exposed to public shame.[113] In several texts he refers to suffering as a constituent part of mortal existence. Philo's imagery of the contest has numerous references to struggle and suffering, for the fate of the athlete is to suffer adversity.[114] Similarly, the suffering in Hebrews is placed within the imagery of the athletic contest (10:32; 12:1-2). In addition, the expectation of suffering is implied for both Philo and Hebrews in the notion of being a πάροικος, for this existence implies the acceptance of mockery from the world.[115]

Faith as "Seeing"

Although πίστις is oriented toward the invisible reality (11:1, 27), it

---

[110a]Windisch, *Hebräerbrief*, 105.

[111] Käsemann, *Gottesvolk*, 24.

[112] R. Völkl, *Christ und die Welt nach dem Neuen Testament*, 353.

[113] This tractate is a report of Jewish persecution by Flaccus, the prefect of Alexandria and Egypt. Because Philo's report is straightforward and historical, lacking any allegorical or theological interpretation, it is of only limited value in giving Philo's theology of suffering.

[114] See *de Cher.* 80-81; *Leg. All.* 3: 201; *de Congress.* 164; *de Jos.* 26, 223; *de Vit. Mos.* 106. Suffering is a part of the life of *askēsis*. Those whose goal is perfection must receive blows like the athlete in the arena.

[115] Völkl, *Christ und Welt*, 354. See especially *de Congress.* 164.

involves the paradoxical existence of "seeing the invisible" (11:27). Thus chapter 11 employs verbs for "seeing." The men of faith died without receiving the promises, according to 11:13, πόρρωθεν αὐτὰς ἰδόντες. According to 11:26, Moses ἀπέβλεβεν . . . εἰς τὴν μισθαποδοσίαν. Such seeing is comparable to "knowing" in 10:34 and 11:3.

R. Williamson incorrectly reduces the "seeing" in Hebrews 11 to "foreseeing."[116] While 11:7 implies that there is an element of "foreseeing" in Hebrews, the language cannot be reduced to that level of experience, for the terminology is rooted also in the Platonic dualism which is implied throughout chapter 11. Thus the idea of "seeing the invisible" is rooted in Platonic epistemology, where a special gift of sight allows one to gaze beyond the phenomenal world.[117]

It is particularly striking that Platonists connected this "seeing" with knowledge, and not with faith.[118] True intellectual striving was always a seeing, made possible by the eye of the soul. In Hebrews and Philo, this "seeing" is connected with faith. Thus Hebrews shares with Philo the use of Platonic epistemological categories to describe faith. Such a tendency to elevate πίστις and to identify it with νόησις was already present among the later Platonists. It was the achievement of Philo, according to D. Lührmann, that the Jewish appreciation of πίστις was combined with Greek philosophical categories, thus giving πίστις a dominant role in the apprehension of reality.[119] The author of Hebrews has made a similar contribution.

Conclusion

It is true, as E. Grässer has argued, that faith in Hebrews is very different from faith in the Pauline literature.[120] It is also true that there are important differences between πίστις in Philo and Hebrews. In fact, the view of faith in Hebrews cannot be equated with that of any source known to us. Hebrews shares with 4 Maccabees the identification of πίστις and ὑπομονή

---

116 Williamson, *Philo*, 340.

117 See Plato, *Symposium* 210-212. With the "eye of the soul" the truth is perceived. Cf. also *Rep.* 7. 527de.

118 R. Walzer (*Galen*, 56) quotes a statement made about Proclus: "Whenever he achieved a direct knowledge of transcendental sights, he no longer inferred the knowledge of those objects by way of syllogism, by discursive reasoning, and demonstration." Cited from Marinus, *Life of Proclus*, 22. In *CH* 7. 3, there is a spiritual and visionary apprehension of higher reality.

119 Philo, *de Mig. Ab.* 183; de *Praem. Poen.* 27, 36, 51, 58; *Leg. All.* 1. 43; 2. 34; *de Eb.* 82-83; *de Mut. Nom.* 81-82. C. Spicq, *Hébreux*, 1. 80; Luhrmann, "Pistis in Judentum," 31.

120 Grässer, *Glaube*, 66.

but has a metaphysical content not found in 4 Maccabees. Hebrews obviously gives πίστις an important role unparalleled in Greek philosophy. Thus it would be a mistake to equate Hebrews' view with that of any extant literature.

Although Hebrews is unique in many respects, the epistle has much in common with Philo. Both writers have taken a category which was relatively unimportant in Greek philosophy and employed it within the framework of Greek metaphysics. For both Philo and Hebrews, πίστις involves living as a stranger on earth and "seeing" a better reality. Thus both writers interpret πίστις within the assumptions of Platonic dualism. In fact, πίστις in Philo and Hebrews is hardly distinguishable from knowledge in the Platonic tradition. Although Hebrews has a future expectation which is not found in Philo, the writer shares the dualistic distinction between the phenomenal and invisible worlds. This distinction is the fundamental presupposition for his view of faith.

CHAPTER V

THE KATAPAUSIS MOTIF IN HEBREWS

Heb 3:7-4:11 has stood at the center of the debate over the conceptual world of the epistle. The passage is formally a midrash on Ps 95:7-11 and Gen 2:2, which are connected by means of the rabbinic interpretative principle, *gezera shawa*. The common word connecting the two passages is κατά-παυσις/καταπαύω, which allows the author to interpret the "rest" of the OT as the fulfillment of eschatological hopes.

While the author's method of employing the rabbinic *gezera shawa* is obvious to the exegete, it is not obvious why he chose to employ the category of "rest" in general. The term appears in only one other text in the NT as a soteriological word (Matt 11:28-30); in Hebrews it is limited to this midrash. It is extremely doubtful, as E. Käsemann has correctly argued, whether the author derives his categories merely from his exegesis of Scripture. It is probable that the OT serves as his anchor for speculation derived from other sources.[1] Scholarship has been sharply divided in determining which sources have made this framework useful for the author in Hebrews.

The motif of "rest" appears in such a variety of biblical and non-biblical sources that it is difficult to assess the parallels to Hebrews. The category belongs to general experience and is often used metaphorically. It is used metaphorically for salvation throughout the literature of antiquity.[2] E. Käsemann argued, on the basis of the word *anapausis* in Gnostic texts, that the *katapausis* speculation in Hebrews was rooted in Gnosticism. Käsemann, however, had few Gnostic texts at his disposal. His argument depended heavily on the assumption that Philo was a representative of a Gnostic movement.[3] Nevertheless, more recent studies have shown that *anapausis* was an important category in the Nag Hammadi texts, leading E. Grässer to affirm that Käsemann's position is "betstätigt."[4] O. Hofius has shown that

---

[1]   Käsemann, *Gottesvolk*, 44.

[2]   See C. Schneider, "Anapausis," *RAC* 1. 415.

[3]   Käsemann, *Gottesvolk*, 40-45. See also C. Colpe, "Philo," *RGG*³ 5. 345. Philo stands under various philosophical influences, including those of Platonism, Stoicism, and Neopythagoreanism. The influence of Gnostic traditions on Philo has not been demonstrated. Cf. O. Hofius, *Katapausis*, 254.

[4]   E. Grässer, "Der Hebräerbrief 1938-1963," *TRu* N.F. 30 (1964) 186.

"rest" and "sabbath" were important eschatological categories in rabbinic and apocalyptic literature, and has argued that the conceptual framework of Hebrews belongs to the apocalyptic matrix. The controversy itself suggests the difficulty of assessing the importance of various parallels.

O. Hofius has expressed his surprise at Käsemann's omission of rabbinic and apocalyptic parallels to Hebrews in his study of the *anapausis* motif. However, a similar criticism has been made of Hofius' work, as Hofius' first edition omitted serious consideration of Philo as a parallel to Hebrews.[5] Thus while parallels to *katapausis* in Hebrews have been collected, the complexity of the problem has been overlooked. Insufficient attention has been given to the conceptual framework within which the parallels function.

"Rest" as a Motif in the OT and in Jewish Literature

Gerhard Von Rad has shown the variety of meanings of *anapausis* (Hebrew מְנוּחָה) in the OT.[6] "Rest" in much of this literature is the promise of salvation from Israel's enemies (Deut 12:9-10; 25:19; Josh 21:43-45; 1 Kgs 8:56). It was later used for God's "resting" at the temple. The God who had given his people rest thus rests in Jerusalem (1 Chr 23:25; 2 Chr 6:41). In Psalm 95 that rest is identified as "God's rest," a gift to which the people of God may receive entry. It is thus a place of salvation, but not the earthly Canaan. This development in Psalm 95 provides a background for the eschatological category of "rest" in later Jewish literature. The "rest" of Psalm 95, which is at the same time "God's rest" and a possibility for the people of God, is no longer the earthly Canaan. Von Rad argues that this development provides the background to the eschatological *katapausis* of Hebrews.

Von Rad's argument would also suggest that the usage in Jewish literature in general has followed the development which he suggests for Hebrews. The importance of rest in this literature has been demonstrated by O. Hofius. Hofius demonstrates that the object of salvation, both in the apocalyptic and in the more "Hellenized" Jewish literature, was identified with rest. In documents which argue for a final catastrophe followed by a new creation (4 Ezra; 2 Baruch; 1 Enoch) and in those which speak of immortality in more Greek terms, salvation is identified with rest. Indeed, Hofius argues that *katapausis* in Hebrews has its closest parallel in 4 Ezra, where the rest of the blessed follows the eschatological catastrophe and the coming of the restored paradise and the new Jerusalem.

Hofius' important work brings together an impressive collection of texts

---

[5] See G. Theissen, *Untersuchungen zum Hebräerbrief*, 125-127.

[6] G. Von Rad, *Gesammelte Studien*, 101-108.

which speak of the eschatological rest. It is impossible within the scope of this chapter to examine the conceptual framework within which this motif appears. Hofius' summary adequately depicts this framework.

> Ganz gleich, ob wir es mit der Erwartung einer endzeitlichen, einer himmlisch-jenseitigen oder einer zwischenzeitlichen Ruhe zu tun haben, —immer gehört zu dieser Erwartung zugleich auch der Glaube an die Existenz eines für die Ruhe bereiteten Ortes hinzu. Häufig wird dieser Ruheort ausdrücklich mit dem Paradies identifiziert, und zwar je nach der eschatologischen Grundanschauung mit dem präexistenten end-zeitlichen Paradics (4 Esr 7:26b, 36, 121-125; 8:52; Test. Dan 5:12), mit dem jenseitigen Paradies (Slav. Hen. 8:3; 9:1; 42:3A; Apok. Sedr. Esdr. 16:5) oder mit dem zwischenzeitlichen Paradies der Seelen (Apok. Esdr. 1:12; rabbinische Literatur). . . . Der alttestamentliche Gedanke, dass das gelobte Land mit der heilige Stadt Jerusalem die Ruhestätte des Volk Gottes ist, lebt—eschatologisch umgeprägt und modifiziert—fort, wenn einige Texte den Ruheort der Seligen in dem neuen, bei Gott schon vorhanden Jerusalem (4 Esr. 7:26b; 8:52; Test Dan. 5:12) bzw. in dem erneuten irdischen Jerusalem (rabbinische Quellen) suchen oder andere Schriften den zwischenzeitlichen Ruheort der Seelen in himm-lischen Jerusalem finden wollen.[7]

"Rest," therefore, is a part of a total framework that includes the traditional apocalyptic, materialistic expectation of a new Jerusalem.

"Rest" as a Category of Greek Philosophy

The terms ἀνάπαυσις and κατάπαυσις appear only occasionally in the works of Greek philosophers, and have no important function in the history of Greek philosophy. Plato occasionally speaks of the repose of the philo-sopher, but the word appears to be unrelated to his metaphysical system. He recognizes the need for a rest from one's normal labors. Consequently, ἀνά-παυσις in *Tim.* 59C is the equivalent of ἡδονή. It is the pleasure which is associated with a pastime. In *Leg.* 1. 625B; 2. 653D; 4. 722C, he uses the verb for a station of repose where one stops on a long journey.[8]

In the *Timaeus*, where Plato distinguishes between the two levels of being, the categories of movement and immutability are important for dis-tinguishing the intelligible and material worlds. Here the material world is characterized by movement (κίνησις), while the world of ideas is ἀκίνητος

---

[7] Hofius, *Katapausis*, 74.
[8] A. J. Festugière, *Contemplation et vie contemplative selon Platon*, 457.

(*Tim.* 38A). The term ἀνάπαυσις, which becomes significant in a later period, is not used by Plato within this framework.

It is in the work of the two Alexandrians, Philo and Clement, that ἀνάπαυσις has a significance which it has neither in the Bible nor in the Greek philosophy of that period. Undoubtedly the significance of the term is at least partially explained by their relationship to each other and their common dependence on the Bible. Both writers cite passages which contain the word ἀνάπαυσις (or κατάπαυσις) and then elaborate on them. Their development of this motif is important as a comparison to the Epistle to the Hebrews, as they indicate one of the ways this biblical category was employed by those who had received philosophical training.

Although ἀνάπαυσις is not one of Philo's most frequently recurring categories, the term has a theological significance in his tractates. In most instances, Philo's use of the term is derived either from an OT citation (Exod 20:10/*de Cher.* 87), from the etymology of Noah's name,[9] or from biblical references to the Sabbath.[10] Thus Philo takes his starting point from Scripture. The significance of ἀνάπαυσις can be seen when one notices the categories with which it is used.

For Philo, ἀνάπαυσις belongs to the nature of God, "For in all truth there is but one thing in the universe which rests, that is God" (τὸ δὲ ἐν τοῖς οὖσιν ἀναπαυόμενον . . . ἕν ἐστιν ὁ θεός).[11] "Rest belongs in the fullest sense to God and to Him alone" (*de Cher.* 90, . . . μόνῳ θεῷ τὸ ἀναπαύεσθαι). These affirmations about God's rest belong to a wider category of Philo's regular argument that God is immutable, a subject to which Philo devoted an entire tractate. Thus Philo's work has consistent appeals to God's immutability. According to *de Post. Cain.* 28, God's nature is repose (ἠρεμία). He is also immovable (ἀκίνητος) and unchangeable (ἄτρεπτος). According to *de Som.* 2. 221, God stands "the same, immutable" (ἑστὼς ἐν ὁμοίῳ καὶ μένων, ἄτρεπτος ὤν). According to *de Som.* 2. 237, God is characterized by stability or fixity (στάσις καὶ ἵδρυσις). Ἀνάπαυσις, which Philo derives from Scripture quotations, is thus Philo's equivalent for other terms for the immutability of God.

Philo's use of ἀνάπαυσις and of the other terms for immutability belong within the matrix of his metaphysic. This fact is apparent in *de Post. Cain.* 28-29, where God's immutability is contrasted with the constant mutability of God's creation. "Quiescence and abiding are characteristic of God, but change of place (μετάβασις) and all movement (μεταβατικὴ πᾶσα κίνησις)

---

9   Cf. *Leg. All.* 3. 77.
10 *De Fug.* 174.
11 *De Cher.* 87.

is characteristic of the creation."[12] Similarly, Philo says in *de Post. Cain.* 23, "That which is unwaveringly stable is God, and that which is subject to movement is the creation" (τὸ μὲν οὖν ἀκλινῶς ἑστὼς ὁ θεός ἐστι, τὸ δὲ κινητὸν ἡ γένεσις).

The "rest" of God is frequently identified with the motif of the Sabbath. According to *de Cher.* 87, the Sabbath of Exod 20:10 is to be interpreted as "rest" (ἑρμηνεύεται δ' ἀνάπαυσις—"θεοῦ"). This interpretation allows Philo to describe the nature of God's immutability, a changelessness which incorporates his ceaseless activity. This connection of Sabbath and rest presupposes an interpretation of the creation story. However, more is involved than Philo's use of the creation story. There is also the Pythagorean number speculation, according to which seven was the symbol of absolute peace. Thus, according to *de Op. Mund.* 100, the number seven has an august and unique dignity.

> It is the nature of 7 alone, as I have said, neither to beget nor to be begotten. For this reason other philosophers liken this number to the motherless and virgin Nike, who is said to have appeared out of the head of Zeus, while the Pythagoreans liken it to the chief of all things; for that which neither begets nor is begotten remains motionless; for creation takes place in movement, since there is movement both in that which begets and in that which is begotten, in the one that it may beget, in the other that it may be begotten. There is only one thing that neither causes motion or experiences it, the original ruler and sovereign. Of Him 7 may be fitly said to be the symbol. Evidence of what I say is supplied by Philolaus in these words: 'There is,' he says, 'a supreme Ruler of all things, God, ever One, abiding (*monimos*), without motion (*akinētos*), Himself (alone) like unto Himself, different from all others.'[13]

In Philo's work, the terms ἀνάπαυσις and ἑβδομάς were symbols for transcendence. According to *Quis Rer. Div.* 216, seven is, as in *de Op. Mund.* 100, ἀμήτωρ. According to *de Ab.* 28, seven is the most peaceful of all numbers. According to *de Fug.* 173-174, a passage which alludes to the creation narrative and to Lev 25:6 ("The Sabbath of the land shall be a food for you"), peace and seven are identical. Thus Philo frequently took these

---

[12] Translations of Philo are taken from the *Loeb Classical Library*.

[13] See John Dillon, *The Middle Platonists*, 156-157. "The quotation from Philolaus is most interesting . . . as being evidence of the influence of Neopythagorean texts on the Platonism on which Philo is drawing." The influence of Pythagorean speculation on the number seven is evident in Alexandrian Judaism prior to Philo. Aristobulus interprets the seventh day of Genesis with Pythagorean number speculation, arguing that it is the principle of the number seven which orders the cosmos. Cf. N. Walter, *Der Thoraausleger Aristobulos*, 73-75. Cf. 150-171 on Jewish Pythagoreanism and the number seven.

terms from the Bible and placed them within the framework of his metaphysics, suggesting that the seventh day of Hebrew tradition was only a
symbol for a higher reality.

Although Philo argued that ἀνάπαυσις and ἑβδομάς were suitable
terms for describing God alone, he nevertheless argued that the Sabbath rest
of God was available to mortals.[14] According to *de Post. Cain.* 23, there is a
general principle that "proximity to a stable object produces a desire to be
like it and a longing for quiescence." Those who have, like Cain, turned to
the material world inhabit the land of "tossing" (σάλος). The foolish man is
averse to rest and quietness (24, ἠρεμία καὶ ἀνάπαυσις). It was only those
who "stood" by God who shared his stability (27-28). Philo finds references
to the "standing" of both Abraham (Gen 18:22-24) and Moses (Deut 5:31) in
God's presence. Thus "rest" and "standing" are equivalent terms for the
stability of those who stand by God.

The belief that mortals can share in God's stability is the background
for those passages which describe the goal of human existence as "resting in
God." According to *de Post. Cain.* 28, it is possible to share God's nature,
ἠρεμία. According to *Quod Deus Immut.* 12, the number seven refers to the
soul which "rests in God" (ἀναπαυομένης ἐν τῷ θεῷ ψυχῆς). According to
de Fug. 174, the most important goal of existence is the "rest in God" (ἡ ἐν
θεῷ ἀνάπαυσις). This rest in God involves the leaving of the unstable creation and the sharing with God in his nature.

These passages which speak of resting in God belong to a broader
context of Philonic thought. We have already observed that ἀνάπαυσις is the
equivalent of ἠρεμία. This motif of sharing in God's stability is to be seen
elsewhere in the Philonic corpus. According to *de Gig.* 49, "True stability
and immutable tranquility (στάσις τε καὶ ἠρεμία ἀκλινής) is that which we
experience at the side of God, who is himself immutable." According to *de
Som.* 2. 237, stability (στάσις) or permanent stability (ἵδρυσις) are possible
for the sage.

The wider context of Philonic thought demonstrates that ἀνάπαυσις
was a synonym for other terms for immutability. Such terms as στάσις and
ἠρεμία were terms used in the Platonic tradition in distinctions between the
immutable heavenly world and the changeable material world.[15] Philo's use
of ἀνάπαυσις belongs clearly within this tradition. His consistent way of
connecting ἀνάπαυσις and ἑβδομάς reflects his dependence on Pythagorean
speculation. The term ἀνάπαυσις, which did not have a corresponding place
in philosophical discussions, reflects Philo's use of the Hebrew Scriptures.

---

[14] On this motif, cf. J. Pascher, *Der Königsweg*, 228-239.
[15] On this theme, cf. R.E. Witt, *Albinus and the History of Middle Platonism*, 123-125,
133. Cf. H. Krämer, *Der Ursprung der Geistmetaphysik*, 232.

He employs the word within a Platonic metaphysical framework. It is therefore unnecessary to place Philo within a Gnostic context.

Philo's understanding of ἀνάπαυσις is continued in the work of Clement of Alexandria. In fact, it is obvious at several places that Clement is
dependent either on Philo or a tradition known to Philo. In other instances,
Clement appears merely to interpret the OT according to a pattern which is
found in Philo. Clement, like Philo, has an interest in OT texts which speak
of the ἀνάπαυσις and of the seventh day. Clement interprets these passages
with his own metaphysical assumptions.

Clement shares with Philo the belief that ἀνάπαυσις is the goal of the
believer. It is the blessed condition of the τέλειος and γνωστικός (*Paed.* 1. 6.
35. 1; *Strom.* 2. 11. 52. 4). The true ἀνάπαυσις is an eschatological concept.
Eternal rest is achieved ultimately in the heavenly Jerusalem (*Paed.* 1. 6. 45),
when the promise is finally fulfilled (*Paed.* 1. 6. 29). Then one receives
ἀνάπαυσις ἐν θεῷ (*Strom.* 7. 12. 68. 5; *Paed.* 1. 12. 102, 3-6).[16]

Ἀνάπαυσις is, as several passages indicate, an important metaphysical
word for Clement. This metaphysical connotation is evident in *Strom.* 6. 14.
108, for instance, where Clement cites Ps 14:1, "They will rest in the mountain of God." Clement then shows that this "rest" is for those who leave the
"seventh seat" (ἐν ἑβδομάδι ἀναπαύσεως) and proceed to the eighth grade
(εἰς ὀγδοαδικῆς). "Rest" is thus identified with both the Hebdomad and the
Ogdoad, the heavenly spheres. In *Strom.* 4. 25. 129, Clement speaks of the
"highest repose" (ἀκροτάτην ἀνάπαυσιν). In *Strom.* 5. 6. 36, Clement gives
an allegorical interpretation of the ark of the covenant in which he declines
to say whether it is symbolic of the κόσμος νοητός. Instead, he says that it
symbolizes the ἀνάπαυσις of the cherubim, who symbolize the number eight
(cf. *Strom.* 4. 25. 158. 4; 4. 25. 159. 30; 5. 6. 36. 3; 6. 14. 108. 1). Ἀνάπαυσις is
thus related to the number symbolism which was known also to Philo and to
the Pythagoreans. The identification of rest with the numbers seven and eight
has developed from the influence of Pythagoreanism on Platonic thought.

In *Strom.* 6. 16. 137-140, the number symbolism is developed in connection with biblical tradition. Clement finds significance in the fact that
God rested on the seventh day. Such a rest was a prelude to the future rest of
the believer. The nature of the rest is indicated by the number seven, which
ἀμήτορα καὶ ἄγονον λογίζονται. [17] Seven is the perfect number, as it symbolizes the highest sphere of being. Consequently, to rest in God is to ascend
beyond this creation and become impassible. Clement writes, ἀπαθεῖς
καθιστάμεθα, τὸ δέ ἐστιν ἀναπαύσασθαι (6. 16. 138). To rest is to share

---

16 Schneider, *RAC* 1. 416.
17 Cf. Philo, *de Op. Mund.* 100. Cf. also Heb 7:3.

God's being, for Clement concludes from God's resting on the Sabbath that God is "unwearied and impassible" (ἄκμητος καὶ ἀπαθής).

Ἀνάπαυσις has an importance for Clement which goes far beyond the significance of the term in the Bible or in Greek philosophy. Clement shares this category primarily with Philo, his Alexandrian predecessor. His use of the term within a metaphysical framework shows that he is influenced by the same Platonic and Pythagorean elements which were known to Philo. For both writers, ἀνάπαυσις and the number seven are biblical categories which are interpreted within a metaphysical framework.

"Rest" as a Gnostic Category

Ernst Käsemann correctly argued that ἀνάπαυσις was a major Gnostic category. Ἀνάπαυσις was frequently identified with the highest aeon, the place from which the individual came and to which the Gnostic will return. It was thus the place of the eschatological salvation. This place was, according to Käsemann, often connected with speculation about the Sabbath as the goal of the eschatological hope. "Die Sabbath-Vorstellung ist demnach hier in kosmisch-metaphysische Spekulationen eingebettet."[18]

While Käsemann's observations about the significance of ἀνάπαυσις in Gnosticism were largely correct, his analysis was severely limited by the paucity of sources at his disposal and by his citation of sources which are not indisputably Gnostic. The publication of the Nag Hammadi texts and subsequent research in other Gnostic materials have allowed a more thorough understanding of ἀνάπαυσις in Gnosticism. The appearance of the word in a variety of texts led E. Haenchen to describe ἀνάπαυσις as a specifically Gnostic concept.[19]

The Gnostic ἀνάπαυσις speculation is so variegated and the Gnostic systems so diverse that it would be difficult to find a consistent Gnostic concept of rest. In many texts, the usage is dependent on the citation of biblical materials. Thus it is one of several biblical categories used by Gnostics. In the *Unknown Gnostic Work* ἀνάπαυσις is one of several biblical terms which are ascribed to those who have γνῶσις. The term is associated with ἐλπίς, ἀγάπη, ἀνάστασις, and πίστις.[20] It can also be associated with eternal life. In the Gospel of Thomas, the term is sometimes dependent on synoptic usage (Matt 8:20/Luke 9:58; Matt 11:28-30). Thus in many

---

[18] Käsemann, *Gottesvolk*, 43.

[19] E. Haenchen, *Die Botschaft des Thomas-Evangeliums*, 72. M. Dibelius *Die Formgeschichte des Evangeliums*, 279-284, argued that ἀνάπαυσις in Matt 11:29 has a Gnostic background.

[20] C. Schmidt, *Koptisch-Gnostische Schriften*, 336, line 18.

instances, the Gnostic usage of ἀνάπαυσις is dependent on biblical and common usage where salvation is described as rest.

Although many texts employing ἀνάπαυσις are dependent on biblical usage, there is a prominence and consistency to the concept that is not found in the NT. This fact allows us to speak of ἀνάπαυσις as a major Gnostic category. In the variety of texts, there are some consistent features to the Gnostic usage.

The word ἀνάπαυσις is often used for God. In the *Unknown Gnostic Work*, ἀνάπαυσις designates the "Urvater,"[21] who is without substance (ἀνούσιος), still (ἤρεμος), and unknown (ἄγνωστος) in all rest. According to the Valentinians He is ἠρεμῶν καὶ ἀναπαυόμενος αὐτὸς ἐν ἑαυτῷ μόνος (Hipp. *Ref.* 6. 29. 5). He is known in the *Gos. Truth* 42:22 as the "one who rests." In other instances Christ is described as "rest" (*Act. Th.* c. 60=177. 10-12). God is frequently addressed in prayer as ἀνάπαυσις.[22] In the *Unknown Gnostic Work*, he is praised in the following terms:

> I praise you, O still One (ἤρεμος) of light
> . . .
> I praise you, O Rest.[23]

In addition to being a term for God, ἀνάπαυσις is also the term for the highest aeon of the heavenly world. "Die 'Ruhe' ist schlechterdings eine rein lokale Grösse, eine himmlische Ortsbezeichnung."[24] According to *Soph. Jes. Chr.* 110:5-7, "The first (aeon) is called "Unity and Rest" (ἀνάπαυσις). According to *Ap. John* 26:6-8, "His aeon is everlasting; he is in rest and rests in silence." In many instances ἀνάπαυσις is connected with speculation about *Hebdomad*, *Ogdoad* or the *Plēroma*.

This understanding of rest is the presupposition for the Gnostic understanding of redemption. This "rest" is the original home of the Gnostic, who now finds himself homeless in the midst of the unrest characteristic of the material world. Ἀνάπαυσις, mediated by the redeemer, is thus the goal of the Gnostic. The Gnostic texts frequently speak of the goal of finding rest. Redemption consists in a return to the *plēroma*, or rest, of the father. According to *Gos. Thom.* 60, "He said to them, 'Seek your resting place.'" In the *Gospel of Philip* 63 we read, "As we find ourselves in this world it is seemly for us to attain the resurrection so that we, when we are unclothed from the flesh, can be found in the place of rest."[25] To "come to rest" is thus

---

[21] Hofius, *Katapausis*, 76.
[22] P. Vielhauer, *Aufsätze zum Neuen Testament*, 224.
[23] *Unknown Gnostic Work* 22; cited in Hofius, *Katapausis*, 76.
[24] Käsemann, *Gottesvolk*, 41.
[25] Cited in E. Grässer, *Der Glaube im Hebräerbrief*, 107.

the Gnostic goal. It involves a return to the divine *plēroma*.

> Die durch 'Gnosis' gewonnene 'Ruhe' ist die in diesem Leben schon vollzogene Rückkehr des Ich zu seinem göttlichen Ursprung, d.h. sich selbst. Sie verleiht dem Gnostiker die Freiheit von der verachteten Welt. . . .[26]

While the Gnostic texts cited above indicate that ἀνάπαυσις was an important concept among Gnostics, they do not show that it was a specifically Gnostic concept. Much of Käsemann's argument for the Gnostic background of the concept of rest depends on his use of Philo and apocalyptic texts, which are cited with the assumption that they belong to a wide Gnostic movement. It appears more likely that the Gnostic use of ἀνάπαυσις has a derivative character. The Gnostic references to ἀνάπαυσις are normally in texts where ἀνάπαυσις stands alongside other biblical terms for salvation. Ἀνάπαυσις is often the equivalent for eternal life, resurrection, peace, and hope. The word also is dependent on biblical usage, as in the citation of Matt 11:28-30. Thus ἀνάπαυσις in Gnostic texts probably depends on biblical materials rather than serving as the direct background for any NT reflections.

If we are to account for the importance of ἀνάπαυσις in Gnosticism, we must observe the consistent metaphysic which the term presupposes in the Gnostic literature. Ἀνάπαυσις is the characteristic only of the highest aeon and of the highest deity. The material world is characterized by unrest, movement, and passions. In the *Acts of Thomas* the world is called "a land of wandering" and the "unresting sea."[27] Thus rest consists in leaving the unstable creation for the heavenly world.

This metaphysical distinction between the stable and the unstable reality is a consistent Gnostic feature. The highest aeon is regularly described as being ἀσάλευτος, ἀκίνητος,[28] and as possessing στάσις.[29] According to *CH* 11.4, the transcendent reality "abides in sameness." Thus ἀνάπαυσις must be seen in a wider context of Gnostic thought.

The description of the highest deity as ἀνάπαυσις also belongs to a wider context. The word appears alongside ἀνούσιος and ἄγνωστος, and thus reflects the familiar negative theology of the Hellenistic Age.[30]

---

[26] Vielhauer, *Aufsätze*, 234.

[27] *Acts of Thomas* 37. Cited in Hofius, *Katapausis*, 79.

[28] Hippolytus, *Ref. Om. Her.* 5. 7. 6. From Paul Wendland, ed., *Die griechischen christlichen Schriftsteller der ersten drei Jahrhunderte* (Tübingen: Mohr, 1906). On ἀσάλευτος as a Gnostic category, see p. 85.

[29] *Gos. Truth* 26:15.

[30] See. H. Krämer, *Geistmetaphysik*, 118-119, 124-125, for the significance of negative theology among Middle Platonists. Cf. Dillon, *Middle Platonists*, 284-285.

The wider context of ἀνάπαυσις indicates that the term is, in Käsemann's words, "in kosmisch-metaphysische Spekulationen eingebettet."[31] What Käsemann does not demonstrate is that the metaphysic is derived from the Middle Platonism of the period. The use of negative theology to describe God was a significant feature of Middle Platonism. The distinction between the stable and unresting worlds was regularly employed by Middle Platonists. Thus the Gnostic literature, which is frequently dependent on Middle Platonism in its view of the structure of the world, is dependent on both biblical and Platonic sources in its description of ἀνάπαυσις. H. J. Krämer has written,

> Das valentiniasche Emanations- und Derivationssystem stellt sich demnach, auf seine innere Bewegung hin betrachtet, als eine mythologisch-anthropomorph überkleidete Form der Geistmetaphysik.[32]

The Gnostic concept of ἀνάπαυσις is to be seen within this framework.

This examination of the category of rest indicates that the word has a soteriological significance in those texts which are dependent on the biblical materials. At the same time its significance in apocalyptic, Alexandrian, and Gnostic texts exceeds its importance in either the OT or NT. The term was thus incorporated in various ways into materials which were dependent on the Bible. In apocalyptic and rabbinic literature, it was connected with the new heavens and new earth and restored Paradise. In Philo, Clement, and in Gnosticism it was brought within a Platonic metaphysic as the equivalent of Platonic terms for immutability. Thus it was not a Gnostic category; it was a useful term for those who read the Bible with Platonic assumptions.

Hebrews

This examination of the ἀνάπαυσις theme in antiquity provides the background for an analysis of κατάπαυσις in Hebrews. This passage (Psalm 95) itself has little significance in apocalyptic texts, and is never cited by Philo or Clement, although von Rad saw in Ps 95:7-11 a transition to a transcendent interpretation of rest.[33] Thus while Hebrews is not directly dependent on any of these traditions in the midrash, it is probable that the author's exegesis relies on assumptions that are closely related to those of other writers of the period. The author's conceptual framework can only be ascertained by careful examination of the assumptions with which he handles OT texts.

The function of Ps 95:7-11 is to be seen in the context of the conditional

---

[31] Käsemann, *Gottesvolk*, 43.
[32] Krämer, *Geistmetaphysik*, 259.
[33] Von Rad, *Gesammelte Studien*, 108.

statement of 3:6, as διό in 3:7 indicates. Διό is a transition, pointing both forward and backward.[34] Verse 3:6 contains both an assurance ("we are his house") and an implication of impending danger ("if we hold fast"). The psalm citation is intended to buttress these two features of 3:6. Thus 3:12-4:2 contains a warning, derived from the psalm, while 4:3-11 offers assurance of encouragement, as in 3:6a. The midrash, with its typological interpretation, therefore, continues the dominant parenetic motifs of warning and promise, which characterize this "word of exhortation" (13:22).

The close parallel between 3:6 and 3:14 suggests in particular the importance of 3:6 as the background determining the function of the midrash, for the indicative, "We are his house" (οἶκός ἐσμεν ἡμεῖς), is the context for the warnings and exhortations which follow. Ἡμεῖς identifies the author with his readers, as in 2:2 and 12:25. The affirmation presupposes the correspondence between the old and new people of God, both of whom have heard the word of promise (4:1-2; cf. 4:11). However, the context of 3:1-5 shows that there is more than typological correspondence between Israel and the new people of God. Only the new people of God are "his house" (i.e., the son's). They thus have a "great salvation" (2:3) based on the metaphysical dignity of the exalted son.[35] Israel's revelation was mediated through servants (1:7, 13; 3:5). "We" (3:6) are the house of the exalted son.

The expression, οἶκός ἐσμεν ἡμεῖς, is one of the affirmations of Hebrews suggesting the extraordinary character of the Christian salvation. It thus has a function in Hebrews parallel to the statements in 3:1, 14; 4:14; 10:19-20. Each of these statements affirms a possession which already exists for the church ("we have . . ."). The description of the church as a house suggests a difference between Hebrews and other NT references to God's house. Οἶκος is used in 3:4 for the created world and in 10:21 for the heavenly sanctuary. In 3:6a, οἶκος refers to God's heavenly residence, of which the readers have become "partakers" (3:1). Through the work of Christ, access to the heavenly world has been granted. Thus the church is God's house as a result of the exaltation of Christ. Christ is the "brother" who has participated in human existence (2:10-17); the church now shares in his heavenly calling.

Οἶκος is to be understood within the dualistic perspective of Hebrews, as the parallel to 3:1 shows.[36] The existence of the church, as a result of the exaltation, does not remain at the level of the "fleshly" (7:16) and "worldly" (9:1), as did Israel's. A particularly significant parallel appears in Philo, for

---

[34] Michel, Hebräer, 186.

[35] The arguments of 1:5-13 and 3:1-6 are closely parallel. The son is the exalted one who is contrasted with servants (angels in 1:5-13 ; Moses in 3:1-6). Thus to be "his house" presupposes a share in this metaphysical dignity (cf. 3:1).

[36] F. J. Schierse, Verheissung und Heilsvollendung, 108-112.

whom the motif οἶκος played an important role. Indeed, Philo frequently appeals to Num 12:7, the passage which provides the basis for Heb 3:1-6.[37] Philo, like the author of Hebrews, speaks of both an earthly and a heavenly house. In several texts, Philo employs this theme in the context of the pilgrimage motif. One leaves the earthly house in order to obtain the heavenly dwelling. God's dwelling is both in heaven and in the soul. In *de Som.* 1. 149, Philo says, ᾧ ψυχή, θεοῦ οἶκος γενέσθαι, ἱερὸν ἅγιον. One becomes God's house when one "goes out" from the house of the senses and returns home to God (*de Ab.* 62). Thus both Philo and Hebrews place the motif of being God's house within a dualist framework. Those who are God's house are κλήσεως ἐπουρανίου μέτοχοι.

The παρρησία καὶ τὸ καύχημα τῆς ἐλπίδος of 3:6b are parallel to the church's role as God's house in 3:6a, as 3:6b also describes an objective fact which has been granted through the entrance of Christ to the heavenly sanctuary. Παρρησία, a Hellenistic word, appears in Hebrews at 4:16; 10:19; and 10:35. The term is connected with access to God (4:16; 10:19) and a purified conscience (10:19-22). "The saving work of Christ, which has penetrated the heavens, has created παρρησία and made its fulfillment possible."[38] It is thus an objective reality which includes access to God through the blood of Christ. It also describes the stance of the believer, including his unchanging certainty, full assurance (6:11; 10:22), and endurance (ὑπομονή, 10:36). Παρρησία is used in Hebrews within the same complex of ideas as one finds in Hellenistic Judaism, particularly in Philo, for whom παρρησία was "the mark of intelligent religion."[39] For both Hebrews and Philo, παρρησία is a term for the certainty with which one approaches God. Philo's models of the religious life, Abraham and Moses, were both models of παρρησία. The friends of God were able to approach God directly with παρρησία and without fear because their consciences were purified.[40]

Καύχημα τῆς ἐλπίδος is parallel both to παρρησία and to other texts in Hebrews where the genitive ἐλπίδος is preceded by the substantive. One may compare πληροφορία τῆς ἐλπίδος (6:11) and ὁμολογία τῆς ἐλπίδος (10:23). Thus, while καύχημα τῆς ἐλπίδος is verbally similar to Rom 5:2 (καυχώμεθα ἐπ' ἐλπίδι τῆς δόξης τοῦ θεοῦ), in Hebrews it refers especially to the cer-

---

[37] *Leg. All.* 2. 67; 3. 103, 204, 228.

[38] H. Schlier, *Παρρησία, TDNT* 5. 884.

[39] James Moffatt, *The Epistle to the Hebrews*, 44.

[40] *Quis Rer. Div.* 21. E. Grässer (*Glaube*, 96) shows that παρρησία in the NT appears only in writings which are associated with a Hellenistic-philosophical background. It occurs only once in the Synoptic Gospels (Mark 8:32). The term occurs only twelve times in the LXX. The connection of παρρησία with a purified conscience was a distinctive and new element in the usage of the word which Hebrews shares with Hellenistic Jewish writers. See G. J.Bartelink, *Quelques Observations*, 10-11. Cf. the discussion on pp. 32-33.

tainty opened up by the Christ event.[41] L.K.K. Dey has shown that Philo uses this terminology in a similar way.[42] According to *de Congress*. 134, the "boast" (αὔχημα) of the exalted soul is to rise above the created world and hold fast to the Uncreated. Thus Philo and Hebrews agree in attributing confidence and boasting to those who stand close to God.

The affirmations of 3:6 have an unmistakable parallel to 3:14. Μέτοχοι γὰρ τοῦ χριστοῦ is both formally and substantively parallel to οὗ οἶκός ἐσμεν ἡμεῖς (3:6) and to κλήσεως ἐπουρανίου μέτοχοι (3:1). Μέτοχοι, a term which is used only once outside of Hebrews (Luke 5:7), is used in a theological sense only in Hebrews. In Hebrews the word is used both for the identification of the earthly Jesus with his people (2:14-17) and for the church's relationship to the heavenly world (3:1). Μέτοχοι τοῦ χριστοῦ in 3:14 obviously refers to the church's relationship to the transcendent world. Γεγόναμεν refers to an event in which the readers became Christ's "colleagues." This motif, which does not play a significant role in Philo, is well-attested in the philosophical literature. Μετέχειν was used for the participation of the lower being in the superterrestrial world and in the deity.[43] The term in Hebrews is used for the church's share in Christ's transcendent existence.

The term ἀρχὴ τῆς ὑποστάσεως is parallel to παρρησία in 3:6 and serves in 3:14 to clarify the meaning of μέτοχοι τοῦ χριστοῦ. Those who are μέτοχοι τοῦ χριστοῦ thus have an ἀρχὴ τῆς ὑποστάσεως. Ὑποστάσεως, a term which is used three times in Hebrews (cf. 1:3; 11:1), is a philosophical term which can best be rendered "reality." The word, derived from ὑφίστημι, refers to the essential reality which "stands beneath" (ὑπό-στάσις) all appearances.[44] Thus ἀρχὴ τῆς ὑποστάσεως is a description of the reality on which the existence of the community rests in the same way that Christ is the reality of God (1:3). It thus stands in contrast to the metaphysically inferior experience of Israel, which was identified with the material and transitory world.[45] This use of ὑπόστασις for the Christ event is indebted to Hellenistic metaphysics, particularly as this term developed among Platonists to describe the reality of the intelligible world.

It is apparent that one function of the midrash in 3:7-4:11 is to reinforce the community's awareness of its certain and stable possession. The affirmations of 3:6, 14 point to the church's present relation to the heavenly world, a fact which distinguishes their experience from that of Israel. Παρρησία,

[41] Michel, *Hebräer*, 178.
[42] L.K.K. Dey, *Perfection*, 197.
[43] H. Hanse, Μετέχω, *TDNT* 2. 830. E.Grässer, *Glaube*, 100.
[44] H. Koester, Ὑπόστασις, *TDNT* 8. 587.
[45] *Ibid.*, 587-588.

καύχημα, and ὑπόστασις together describe this stable existence. The terms are to be seen in the context of other words in Hebrews which suggest the stability of the Christian possession. The work of Christ has given the church an objective reality, an "unshakable kingdom" (12:28), and an "abiding possession" (10:34). The author of Hebrews agrees with Philo in affirming that παρρησία, καύχημα, and ὑπόστασις are the possessions of those who approach God. The relationship to God provides a stable existence.

The second function of the midrash is indicated by the conditions of 3:6, 14: ἐάν(περ)[46] . . . κατάσχωμεν. The condition is stated more fully in 3:14, ἐάνπερ τὴν ἀρχὴν τῆς ὑποστάσεως μέχρι τέλους βεβαίαν κατάσχωμεν. The stable possession must be "held fast." Κατέχω, "hold fast," is used at times in the NT for the holding fast of spiritual values or traditions.[47] The word has a special place in Hebrews, where it appears three times (3:6, 14; 10:23) in theologically significant places. In 3:14 and 10:23 the word is accompanied by terms suggesting stability (βεβαία in 3:14; ἀκλινής in 10:23). Closely related to κατέχω in Hebrews is the use of κρατεῖν in 4:14; 6:18. The community is encouraged in 6:18 to "grasp" (κρατεῖν) its hope which ὡς ἄγκυραν ἔχομεν τῆς ψυχῆς ἀσφαλῆ τε καὶ βεβαίαν . . . The function of the midrash, as with the cultic material of 7:1-10:18, is to provide the basis for the church's unwavering steadfastness. The metaphysical "reality," made available by Christ's entry into the heavens, provides the basis for Christian steadfastness.

Βεβαίαν κατάσχωμεν, along with the parallel expressions in 6:18-19, 10:23, belongs to a complex of ideas which distinguishes Hebrews from other NT literature. The root βεβαι-, as H. Braun has pointed out, occurs seven times in Hebrews (2:2; 3:14; 6:19; 9:17; 2:3; 13:9; 6:16), "genauso häufig wie in dem Römerbrief, den beiden Korintherbriefen und dem Philipperbrief zusammen" (Rom 4:16; 2 Cor 1:7; Rom 15:8; 1 Cor 1:6, 8; 2 Cor 1:21; Phil 1:7).[48] In addition, the image of the anchor (6:19) and of "drifting away" (παραρρέω, 2:1) occur only in Hebrews, as does the term ἀκλινής (10:23).

These images have their closest parallel in the work of Philo. Philo also employed the nautical image to distinguish between those whose unstable nature involved "tossing" (σάλος) and those who had found the security of an anchor (cf. *de Post. Cain.* 22-23). In addiiton, βεβαι- is an important category for Philo, for whom the βεβαίωσις of man presupposes his relation

---

[46] The reading ἐάν in 3:6, which is attested by p[13] B, is preferable to ἐάνπερ, although the latter has the attestation of p[46] AC. Similarly, the omission of μέχρι τέλους βεβαίαν is to be preferred, despite the attestation of A C D. Both textual problems are to be explained by the copyist's assimilation of 3:6 and 3:14.

[47] H. Hanse, Κατέχω, *TDNT* 2. 289; Luke 8:15; 1 Cor 11:2; 15:2; 1 Thess 5:21.

[48] H. Braun, "Die Gewinnung der Gewissheit," 321.

to the immutable God.[49] In Philo's work, βεβαι- is one of several words which appear to be used interchangeably for the immutability of God in which men share.[50]

The category of "holding fast," which has an important role in Hebrews, is also attested in Philo in a framework similar to that of Hebrews. According to *de Congress.* 131-134, Moses was able to "soar above created being" and "hold fast to the Uncreated alone" (μόνον τοῦ ἀγενήτου περιέχεσθαι), having followed the biblical injunction to "cling to him" (ἔχεσθαι αὐτοῦ, Deut 30:20).[51]

The function of the midrash in 3:7-4:11 is indicated by the conditional clauses of 3:6, 14. The author intends to give a basis by which the readers can "hold fast" to the stable possession. Using categories known also to Philo, the author develops the midrash with the intention of reaffirming the quality of the Christian experience and of warning against its neglect. Thus the midrash is intended to make explicit what is implicit in 3:6, 14.

Warning: 3:12-4:2

The conditional nature of salvation and the need for "holding fast" are shown in the first part of the midrash, 3:12-4:2. The author of Hebrews, like Paul in 1 Cor 10:1-13, derives a severe warning for the church from the experience of Israel in the wilderness. Their experience serves as a ὑπόδειγμα, and thus it is analogous to the experience of the church. A historical retrospect over Israel's past is given in 3:15-19, while 3:12-13 and 4:1-2 address the church. The assumption behind this combination of historical retrospect and personal address to the church is the fact that both communities have heard the word of promise (4:1-2).

In 3:15-19, Israel is the negative example for what it means to "hold fast" (cf. 1 Cor 10:5). The threefold question τίνες . . . τίσιν . . . τίσιν divides the retrospect into three sections in the form of a diatribe.[52] Each question reflects the language of the psalm.[53] Unlike Paul, the author does not mention the faithful minority (cf. 1 Cor 10:7-8), for the argument of

---

[49] Dey, *Perfection*, 133.

[50] See E. Grässer, *Glaube*, 33. The image of the anchor is unknown in the OT and in rabbinic literature. Ἀσφαλής is also an important word for Philo (cf. *Quis Rer. Div.* 314; *de Conf. Ling.* 106).

[51] Dey, *Perfection*, 197. Cf. *de Post. Cain.* 12.

[52] Moffatt, *Hebrews*, 48. Michel, *Hebräer*, 190, calls it a catechetical style.

[53] Παρεπίκραναν in 3:16 refers to παραπικρασμός (cf. Heb 3:8); προσώχισεν refers to προσώχθισα, Heb 3:10; 3:18 refers back to 3:11. O. Hofius (*Katapausis*, 134-137) points to features of the author's interpretation of the psalm which suggest that Numbers 14 has influenced the reading of the text.

4:3-10 presupposes the total failure of Israel. Thus πάντες, which appears only in 3:16, is assumed in the following verses.

The emphasis of the historical retrospect is on the verbs παρεπίκραναν, ἁμαρτήσασιν, and ἀπειθήσασιν, all of which elaborate the motif of κατέχω in 3:6, 14. Israel was therefore characterized by its failure to "hold fast." Such a failure is characterized by ἀπιστία in 3:19, which summarizes the point of 3:16-18. The author also ascribes Israel's failure to its lack of faith in 4:2. Thus for Hebrews ἀπιστία is the equivalent of disobedience (cf. 4:6, 11; 11:31) to God's word (4:2). Its opposite is πίστις, which in Hebrews is connected with obedience, patience (μακροθυμία, 6:12), endurance (ὑπομονή, 10:36-39), and παρρησία (10:35-39). Faith is thus "holding fast" to the "things unseen" (11:1). Israel is thus the negative example of the very behavior which is the temptation of the readers (cf. 2:1-4; 6:4-6; 12:12). Unlike the faithful models (cf. μιμηταί, 6:12) of chap. 11, Israel is the example of ἀπιστία (3:19), the failure to "hold fast."

The experience of Israel is the basis for the warning to the readers in 3:12-13; 4:1-2. The ἀπιστία of Israel is the background to the warning, βλέπετε, ἀδελφοί, μήποτε ἔσται ἔν τινι ὑμῶν καρδία πονηρὰ ἀπιστίας ἐν τῷ ἀποστῆναι ἀπὸ θεοῦ ζῶντος. This warning is parallel to 4:1, φοβηθῶμεν οὖν μήποτε καταλειπομένης ἐπαγγελίας . . . τις ἐξ ὑμῶν ὑστερηκέναι. In contrast to the πάντες of Israel (3:16), the author is concerned in 3:12; 4:1 with "any" (τις) of the community (cf. 12:13-15). The warnings develop the meaning of ἐάν . . . κατασχῶμεν (3:6, 14). Βλέπετε appears in 12:25 in a similar warning. It is parallel to 2:1, δεῖ . . . προσέχειν ἡμᾶς τοῖς ἀκουθεῖσιν, μήποτε παραρυῶμεν. In each instance (3:12; 4:1; 2:1), μήποτε suggests the danger to the community.

The danger to the community is especially acute because of the nature of the salvation which is now offered. Βλέπετε (3:12) and φοβηθῶμεν (4:1) thus presuppose not only a parallel between Israel and the church (cf. 4:2), both of whom have received the "word of hearing" (ὁ λόγος τῆς ἀκοῆς). What "we have heard" (2:1) in Jesus Christ (1:2) is a "great salvation" (τηλικαύτη σωτηρία, 2:3). It includes not only the proclamation of the earthly Jesus and those who heard him (2:3). It is a "better promise" (8:6) and a personal address of the one who speaks ἀπ' οὐρανῶν, unlike the original word ἐπὶ γῆς (12:25). The "word" in Hebrews is the revelation of the exalted one,[54] and thus metaphysically superior to the older revelation. This superior word presents a greater responsibility and danger to the church than the previous word (2:1-4; 12:25).[55] "Die Überlegenheit Jesu gewährt

54 See E. Grässer, "Das Heil als Wort," 265.
55 Grässer, "Heil," 272.

eine überlegene Gewissheit, aber auch eine überhöhte Gefährdung."[56] Thus the warning of 3:12; 4:1 presupposes the quality of the Christian message, as in 2:1-4.

The parallelism between sin and unbelief, which has been seen in 3:17-19, also appears in 3:12-13. Ἁμαρτία (3:13) is equivalent to ἀπιστία (3:12). The meaning of these terms is to be seen in the verbs ἀποστῆναι (3:12) and ὑστερηκέναι (4:1). The two words are equivalent to other verbs in Hebrews which describe the temptation of the community: παραρυῶμεν (2:1), παραπέσοντας (6:6), ἐγκαταλείπειν (10:25), ἀποβάλλειν (10:35), and ὑποστέλλειν (10:38-39). They describe the nature of ἀπιστία as lack of stability, certainty, and endurance. Ὑστερεῖν, "fail to reach,"[57] suggests the image of the pilgrimage to the heavenly homeland (cf. 12:15, ὑστερεῖν; 12:1-2), which the pious may either enter or fail to reach. It is thus the opposite of εἰσελθεῖν in 3:19. Philo employs the image in Frag. Mang. 1. 656:

> As those who are not able to proceed with firm feet, but remain back (ὑστερίζουσαν) stumbling and worn out a long way from the goal of the way, so the soul is also hindered from completing the way leading to piety, when it hits against the impassable stretch of godlessness, because of which the reason falls short (ὑστερίζει), wavering on the natural way.[58]

Both Hebrews and Philo thus employ images of pilgrimage toward the heavenly homeland. Πίστις is the steadfastness of the believer (cf. 10:36-39; 12:1-2) on the way to the heavenly homeland. Ἀπιστία involves the failure to hold fast to the certainty granted by Christ (3:14). In the exhortation to "encourage one another" (3:13; cf. 10:25), the author emphasizes the communal nature of Christian existence. Both exhortations to mutual encouragement are given in the context of the demand to "hold fast."

The Promise: 4:3-11

The warning of 3:12-4:2 is the background of the promise which is affirmed in 4:3: "We who have believed enter that rest" (εἰσερχόμεθα γὰρ εἰς τὴν κατάπαυσιν οἱ πιστεύσαντες). The affirmation is parallel to 4:9, "There remains a sabbath rest (σαββατισμός) for the people of God." This affirmation of 4:3, 9 is the thesis statement of 4:3-11, as 4:4-8 provides the supporting argument for the affirmation and 4:11 gives the concluding exhortation. The parallel between 4:3 and 4:9 suggests that "the people of God" (4:9)

---

[56] Braun, "Gewissheit," 325.
[57] BAG, 856.
[58] Cited in Michel, *Hebräer*, 191-192.

and "we who have believed" are identical; κατάπαυσις is equivalent to σαββατισμός.

The main statement contrasts the situation of the new people of God with Israel. The fact that the church "enters" (εἰσερχόμεθα) is contrasted to Israel's failure to enter (3:19), just as the ἀπιστία of Israel is contrasted to the church as the community of believers (πιστεύσαντες). Thus 4:3, 9 present affirmative statements suggesting to wavering members the greatness of the Christian salvation. Like the other important affirmations of Hebrews (3:6, 14; 4:14; 10:19-22), the purpose of the affirmation is to encourage the church to "hold fast."

Πιστεύσαντες in 4:3, which is distinguished from ἀπιστία in 3:19, is parallel to κατάσχωμεν in 3:6, 14. Israel's ἀπιστία was its failure to hold firm in the midst of temptation. In Hebrews, πίστις/πιστεύω describes the un-wavering certainty in the existence of the unseen reality which allows one to remain firm throughout the temptation to waver.[59] Thus "we who believe" are those who fulfill the demand for "holding firm" in 3:6, 14. This affirma-tion is thus closely identified with those of 3:6, 14.

The nature of the κατάπαυσις is indicated both by the verb εἰσερ-χόμεθα and by the argument of 4:4-5. The verb εἰσερχόμεθα indicates that κατάπαυσις is to be understood in spatial terms. In fact, with only one exception (10:25) outside the midrash, the verb is used in Hebrews for entry into the heavenly world (6:19, 20; 9:12, 24, 25). Thus entry into the κατάπαυ-σις is entry into heaven. A major theme of Hebrews is the access to God made available through the death of Jesus. Thus the entry of the church into the κατάπαυσις presupposes the entry of Christ into the transcendent world (cf. especially 10:19-22). Εἰσέρχομαι is parallel to προσέρχομαι, which is used for the church's access to God (4:16; 10:22; 12:18) through Jesus Christ.

The entry into the κατάπαυσις is the fulfillment of the eschatological hope, as it is still a promise (4:1) that "remains open" (καταλείπω, 4:1, ἀπολείπω, 4:9). Nevertheless, this entry is also a present reality, as the exhor-tations of 4:16; 10:22 and the affirmation of 12:18 show. The "partakers of a heavenly calling" have already "drawn near" to the heavenly world (12:18) and become members of "God's house" (3:6).

Εἰσέρχομαι is also to be seen in the context of the author's frequent use of ἐξέρχομαι for the existence of the believer. Just as faith is the presupposi-tion for entry into the heavenly world (4:3; cf. 10:22; 11:6), it also involves "going out," as exemplified by Abraham (11:8). In fact, the author urges his readers both "to hasten to enter" (σπουδάσωμεν οὖν εἰσελθεῖν, 4:11) and to "go outside" (13:13). The imagery thus belongs to the motif of pilgrimage. Faith (πιστεύσαντες) involves the recognition that one's homeland is not in

---

59 See Grässer, Glaube, 19-24.

the material world and a certainty that one's κατάπαυσις, or πόλις, is the heavenly world. Thus to "enter his rest" is also to "go outside the camp" (13:13) of the material world. This entry occurs both now, in being partakers of the heavenly calling, and later, in the coming age.

The nature of the κατάπαυσις is indicated by the *gezera shawa* argument of 4:4-5, 10. The eschatological κατάπαυσις of Ps 95:11 is identical to God's "rest" (κατάπαυσις) on the seventh day (Gen 2:2; Heb 4:4-5). This connection between the two passages from the OT is restated in 4:10, where κατάπαυσίς μου of Ps 95:11 becomes κατάπαυσις αὐτοῦ. The believer enters "his rest." The "rest" of the believer is thus parallel to God's rest (cf. ὥσπέρ, 4:10), if not identical. Κατάπαυσις is, therefore, not only a place; it is also a status.[60] The transcendent world at God's side is the place of rest.

O. Hofius has argued that the place of rest in Hebrews is most closely related to the perspective of the Jewish apocalypses, especially 4 Ezra. In 4 Ezra the place of rest is entered by the pious at the end time. It appears after the dissolution of this world when the new world appears. Thus, according to Hofius, κατάπαυσις in Hebrews is identical with the place of rest in Hebrews.[61] While Hofius correctly sees that in both Hebrews and apocalyptic literature rest is an eschatological concept, he overlooks the metaphysical foundation of the argument in Hebrews. The identification of the believer's rest with God's rest has its closest parallels in Philo and Clement of Alexandria, those writers who were influenced by Platonic metaphysics.

It is commonly agreed that κατάπαυσις is the author's equivalent for other terms describing the goal of the believer: πατρίς (11:11, 14), πόλις (11:10, 16; 12:22; 13:14), τὰ μὴ βλεπόμενα (11:1), βασιλεία ἀσάλευτος (12:28), and ὕπαρξις μένουσα (10:34). These terms are used within a dualistic world view, and connote both transcendence and stability. I have shown that the view of the end given in Heb 12:27-28 employs metaphysical categories not present in the apocalyptic literature.[62] The new world of 4 Ezra is a new creation described in materialistic terms. In Hebrews there is no new creation. When the material world disappears, the unshakable kingdom remains (12:28). Κατάπαυσις, with its suggestion of immutability, is parallel in Hebrews to the other terms suggesting the stability of the heavenly world. Just as Philo, Clement, and the Gnostics took the biblical category of ἀνάπαυσις and equated it with Platonic categories for the stability of the heavenly world, Hebrews equates κατάπαυσις with the abiding and unshakable

---

60 G. Theissen, *Untersuchungen*, 128.
61 Pp. 91-94.
62 See pp. 50-52.

kingdom. These categories function within a metaphysic that is dependent on the Platonic tradition.

O. Hofius has described the imminent eschatology which characterizes the perspective of this midrash, as the "today" of the psalm becomes the "today" of the church.[63] The members of the community are to encourage each other "while it is called today" (3:13). This argument is based on the statement of 4:8, according to which the psalm refers to "another day," the time of the church. Such an argument is frequently used in Hebrews to show that the OT itself assumes its own imperfection and points toward a new day (cf. 7:11; 8:7). However, the new "today" in Hebrews is different from the Pauline νῦν (2 Cor 6:2; Rom 13:11-14). The "today" of Hebrews (σήμερον) is the period of the last days (1:2). Σήμερον is especially connected with the exaltation of Christ (1:4; 5:5). It is the time of the church's new opportunity for obedience. The final salvation lies in the future (9:27; 10:25; 12:25-29), and one's response "today" determines that future.[64]

While Hebrews refers in one instance to the approaching end (10:25), the emphasis has shifted to the reliability of the future possession.[65] This fact is to be seen in the midrash. The thesis statement of the midrash (4:3, 9) affirms the certainty of the eschatological gift. These affirmations have a function similar to other statements in Hebrews (cf. 4:14; 10:19-22; 13:14). It is to reaffirm the certainty of the transcendent world for the community. This certainty is the basis for the community's endurance. Those who are wavering (12:12; 13:9) now "hold fast" to the heavenly possession through faith.

While the eschatological nature of κατάπαυσις has similarities to this category in the Jewish apocalypses, this motif functions in a way that is most analogous to the work of those who read the Bible with Platonic assumptions. Just as the biblical words ἀνάπαυσις and ἑβδομάς in Philo and Clement were placed in the service of a Platonic metaphysic, κατάπαυσις in Hebrews is associated with the essential reality (i.e., ὑπόστασις) of the heavenly world. The author's connection of God's rest with the believer's rest also indicates his proximity to Philo and Clement. In addition, the use of the term κατάπαυσις in order to encourage the community to "hold fast" indicates his agreement with Philo that proximity to a stable object confers stability.

The fact that κατάπαυσις is the term employed by Hebrews instead of the common term ἀνάπαυσις, which appears normally in Gnostic texts and in Philo, does not diminish the relationship between Hebrews and the other

---

[63] Hofius, *Katapausis*, 142.

[64] E. Grässer, "Hebräer 1.1-4. Ein exegetischer Versuch," *Text und Situation*, 210-211.

[65] G. Theissen, *Untersuchungen*, 106-110. This fact is especially evident in 12:25-27, where the emphasis is on the quality of the eschatological possession. Cf. 10:34.

literature where biblical and Platonic traditions were combined.[66] The words are synonymous, as is apparent in Clement, *Strom.* 6. 16. 141-142; 6. 14. 108, where Clement uses the words interchangeably. The category was useful in Greek literature primarily in texts which depended both on the Bible and Platonic metaphysics. While Hebrews has definite eschatological features not found in Philo, the author shares metaphysical assumptions which are present also in Philo.

---

[66] A major argument of Hofius is that *anapausis*, and not *katapausis*, is the term always cited as a parallel in Gnosticism (pp. 98, 256). The parallels cited by Hofius, however, are primarily in either Hebrew or Latin texts (4 Ezra). Thus it is unknown how these terms would have been rendered in Greek.

CHAPTER VI

HEBREWS 9 AND HELLENISTIC CONCEPTS OF SACRIFICE*

The author of Hebrews, in contending that the blood of animals is not an adequate sacrifice, was making an argument that would have been widely accepted in the Hellenistic world. There was an old Palestinian tradition extending to the Psalms and Prophets which had condemned any belief in the automatic efficacy of sacrifices, demanding in its place a "sacrifice of thanksgiving" or deeds of mercy.[1] The events of the Hellenistic Age led to the further reinterpretation of the demand for sacrifice in Palestinian circles. At Qumran, the belief that the Jerusalem temple was defiled led to the renunciation of its cultus and the reinterpretation of sacrificial language, so that the appropriate sacrifices now included prayer and praise.[2] The old prophetic tradition of questioning the validity of sacrifice later became useful after the destruction of Jerusalem, for Yohanan ben Zakkai could respond to this disaster by calling for acts of mercy to replace the old cultus.[3]

Within the context of Greek speculation, it had become commonplace to question the efficacy of sacrifice on metaphysical gounds. The Hellenistic enlightenment had led to the widespread belief that true sacrifice demands neither the blood of animals nor a physical sanctuary.[4]

This widespread tendency toward the "spiritualization" or reinterpretation of the concept of sacrifice is the background for analyzing the intellectual framework of the author of Hebrews. Just as the *religionsgeschichtliche* background of the book has been a matter of dispute, the author's understanding of sacrifice has also been associated with several possible origins. In an article in the 1933 *Theologische Blätter*, von Loewenich argued that

---

*Originally appeared in *JBL* 98 (1979)

[1] Amos 5:21-24; Mic 6:6-8; Isa 1:10-17; Ps 50:7-15.

[2] See G. Klinzing, *Die Umdeutung des Kultus in der Qumrangemeinde und im Neuen Testament*. Cf. Elisabeth Schüssler Fiorenza, "Cultic Language in Qumran and in the New Testament." For Qumran texts which call for a sacrifice of praise, see 1QS 9:4-5, 26; 1QS 10:18, 22.

[3] According to Aboth de R. Nathan, the sight of the temple in ruins led R. Joshua b. Hananiah to say, "Woe to us, for the place where the iniquities of Israel were atoned is destroyed!" Yohanan replied, "Do not grieve, my son, for we have an atonement which is just as good, namely deeds of mercy, as the Scripture says, 'For I desire mercy and not sacrifice'" (Hos 6:6). Cited in G.F. Moore, *Judaism in the First Centuries of the Christian Era* 1. 503.

[4] Frances M. Young, "Temple Cult and Law in Early Christianity," 325.

Hebrews' understanding of sacrifice is a development of the prophetic critique of the cultus.[5] Otto Michel has denied any relationship between Hebrews and Hellenistic philosophy at this point.[6] Valentin Nikiprowetzky, on the other hand, has argued in an article dealing with Philo's view of sacrifice that Hebrews is even closer to Hellenistic critiques of sacrifice than is Philo.[7] It is the purpose of this chapter to analyze the force of the author's statements on sacrifice in Heb 9:11-14 in order to understand the intellectual framework of the author.

The discussion of sacrifice in Hebrews 9-10 appears in the context of the larger cultic section in 7:1-10:18. Although the author has previously reflected his interest in cultic language in the epistle (2:17; 4:14-16; 5:1-10; 6:19-20), it is not until 7:1-10:18 that he discusses the cultus in great detail. A dominating motif of this cultic section, as in the rest of the material, is the motif of comparison, which Schierse calls "Entsprechung und Überbietung."[8] The new possession of the church both corresponds to and surpasses the possession of the earthly Israel. The order of Melchizedek, to which Christ belongs, is "better" than the old (8:6). This discussion sets the stage for the author's description of the "better sacrifices" mentioned in 9:23.

The grounds on which the sacrifice of Christ is "better" is explained in 9:1-14. That the author intends to continue the motif of comparison is suggested by the μέν . . . δέ construction of 9:1, 11. The points of comparison, as 9:1 indicates, are the δικαιώματα λατρείας τό τε ἅγιον κοσμικόν which are to be found under the first covenant. Λατρεία is the author's word for the sacrificial ministry (cf. 9:9, 14; 8:5).[9] Its close connection with ἅγιον κοσμικόν suggests that the author chooses to discuss the sanctuary and the sacrifice together. This connection is maintained in 9:11-12, where the δέ clause points to the corresponding sanctuary and sacrifice of the new high priest.

The description of the sacrificial ministry of the earthly sanctuary appears to supply the foil for the author's description of the superior work of Christ in 9:11-14.[10] Consequently the emphasis of 9:1-10 is on the defects of the levitical cultus as the μήπω and μή of 9:8, 9 and the μόνον of 9:10 suggest. These defects of the cultus are related to its material nature, as the

---

5   "Zum Verständnis des Opfergedankens im Hb," 167-172.

6   *Der Brief an die Hebräer*, 328. The important monograph by H. Wenschkewitz, *Die Spiritualisierung der Kultusbegriff*, on p. 145 contains the argument that the thought of Hebrews on this subject is not explicable against the background of Hellenistic philosophy.

7   Valentin Nikiprowetzky, "La Spiritualisation des Sacrifices et le Cult Sacrificiel au Temple de Jérusalem chez Philon d'Alexandrie," 114.

8   F.J. Schierse, *Verheissung und Heilsvollendung*, 49.

9   H. Strathmann, Λατρεία, *TDNT* 4. 63.

10   Wenschkewitz, *Spiritualisierung*, 135.

author indicates by his use of pejorative terms describing both the sanctuary and the ministry.[11] The sanctuary is κοσμικός, and the regulations are δικαιώματα σαρκός. Κοσμικός is not used here to mean "cosmic."[12] It denotes something "which belongs to this world," with a suggestion of the transitoriness characteristic of the cosmos, and it is equivalent to ἐπὶ γῆς in 8:4.[13] The expression δικαιώματα σαρκός is reminiscent of the author's statement in 7:16 that the levitical priesthood was founded upon a commandment that was σαρκίνη. Thus in 9:10 the author offers a fundamental critique of the levitical cultus which is similar to his regular criticism of the institutions of the old covenant. Because these institutions are material, they are not efficacious.[14] Rites offered in the earthly sphere cleanse the flesh, but not the conscience. Thus "better sacrifices" are required.

The δέ of 9:11 refers back to the corresponding μέν in 9:1, indicating that the following material contrasts the sacrifice and sanctuary of Christ with the old cultus. This statement consists of two long sentences, in which the first (9:11-12) describes an event (εἰσῆλθεν, 9:12), and the second describes the significance of the event for salvation (ἁγιάζει, 9:13; καθαριεῖ, 9:14).[15] The section 9:11-14, as a contrast to 9:1-10, is thus intended to contrast the new event and its effects with those which occurred in the levitical cultus. The event, as the main clause of 9:11-12 indicates (χριστὸς δὲ παραγενόμενος ἀρχιερεύς . . . εἰσῆλθεν . . . εἰς τὰ ἅγια), is the exaltation of Christ. Παραγενόμενος is reminiscent of γενόμενος elsewhere in Hebrews (1:4; 2:7; 5:5, 9) for the event of Christ's exaltation and installation as high priest. The exaltation is frequently described as an entry into the heavenly sanctuary (cf. 6:19-20; 9:24-25). The event is further described with the chiastic balancing of positive and negative statement in 9:11-12:

διὰ τῆς μείζονος καὶ τελειοτέρας σκηνῆς
οὐ χειροποιήτου, τοῦτ' ἔστιν οὐ ταύτης τῆς κτίσεως
οὐδὲ δι' αἵματος τράγων καὶ μόσχων,
διὰ δὲ τοῦ ἰδίου αἵματος.[16]

The superiority of Christ's offering rests on the nature of his sanctuary and his sacrifice, as the parallelism of positive and negative statements indicates. The two negative statements indicate that the work of Christ has none of the defects of the levitical cultus. In the positive statements, the author has

---

[11] C. Spicq, *L'Épître aux Hébreux*, 2. 255. Cf. James Moffatt, *The Epistle to the Hebrews*, 112.

[12] Cf. Philo, *De Spec. Leg.* 1. 66; *De Vit. Mos.* 2. 77-78 for the "cosmic" sanctuary.

[13] H. Sasse, *TDNT* 3. 896.

[14] See Chapters VII and VIII.

[15] Michel, *Hebräer*, 309.

[16] This arrangement is taken from O. Hofius, *Der Vorhang vor dem Thron Gottes*, 66.

brought together two balanced *dia* clauses for rhetorical effect. This use of διὰ τῆς . . . σκηνῆς alongside εἰσῆλθεν . . . εἰς ἅγια provides two different images of the exaltation, both of which are common in Hebrews. On the one hand, it is an entry through the heavenly world, as the author frequently suggests (cf. 4:14; 10:20). On the other hand, it is an entry into the heavenly world, as the author suggests in several places (cf. 9:23f.; 6:19-20).[17] Both images are used regularly to describe the transcendence of Christ and to contrast his work with the earthly nature of the institutions of the old covenant.

The sacrifice of Christ is "better," as the first two lines indicate, because it was offered "through" the superior tent.[18] The author assumes, according to 8:5 and 10:1, that the earthly temple is a copy of the heavenly model. This fact does not, however, legitimate the earthly tent, as the pejorative term κοσμικός in 9:1 indicates.[19] Μείζονος and τελειοτέρας in 9:11 are used in contrast to κοσμικός in 9:1, and are reminiscent of the author's frequent use of κρείττων for the superiority of the work of Christ.[20] The "greater and more perfect tent" of 9:11 is equivalent to the "true tent which the Lord made" in 8:2 and to the "true" sanctuary of 9:24. It is "greater and more perfect" because it is not material, as the contrast to κοσμικός in 9:1 suggests. The sanctuary of Christ, according to 9:24, is "heaven itself."

That the "greater and more perfect tent" is metaphysically superior to the old tent is further demonstrated by the negative phrase οὐ χειροποιήτου, οὐ ταύτης τῆς κτίσεως. The earthly sanctuary is characterized as "hand made" in 9:11 and 9:23, and as "man-made" in 8:2. Χειροποίητος, which is parallel to κοσμικός in 9:1, has a pejorative connotation throughout Jewish literature.[21] In Hebrews the term means "material," as is suggested by the

---

[17] Otto Kuss (*Der Brief an die Hebräer*, 118) has correctly observed that the author possesses no consistent picture of the heavenly geography. Thus we need not distinguish between the tent and the heavenly sanctuary in 9:11. James Swetnam ("The Greater and More Perfect Tent," 97) and A. Cody (*Heavenly Sanctuary and Heavenly Liturgy*, 161) have argued that the "greater and more perfect tent" is the body of Christ. Thus, according to Swetnam, the first *dia* has an instrumental sense in parallelism to the second *dia*. This arrangement would give the two *dia* clauses the parallel meaning "through his body" and "through his blood." This view does not account adequately for the parallelism between the tent of 9:11 and 8:2 and to other passages where the real issue is the access to God in the heavenly world (cf. 10:19-20; 12:18-22). Cf. Paul Andriessen, "Das grössere und vollkommenere Zelt," 83.

[18] Hofius, *Vorhang*, 66.

[19] G. Theissen, *Untersuchungen zum Hebräerbrief*, 102.

[20] Κρείττων is used 19 times in the NT, of which 13 occurrences are in Hebrews. What is "better" in Hebrews is, in most instances, metaphysically superior. Cf. chap. VIII.

[21] Χειροποίητος was normally used in Jewish literature for idols. In the LXX it is used in Lev 26:1; Isa 46:6 (cf. *Sib. Or.* 3. 606). The term was developed further in the NT, where it was applied to Jewish institutions (cf. Mark 14:58; Acts 7:48; Eph 2:11). In Acts 17:24 it is used with reference to pagan temples. Philo uses the word for the Jewish temple (*De Vit. Mos.* 2. 88) in

additional phrase, οὐ ταύτης τῆς κτίσεως. These pejorative expressions are to be compared to other terms which Hebrews uses to suggest that the material world cannot bring salvation: ψηλαφημένος (12:18), πεποιημένα (12:27), τὸ βλεπόμενον (11:1-3).[22] What is created, according to Hebrews, cannot bring salvation. The institutions of the old covenant are regularly identified with *Sinnlichkeit*, as H. Windisch observed, and thus they do not mediate salvation.[23] There is thus a fundamental criticism of earthly sanctuaries in Hebrews, a criticism that is made on metaphysical grounds.

The contrast between tents in 9:11 corresponds to the contrast between the "blood of bulls and goats" and the "blood of Christ" in 9:12. That a sacrificial ministry requires the offering of blood is well-known to the author (9:7, 18-25; 13:11), necessitating the offering of the blood of Christ in a genuine sacrificial cult (9:25; 10:19; 13:12). Nevertheless, there is a qualitative distinction between the two offerings. The negative evaluation of the "blood of bulls and goats" is suggested in 10:4 by the expression, ἀδύνατον γὰρ αἷμα ταύρων καὶ τράγων ἀφαιρεῖν ἁμαρτίας. Ἀδύνατον suggests the impotence of cultic rites.[24] This negative evaluation extends to all cultic acts on earth, for the author reflects negatively on those "foods and drinks and baptisms" that belong to the earthly temple. In 13:9 he says that "foods do not benefit the worshiper." There is therefore a metaphysical critique of all rites in earthly places, for they are incapable of dealing with the human problem.[25] "Better sacrifices" are necessary, as 9:23 reminds us.

The nature of this superior sacrifice is indicated by the contrasting phrase διὰ δὲ τοῦ ἰδίου αἵματος αὐτοῦ, which suggests that Christ is the offering as well as the high priest. The author knows a limited period in Jesus' life when he "shared flesh and blood" (κεκοινώνηκεν αἵματος καὶ σαρκός, a time otherwise known as the "days of his flesh" (5:7). This period ended at Jesus' death, when the way into heaven was opened ἐν τῷ αἵματι Ἰησοῦ (10:19) and when he entered "through the curtain, which is his flesh" (10:20).[26] The death of Jesus is thus an event which spans earth and heaven.

---

contrast with the whole cosmos. Throughout classical literature the word was used with a pejorative connotation to emphasize the inferiority of a thing, and to contrast it with what is real (cf. Plato, *Rep.* 3. 405a for χειροτέχνης). Cf. E. Lohse, Χειροποίητος, *TDNT* 9. 436; C. Spicq, *Hébreux*, 2. 255; F.J. Schierse, *Verheissung*, 42.

[22] G. Theissen, *Untersuchungen*, 121. On ψηλαφημένος, see Chapter III.

[23] *Der Hebräerbrief*, 112.

[24] Schierse (*Verheissung*, 38) suggests that the author is giving a metaphysical basis for the inadequacy of the cult. The word ἀδύνατον distinguishes Hebrews from the prophetic demand for mercy alongside sacrifice.

[25] G. Theissen, *Untersuchungen*, 77.

[26] E. Käsemann, *Gottesvolk*, 148. "The sacrificial death of Jesus, by which he offered his fleshly body, is . . . at the same time the *eisodos* into heaven."

It was the time of his leaving the sphere of matter and entering into the heavenly world, as the death and exaltation form one event for the author of Hebrews. As Ulrich Luck has said, "For Hebrews the suffering of Jesus is already his ministry in the sanctuary."[27] The language throughout chap. 9 indicates that the blood of Jesus was actually offered in the heavenly tabernacle. It is this fact which gives Jesus' sacrifice a metaphysical superiority to the blood of bulls and goats. The sacrifice of Christ is qualitatively superior because it is not material.

The parallel passage in 9:14, 25-26 provides a suggestion for what the author means by "the blood of Christ." The author understands Jesus' death as "the sacrifice of himself." Thus "blood" does not refer to a substance in this instance. It is used to describe Christ's self-giving at the cross. This sacrifice is of such superior quality that it provides an "eternal redemption," in contrast to the levitical δικαιώματα σαρκός.

This "eternal redemption" is further described in the *qal wachomer* argument of 9:13-14, which now contrasts the effects of the two sacrifices. The blood offered on earth ἁγιάζει πρὸς τὴν τῆς σαρκὸς καθαρότητα, the blood offered in heaven καθαριεῖ τὴν συνείδησιν. The purification of the conscience is the equivalent of the eternal redemption of 9:12. The contrast between the two tents now corresponds to the distinction between flesh and conscience. This contrast between flesh and conscience was also suggested in 9:9-10, where the rites of the earthly cultus "are not able to perfect the worshipper with respect to conscience," but deal only with "fleshly ordinances." This metaphysical distinction probably also lies behind the statement in 10:4 that "it is impossible" for the blood of bulls and goats to take away sin.

Σάρξ and συνείδησις constitute the two sides of human existence for the author. Σάρξ refers to the earthly sphere of human existence.[28] The author assumes a dualistic anthropology which corresponds to his dualism of heaven and earth. The earthly side of human existence can be cleansed by an earthly cultus.[29] But the συνείδησις is the heavenly side of human existence, which requires a superior sacrifice. Συνείδησις refers to the "consciousness" (10:4), which can be cleansed only by the entrance of Christ into the heavenly tent (cf. 10:22). This heavenly nature of the conscience is indi-

---

[27] "Himmlisches und irdisches Geschehen im Hebräerbrief," 211.

[28] E. Schweizer, Σάρξ, *TDNT* 7. 143.

[29] The dualistic anthropology is to be seen at several places in Hebrews. In 12:9, the author distinguishes between the "fathers of the flesh" and the "fathers of spirits." In 13:3 he compares imprisonment to the life "in the body." See R. Völkl, *Christ und Welt nach dem Neuen Testament*, 345. F.J. Schierse (*Verheissung*, 119) has said that the key to the understanding of redemption in Hebrews is that "der Mensch seinem πνεῦμα nach, seiner συνείδησις nach, wesentlich zur himmlisch-unsichtbaren Schöpfung gehört."

cated, as F. J. Schierse has shown, by the parallelism of 9:13 and 9:23. The purification of the flesh in 9:13 corresponds to the cleansing of the "copies" in 9:23. Thus if the conscience is that part of man which belongs to a higher world, the perfection and cleansing of the conscience can occur only when the way is opened into the heavenly world.[30]

The author has thus supplied a metaphysical ground for his argument that the sacrifice in the heavenly tent is more effective than the bloody sacrifices in the earthly temple. His argument assumes not only that material sacrifices have been superseded, but also that they were impotent, having been offered in the sphere of the flesh. Such an argument implies a radical critique of any material cult and the anthropological dualism of flesh and conscience.

Sanctuary and Sacrifice in the Hellenistic World

This metaphysical critique of the cult is to be compared to the other literature of the period. The author's radical rejection of an earthly cult is at a considerable distance from the prophetic critique of the cult, for there is no evidence that the prophets ever rejected the Jerusalem cultus entirely.[31] Nor did the Qumran community's rejection of the cultus rest on the dualistic assumptions that are found in Hebrews, as we can ascertain from the studies of G. Klinzing and E. Fiorenza, for the community never rejected animal sacrifices in principle.[32] Nor is there any metaphysical argument against sacrifice in rabbinic Judaism[33] or in apocalyptic texts,[34] for we frequently find in this literature the hope for a resumption of animal sacrifice in a rebuilt temple.

---

[30] Schierse, *Verheissung*, 40.

[31] See G. von Rad, *Old Testament Theology*, 2. 186. Cf. J.R. Brown, *Temple and Sacrifice in Rabbinic Judaism*, 13.

[32] The basis for Qumran's rejection of the Jerusalem cultus, according to Fiorenza, is the fact that the temple of Jerusalem had been polluted. "Cultic Language," 162. Klinzing (*Umdeutung*, 146) has said that there is no rationalistic critique of sacrifice at Qumran that is comparable to the polemic of Hellenistic philosophers.

[33] The rabbinic devotion to the cultus, even after A.D. 70, is indicated by the expressions of grief over the loss of the temple and by the continued rabbinic discussions of the regulations of the temple, as recorded by Mishnah *Yoma*. cf. Brown, *Temple*, 4. That the rabbis refused to question the efficacy of the cultus on rationalistic grounds is suggested by the famous story of the Gentile who asked R. Yohanan how the ashes of a red heifer could have purifying effects. When Yohanan's answer seemed evasive, his disciples pursued the matter further. Yohanan answered: "By your life! The corpse does not defile, nor do the waters (mixed with the ashes of a red heifer) purify. It is a decree of the King of Kings. The Holy One, Blessed be He, said, 'I have ordained a decree; no mortal is entitled to transgress it.'" *Pesikt. R. Kahana* 40b. Cited in A. Büchler, *Studies in Sin and Atonement*, 36.

[34] See *2 Bar.* 6:9; 68:4, 5; *1 Enoch* 25:6; 90:29; *Sib. Or.* 3. 294, 575, 772; 5. 247-254.

Otto Michel has observed that the distinction in Hebrews between the cleansing of the flesh and the conscience is also unique when it is compared with the literature of the Judaism of this era.[35] The rabbinic literature, according to Michel, neither emphasizes nor excludes the inner man in its references to the atonement. Thus there are several unique assumptions in Hebrews' view of the sacrificial atonement which have no analogy in the literature of Qumran, the rabbinic literature, or in the OT. Consequently, we shall turn to the literature which bears the stamp of Greek rationalism in order to look for analogous views of earthly sanctuaries, sacrifices, and the dualism of flesh and conscience.

The objection to hand-made sanctuaries and to bloody sacrifices is a frequent theme in the Greek literature extending from distant antiquity into the Christian era. At times the argument is made in terms that are reminiscent of the language of the OT, as when it is sometimes argued that no house is adequate for the deity (cf. Isa 66:1-2).[36] In other instances, the criticism of cultic activities was based on grounds that were strange to Judaism. Some, including Euripides and Plato, considered sacrifice an attempt to bribe the gods.[37] Others pointed to the innocence of the animal. Pythagoras and his followers appear to have rejected animal sacrifice on the basis of the doctrine of the solidarity between creatures.[38] Heraclitus argued that it is no more plausible to believe that one can be purified by the blood of a sacrifice than to think that one who was soiled with mud could be cleansed with mud (μὴ πηλῷ πηλὸν καθαίρειν).[39] A frequent theme in the history of Greek thought was that the deity does not need anything, a view that is repeated in all of the schools of Greek philosophy until the Neopythagoreans and the Neoplatonists and is echoed in the NT (cf. Acts 17:25).[40] This criticism of the

---

[35] Michel, *Hebräer*, 313.

[36] J. Geffcken (*Zwei griechischen Apologeten*, 186) cites a text from the fourth letter of Heraclitus: διδάξετε πρῶτον ἡμᾶς τί ἐστιν ὁ θεός . . . ποῦ ὁ θεός; ἐν τοῖς ναοῖς ἀποκεκλεισμένοις; . . . οὐκ ἴστε, ὅτι οὐκ ἔστι θεὸς χειρόκμητος . . . ; cf. the statement from Euripides, frag. 968: "What house made by workmen could enclose the divine form by layers of walls?" Cf. the statement of Plutarch: "For the universe is a most holy temple and most worthy of a god; into it man is introduced as a spectator at birth, not of hand-made or immovable images, but of those sensible representations of knowable things that the divine mind, says Plato, has revealed" (*de Tranquil. animi* 477c). Cited in S. Sowers *The Hermeneutics of Philo and Hebrews*, 55.

[37] See Plato, *Laws* 10. 885b. One form of atheism is the belief in the unconditional efficacy of sacrifices accompanied by no proper moral disposition.

[38] Nikiprowetzky, "Spiritualisation," 98.

[39] Nikiprowetzky, "Spiritualisation," 99.

[40] According to Euripides, *Herc.* 1346, δεῖται γὰρ ὁ θεός, εἴπερ ἔστ᾽ ὀρθῶς θεός, οὐδενός. The Sophist Antiphon says in *Aletheia* 98 that the deity οὐδενὸς δεῖται οὐδὲ προσδέχεται οὐδενός τι ἀλλ᾽ ἄπειρος καὶ ἀδέητος. Stoics spoke of God as ἀπροσδεῆ and αὐτάρκη (Plutarch, *de Stoic. Rep.* 39 p 1052d). Cited in J. von Arnim, *Stoicorum Veterum Fragmenta*

cult, coming from a variety of assumptions, was normally far more radical than the polemic found among the OT prophets.

It is in the literature subsequent to Plato that we meet systematic attempts to deny the validity of hand-made temples and bloody sacrifices. Plato had raised questions about material sanctuaries in the *Laws*, where he had objected to sanctuaries made of gold, silver or ivory (12. 955e) on the grounds that they were too costly.[41] This text, handed on and interpreted in the Platonic schools, was often interpreted as a prohibition of material sanctuaries.[42] Clement of Alexandria, in his attempt to show that Christianity is a grand philosophy, appeals to Moses, the NT, and Plato in demonstrating the common rejection of a material sanctuary. In citing the text from Plato's *Laws*, he concludes that we must approach God by reason and not by sense-perception (ἄνευ πασῶν τῶν αἰσθήσεων διὰ τοῦ λόγου).[43] Eusebius claims a dependence on both Plato and Plutarch when he argues that nothing made of a material substance is appropriate for God.[44] According to several sources, Zeno rejected material temples, arguing that they are inappropriate for the deity.[45] Thus there was a widespread rejection of material temples among Greek philosophers. Their criticisms, based on metaphysical grounds, were especially useful to Christian apologists who rejected the Jewish cult.[46]

The rejection of animal sacrifices was apparently closely connected to the rejection of hand-made temples in the philosophical literature, for both the temple and the sacrifices had to be appropriate to God. Thus there was the widespread rejection of material sacrifices in the Platonic literature. In the Hermetica, for instance, it is argued that even the burning of incense, the

(Leipzig: Teubner, 1903) 2. 604. This passage attributes self-sufficiency explicitly to the *kosmos*. However, one may compare *SVF* 2. 528, where the *kosmos* is equivalent to God.

[41] See Leonard Ramaroson, "Contre les 'Temples Faits de Main d'Homme,'" 217-238. The offerings recommended by Plato are of the simplest and least expensive kind.

[42] Cicero (*De Leg.* 2. 18) understands the text to be a prohibition of luxury in the cult. Apuleius (*Apol.* 61) understands the Platonic text as a prohibition of private sanctuaries. Lactantius (*De Divinis Institutionibus* 6. 25, 3) understands the Platonic text as a prohibition of corporeal gifts offered to the incorporeal deity. Christian writers such as Eusebius and Theodoret understand the text as a prohibition of both temples and idols.

[43] Clement, *Strom.* 690 (PG 9, 112B).

[44] *Prep. Evang.* 3. 18 (οὐδὲν εἶναι σεμνόν, οὐδὲ προσεοικὸς θείᾳ φύσει ἐν χρυσῷ, καὶ λίθοις, καὶ ἐλέφαντι, τοῖς τε ἐξ ὕλης ἀψύχου κατασκευάσμασιν).

[45] Plutarch, *De Stoicorum Repugnantiis* 1034B; Diogenes Laertius 7. 1. 32-33; Clem. Alex., *Strom.* 5. 11. 76; Origen, *Contra Celsum* 1. 5 (324); Stoabeus, *Anthology* 4. 1. 88.

[46] Ramaroson ("Temples," 224-232) demonstrates that the arguments worked out by the philosophers were soon employed by Christian thinkers. J. Geffcken (*Apologeten*, 186) demonstrates the usefulness of these arguments to Justin and Athenagoras. Justin seems to be following the philosophical tradition when he argues that worship that is worthy of God is not destruction of his gifts by fire, but prayer, praise, and thanksgiving (*Apology* 1. 13).

purest form of material sacrifice, is an abomination to the God who is above all matter. Material sacrifices are to be replaced by λογικαὶ θυσίαι, which are variously interpreted in terms of religious ecstasy and moral qualities.[47] Apollonius of Tyana, who exhibits some dependence on the Platonic tradition, argues that, because God is separate from everything, one may not sacrifice to him, nor offer an animal to him, nor use anything material in connection with him; one turns to him through the *nous*, which requires no human instrument. "Through the most beautiful part of our existence we should succeed to the Good."[48]

The Neoplatonists in particular had raised questions about material sacrifices on the grounds that sacrifices must be worthy of God. Porphyry, having rejected animal sacrifices, distinguished between different grades of deity to whom sacrifices would be proper. To the supreme god he would not sacrifice at all, for even a word is too material.[49] Iamblichus, by contrast, accepted the notion of sacrifice, but his philosophical background demanded of him a sophisticated rationalization of the notion of material sacrifice. Consequently, he argued that fire destroys matter, purifies it, and makes it suitable for the gods.[50] Thus, while some in the Platonic tradition rejected all material sacrifices and others found a place for it in their system, all appear to be aware of the problem of offering a material sacrifice to the deity.

The genuine worship to God, according to the Platonic tradition, was a communion with God by means of the higher aspect of human existence and without a physical cult. We have noticed Apollonius' demand that we worship God with *nous*. A similar perspective is to be seen in Cicero's *De Legibus*, which is modeled upon Plato's *Laws*. Cicero distinguishes radically between the purity of mind and the purity of the body, arguing that a mental stain cannot be removed or washed away by the sprinkling of water. Seneca expresses the spirit of this age also when he says that God is not worshipped with sacrifices and much blood, but rather with a pure mind, and with a good and honest intent.[51] In place of the material cult, the philosophers regularly describe the appropriate way in which the inner man can approach God. He is approached by the singing of hymns, prayer, and in the moral life. In this way the rational part of man serves the incorporeal deity.

[47] *CH* 12. 22, 23; 13. 19, 23. See Frances M. Young, "Temple Cult and Law," 328.

[48] Eusebius, *Prep. Evang.* 4. 13. Cited in M. Nilsson, *Geschichte der griechischen Religion*, 2. 420.

[49] Porphyry, *de Abstin.* 2. 34. See Frances M. Young, "The Idea of Sacrifice in Neoplatonic and Patristic Texts," 278. Cf. Andrew Smith, *Porphyry's Place in the Neoplatonic Tradition*, 96.

[50] *De Myst.* 5. 9, 12, 26. 6. 3. Frances M. Young, "The Idea of Sacrifice," 278; Nilsson, *Geschichte*, 452.

[51] Frag. 123; cited in Wenschkewitz, *Spiritualisierung*, 51.

These texts suggest that the rejection of material sacrifices was common in the philosophical texts of the Hellenistic Age. This critique was frequently based on the metaphysical dualism which distinguished between the material and immaterial worlds. The true cult, according to the Platonic tradition, consists in the relationship of the inner, or higher, part of man with the deity.

Philo of Alexandria. Philo of Alexandria is important for our study not only because of the traditional discussion of his relationship to Hebrews, but also because he stands at an interesting place in the history of philosophy. He shares an appreciation for both the ancestral faith and for the assumptions of Middle Platonism, as we can ascertain in his view of the cult. On the one hand, he is an apologist for the Jerusalem cultus. He is faithful to the law, and he participates in pilgrimages to Jerusalem in order to offer sacrifice.[52] Thus we cannot expect from him the radical critique of sacrifice and of temples that we find among the Greek writers. Nevertheless, the influence of the Hellenistic enlightenment is very evident.

As a loyal Jew, Philo does not question the beauty or the importance of the Jerusalem temple. It is the most beautiful temple in the world (*Leg. ad Gaium* 198); the holy of holies exhibits inexpressible splendor (*de Spec. Leg.* 1. 72). It is for Philo, as for Hebrews (8.5), a copy of the heavenly original. Yet Philo knows that the Jerusalem temple is not adequate for the practice of the true cult. According to *De Plant.* 126, "It is not possible to express our gratitude by means of buildings and oblations and sacrifices, for even the whole world were not a temple adequate for him." The true temple is the cosmos (*De Spec. Leg.* 1. 66), of which the earthly altar and tabernacle are only symbols. Indeed, Philo speaks of the artificial nature of the earthly temple as compared to the universe. He describes it with the pejorative epithet χειρόκμητον, a term that is used also for idols.[53] Thus, while the temple is not rejected, its value lies in its being a symbol of the non-material tabernacle.

Just as the earthly tabernacle is valuable only as a symbol, the blood of animals is not inherently valuable as a sacrifice, for what really matters is the intention of the worshiper. When the worshiper comes with impure motives, his sacrifice is nothing more than a reminder of past sins (*De Vit. Mos.* 2. 108; cf. Heb 10:3). God has no need of sacrifice, Philo frequently tells us (*De Dec.* 41; *De Spec. Leg.* 1. 293; *QE* 2. 50), for God abhors external approaches (*Quod Det.* 21, 107). Sacrifice represents only a condescension of God to the coarse spirit of man. Thus Philo is uncomfortable with the Jerusalem cultus, although he does not reject it totally.

---

[52] *De Providentia* 2. 64.
[53] Nikiprowetzky, "Spiritualisation," 110.

The value of the Jerusalem cultus lies in pointing to a better tent and to a better sacrifice. Philo, like the author of Hebrews, distinguishes between the purification of the higher and lower aspects of human existence.[54] He concedes that the ablutions of the levitical cultus are effective for the cleansing of the body, but the cleansing of the soul is far more important.[55] According to *De Ebrietate* 87, the levitical high priest may seem to be preoccupied with the affairs of the flesh when he stands outside the holy of holies; but when he stands at the invisible altar, he is occupied with things of the spirit which are without blood, flesh, and body. Thus the material cult cannot cleanse the soul. Philo is in the position of arguing that one may have a pure soul without any material cult; i.e., if he comes with a pure intent.[56] But if one offers all of the oblations and sacrifices of the temple, his soul may yet be impure. Thus Philo would agree with the author of Hebrews in asserting that the levitical sacrifices purify the earthly, but not the heavenly, aspect of human existence.

There is an echo of Heb 10:19-22 when Philo says that only those who have pure souls may come to the altar.[57] He speaks at different times of the need for the purity of the πνεῦμα λόγικον,[58] the ψυχή,[59] and the συνείδησις.[60] All of these terms appear to be used in connection with the idea of the divine *logos* whom God has planted in the human soul.[61] According to *Quod Det. Pot.* 145-146 the συνείδησις . . . τῶν ἀδικημάτων is equivalent to the divine *logos* which is sent into the human mind. The conscience, according to *De Decal.* 87, is the accuser (ἔλεγχος) who has been planted in the soul. In *De Fuga* 117-118, conscience/ἔλεγχος is identified with the most holy *logos*, whose presence in the soul prevents even voluntary sin from entering her. Its function is to accuse the soul and bring to light its transgressions.[62] It is this

---

[54] Cf. *Quod Det. Pot.* 20. "A man may submit to sprinklings of holy water and to purifications, befouling his understanding (διάνοια) while cleansing his body" (σῶμα)." Translation of F. H. Colson, *Philo* in LCL.

[55] See *De Spec. Leg.* 1. 259-269 for the distinction between the cleansing of σῶμα and ψυχή. The former is cleansed by the prescribed ritual ablutions, while the latter is cleansed by the reformation of conduct (1. 260) and by contemplation (1. 269). Philo says explicitly that the soul is the higher and dominant element in ourselves.

[56] *De Spec. Leg.* 1. 271; *De Vit. Mos.* 2. 106-107; *De Plant.* 108.

[57] *De Spec. Leg.* 1. 270. Heb 10:19-22 encourages those who have pure consciences to come before God with boldness.

[58] *De Spec. Leg.* 1. 277.

[59] *De Spec. Leg.* 1. 259, 269.

[60] *De Spec. Leg.* 1. 203; *Praem. Poen.* 84.

[61] C. Mauer, Συνείδησις, *TDNT* 7. 913. See E. Brehier, *Les Idées Philosophiques et Religieuses de Philon d'Alexandrie*, 302. Cf. Richard Wallis, "The Idea of Conscience in Philo of Alexandria," 27-35.

[62] For this accusing function of conscience, see *Quod Deus Immut.* 126-135.

side of human existence which can be cleansed only by a spiritual cult which is offered by the soul to God. According to *De Spec. Leg.* 1. 272, the best sacrifice is the oblation of noble living "with hymns and songs of praise," for this sacrifice is offered by the soul alone. Philo thus agrees with many representatives of the Hellenistic enlightenment in insisting on a nonmaterial cult in which the inner man approaches the deity.

Conclusion. This study of the philosophical critique of sacrifice in Philo and among his contemporaries allows us to observe the relationship between these works and the epistle to the Hebrews. While there are some aspects of the Epistle to the Hebrews which are unlike the viewpoint of the Hellenistic philosophers, there are metaphysical assumptions in Heb 9:11-14 which are shared with the writers of the Platonic tradition. These assumptions include the belief that a material sanctuary is inadequate for a true sacrifice. There is the corollary belief that genuine cleansing cannot be effected by means of the blood of animals. Finally, there is the dualistic anthropology which insists that we approach God with the purity of the heavenly aspect of human existence, the conscience. Probably it is because the author of Hebrews shares these assumptions about the inadequacy of an earthly cult that he, like Philo, the Hermetica, and others in this period, affirms that the only genuine sacrifice which the worshippers may offer is the sacrifice of good deeds, fellowship, and praise (cf. Heb 13:15-16).

It is likely, as Valentin Nikiprowetzky has argued,[63] that the author of Hebrews proceeds beyond Philo in his criticism of the material cult. Like the later apologists, he was under no obligation to defend it. The author shares with Philo the uneasiness with the earthly cult, but he proceeds beyond him at some points in the direction of those who would allow no earthly cult. The common feature in these Hellenistic texts is the denial of the validity of any cult on metaphysical grounds.

---

[63] "Spiritualisation," 114.

CHAPTER VII

The Conceptual Background and Purpose of the Midrash in Hebrews 7*

Interpreters have been in general agreement that Hebrews 7 has the form of a midrash homily based on Gen 14:18-20 and Ps 110:4, the only texts of the OT which refer to Melchizedek. It is generally recognized also that this midrash is employed to develop the affirmation about the high priesthood of Christ which has been anticipated earlier in the epistle (2:17; 5:5). However, there has been no consensus on attempts to come to a more precise understanding of the conceptual framework to which the midrash belongs. J. Cambier has argued that Hebrews 7 is best understood against the background of the exegetical method and speculation in Philo.[1] H. Rusche has argued, by contrast, that the treatment of Melchizedek in Hebrews is not characterized by the extreme allegorical speculation of Philo, but lies within the matrix of Jewish apocalyptic thinking.[2] It is the purpose of this chapter to analyze this disputed passage in an attempt to ascertain the conceptual background of the treatment of Melchizedek in Hebrews 7.

Because Melchizedek was the subject of much speculation in the period contemporaneous with the author of Hebrews, the task of ascertaining the conceptual framework to which the treatment of Melchizedek in Hebrews 7 belongs is especially difficult. There is an interest in Melchizedek in apocalyptic expectation, where Melchizedek appears as heavenly judge (11Q Melch), and in Philo. Thus if we are to understand the conceptual background of Hebrews 7 more precisely, we must see how the Melchizedek tradition functions in Hebrews 7 in comparison with the literature of the period. One must ascertain whether the author's interests and presuppositions in handling the references to Melchizedek correspond more to the apocalyptic or Philonic tradition.

The Context of the Midrash

The midrash in chap. 7 is to be understood in the general context which

*Appeared originally in *NovT* 29 (1977).
[1] J. Cambier, *Eschatologie ou Hellénisme dans l'Épître aux Hébreux*, 20.
[2] Helga Rusche, "Die Gestalt des Melchisedek," 238-244.

begins in 5:1-10, the author's description of the high priestly status of Christ. This high priesthood is connected in 5:6, 10, through the allusion to Ps 110:4, with the high priesthood κατὰ τὴν τάξιν Μελχισέδεκ. The presupposition for the author's understanding of this high priesthood is, as 5:5-10 makes clear, the exaltation of Christ (cf. 4:14). Indeed, 5:1-10 argues that the exaltation was the time at which Christ was installed both as υἱός (5:5) and ἀρχιερεύς (5:5-10). Moreover, the climax in 5:10 places the emphasis on the exaltation as Jesus' installation (προσαγορευθείς) as high priest κατὰ τὴν τάξιν Μελχισέδεκ. Thus, just as 1:1-13 presents Christ as the exalted son, 5:10 argues that Christ is the exalted high priest.[3] This affirmation, which is interrupted by the exhortation in 5:11-6:19, is resumed in 6:20, thus providing the background for the midrash in 7:1-28. It is thus because of the exaltation that Christ is the high priest after the order of Melchizedek.

That the midrash in Hebrews 7 assumes the exaltation of Christ is also indicated in the discussion of ἐλπίς in 6:19-20. The community, which has lacked a firm ἐλπίς (cf. 3:6; 6:11; 10:23), is encourged κρατῆσαι τῆς προκειμένης ἐλπίδος (6:18). This hope is described as an ἄγκυρα τῆς ψυχῆς ἀσφαλῆ καὶ βεβαία.[4] Both adjectives suggest stability and certainty, qualities which the author repeatedly emphasizes to his readers (on βεβαία, cf. 2:2; 3:6, 14; 6:16; 9:17).[5] This ἐλπίς is the ἄγκυρα . . . εἰσερχομένη εἰς τὸ ἐσώτερον τοῦ καταπετάσματος (6:19), and is established by the exaltation of Christ. The stability of the hope rests on the fact that Christ, who is now exalted and installed as heavenly high priest, is now εἰς τὸν αἰῶνα (6:20). The use of Ps 110:4 in Hebrews 6:20 to describe Christ as the heavenly high priest sets the stage for the midrash which follows. The midrash concerns the one who, by his exaltation, has given certainty to the Christian hope.

Specific Interests of the Author

The interests of the author in the Melchizedek tradition become clear in 7.1-3, where he brings together those features of Gen 14:18-20 and Ps 110:4 which are useful for his claim that Melchizedek is a divine figure. The predicates with which Melchizedek is described are messianic predicates, intended

---

[3] Both 1:1-13 and 5:1-10 refer to Jesus' earthly life and death, followed by the exaltation. This fact supports O. Michel's view that the confessional statement of 1:3 is of decisive importance in Hebrews.

[4] The anchor is a well-known image of stability and hope. Cf. Heliodor. 7. 25. 4, πᾶσα ἐλπίδος ἄγκυρα, cited in E. Grässer, *Glaube*, 33. This image is totally unknown in the OT and in rabbinic literature. Ἀσφαλῆ καὶ βεβαία is a well-known Hellenistic phrase (Wis 7:23; Philo, *Quis Rer. Div.* 314; *de Conf. Ling.* 106). See J. Moffatt, *Epistle to the Hebrews*, 89.

[5] H. Braun ("Die Gewinnung der Gewissheit" 320) has reconigzed the crucial importance of words suggesting stability in Hebrews. The place of βεβαι- in Hebrews is discussed above, pp. 95-96.

to show that Melchizedek is the one who is ἀφωμοιωμένος τῷ υἱῷ τοῦ θεοῦ, and are intended as a basis of comparison between Melchizedek and Jesus.[6] The remainder of the chapter is an elaboration of 7:3, in which the author uses the superiority of the priesthood of Melchizedek over the levitical priesthood as a means of demonstrating the superiority of the high priesthood of Jesus over the levitical priesthood. This superiority is shown by the fact that Christ "lives" (7:4-10); that his τάξις is heavenly and living (7:11-19); and that his priesthood is "abiding" (7:23-28).[7] All of these reflections are derived exegetically from the christological use of Ps 110:4, the author's text.[8] The author is not interested merely in speculations about Melchizedek; he has used the figure of Melchizedek to point to the character of the τάξις to which he belongs.

The character of the τάξις is established by the use of Ps 110:4 throughout the midrash. This usage is first to be observed at 7:3, where it is said that Melchizedek, ἀπάτωρ, ἀμήτωρ, ἀγενεαλόγητος, μήτε ἀρχὴν ἡμερῶν μήτε ζωῆς τέλος ἔχων, ἀφωμοιωμένος δὲ τῷ υἱῷ τοῦ θεοῦ, μένει ἱερεὺς εἰς τὸ διηνεκές.[9] This passage is often explained as an example of the rabbinic and Philonic hermeneutical principle, *quod non in Thora, non in Mundo.*[10] However, as Käsemann has rightly argued, the author is not merely an independent exegete but one who comes to his text with an important *Tendenz.*[11] Thus his use of the rabbinic hermeneutical device is intended to develop a motif which is important for him. In the author's text of Ps 110:4 are the words εἰς τὸν αἰῶνα which, as 6:20 shows, were of great significance for him. To this phrase the author adds μένει in 7:3d. The rest of this *feierliche* statement is to be understood as an interpretation of 7:3d, which stood in the author's text. The phrases in 7:3a (ἀπάτωρ, ἀμήτωρ, ἀγενεαλόγητος) and 7:3c (ἀφωμοιωμένος δὲ τῷ υἱῷ τοῦ θεοῦ) are divine predicates based on the Scripture text in 7:3d. The phrase in 7:3b (μήτε ἀρχὴν ἡμερῶν μήτε ζωῆς τέλος ἔχων) is parallel to 7:3d and serves to interpret the Scripture cited from Ps 110:4.

---

6   Cf. Zech 9:9; Mal 3:20; Jer 23:5; Dan 9:24; Isa 9:5; Mic 5:4 for "righteousness" and "peace" attributed to the Messiah. Cf. H. Zimmerman, *Die Hohepriester-Christologie des Hebräerbriefes,* 13.

7   F. Schröger, *Der Verfasser des Hebräerbriefs als Schriftausleger,* 133.

8   O. Michel, *Der Brief an die Hebräer,* 256.

9   G. Theissen (*Untersuchungen,* 21) has argued that 7:3 was a hymn which the author has taken over. This view is unlikely. The last line is obviously taken from Ps 110:4, a text which the author uses elsewhere (6:20; 10:5-10); 3b is an interpretation of this text; and 3a is composed of divine predicates which were common in the author's day.

10   See Str-B 3. 694-95. For Philo's use of this hermeneutical device, see *Quod Det. Pot.* 48; *de Eb.* 14.

11   E. Käsemann, *Gottesvolk,* 134.

The divine predicates, ἀπάτωρ and ἀμήτωρ, are well known in the Hellenistic world.[12] One may compare here especially Philo's description of Sarah as ἀμήτωρ (*de Eb.* 14). She, as ἀμήτωρ, had no connection with the senses. Philo implies also that Melchizedek is "without parents," for he contrasts Melchizedek to the Moabites and Ammonites whose parents are νοῦς and αἴσθησις (*Leg. All.* 3. 79-82).[13] Thus for both Hebrews and Philo, Melchizedek is a heavenly being, not a part of the world of sense perception (cf. 7:16). Similarly, Plotinus claims that Aphrodite, who has her home in the intelligible world, is ἀμήτορα; and because she has no contact with matter, she is immutable (ἐφ᾽ ἑαυτῆς μένουσαν).[14] In the Pistis Sophia ἀπάτορες is regularly used for heavenly beings.[15] These texts present an interesting parallel to Hebrews, inasmuch as each of these texts uses the term ἀπάτωρ (or ἀμήτωρ) for transcendent beings who have no contact with sense perception. Such honorific terms, which were on occasion used for pagan deities, would have no place in an apocalyptic work like 11Q Melch. Such terminology indicates the proximity of Hebrews 7 to the conceptual framework of Philo. One may also observe that the term ἀγενεαλόγητος is not chosen merely because of the author's adherence to rabbinic exegetical principles. One may compare Philo, *de Congress.* 43-46, where Philo says that in relating the OT narratives about Abraham's two wives, he is dealing with ideal types or symbols, οὐχ ἱστορικὴ γενεαλογία. Similarly, in *de Ab.* 31, Philo says that Moses extols the sage by not giving his genealogy, for the sage has no family except virtues and virtuous actions.[16] Thus for both Philo and Hebrews, not to have a genealogy is the characteristic of the man of God.

The next phrase, μήτε ἀρχὴν μήτε ζωῆς τέλος ἔχων, accents the eternity of Melchizedek and is an appropriate transition to 7:3d. That which is divine (ἀπάτωρ, ἀμήτωρ) is eternal. The phrase has its clearest analogies in the Hellenistic metaphysical speculation. Aristotle, who argues (against Plato) that the world was not generated (οὐ γέγονεν), maintains that it is eternal, adding the words· ἀρχὴν μὲν καὶ τελευτὴν οὐκ ἔχων τοῦ παντὸς αἰῶνος.[17] This formulation is to be compared with Plutarch's description of God as the one who is οὐ γεγονὸς οὐδ᾽ ἐσόμενον, οὐδ᾽ ἀρξάμενον οὐδὲ

---

[12] The context makes it clear that the author does not use ἀπάτωρ and ἀμήτωρ in the pejorative sense of "orphan" or "illegitimae child," as was common in Judaism. Rather the terms carry the meaning of the divine being of Hellenism. Cf. Euripides, *Ion.* 109; Plato, *Symp.* 180d. See G. Schrenk, Ἀπάτωρ, *TDNT* 5. 1021-1022. J. Moffatt, *Hebrews*, 92.

[13] G. Theissen, *Untersuchungen*, 27.

[14] Plotinus, *En.* 3. 5. 2. 15-17.

[15] See the text of C. Schmidt, *Koptisch-gnostische Schriften*, 141, 142-144.

[16] See Lala Kalyan Kumar Dey, *The Intermediary World and Patterns of Perfection in Philo and Hebrews*, 91.

[17] *de Caelo* 1. 9. 283 b 26.

παυσόμενον.[18] Similarly, the αἰών inscription of Eleusis speaks of the αἰών as ἀρχὴν μὲν καὶ τελευτὴν οὐκ ἔχων τοῦ παντὸς αἰῶνος.[19] It is obvious that the terminology of Heb 7:3b has a long history in Greek metaphysics and piety. Hebrews stands in agreement with Plutarch, who adapted the philosophical expression into his piety. Just as Plutarch uses the expression to describe his god who is separated from matter, Hebrews uses the terminology as a description of a heavenly being.

It is striking that the author, in the next line, compares Melchizedek to the υἱός, although the psalm appears to suggest that the υἱός (the σύ) is to be compared to Melchizedek. Ἀφωμοιωμένος τῷ υἱῷ is parallel to κατὰ τὴν τάξιν Μελχισέδεκ in the psalm, with ἀφωμοιωμένος serving as the author's interpretative word for τάξιν. Thus as the midrash later makes clear, the author is not interested in Melchizedek for his own sake. Rather, his interest is to delineate the features of the τάξις to which Melchizedek and Jesus belong.

The particular characteristic of this τάξις of Melchizedek lies in its eternity, for the author concludes here, as in 7:23-24, with the claim that the priesthood of Melchizedek μένει εἰς τὸ διηνεκές. Ps 110:4 is obviously an exaltation text for the author, as 1:3, 13; 6:20 indicate. As in 1:5-13, the author understands the exaltation to mean that Christ, in the heavenly world, "remains" (διαμένει, 1:11). The interest is not in the person of Melchizedek, but in the τάξις to which he belongs. This τάξις, because it is in the heavenly sphere, is characterized by the verb μένει. It is this characteristic which dominates the *feierliche* statement of 7:3, and subsequently the entire midrash.[20] Thus the author's interest in the exaltation (6:20) is that Christ has become the divine being who abides. Μένειν is thus understood within a spatial framework as a quality resulting from the exaltation.

Erich Grässer has written, "Es fällt auf, wie oft Hb das hohepriesterliche Wirken Jesu also eines *in aeternum* qualifiziert (5:6; 7:17, 21, 24f., 28; 13:8; 6:20; 7:3).[21] This fact has been noted by other interpreters.[22] Although chaps. 1 and 7 employ diffferent titles for the exalted one, the two chapters both appeal to the category of "abiding" in demonstrating his superiority to earthly beings. There is never any reference to the abiding of Melchizedek at Qumran. Whereas Melchizedek appears at Qumran as avenger and judge, the significant feature about Melchizedek in Hebrews is that he abides.

---

[18] *The E at Delphi* c. 20.

[19] For the text of the Αἰών inscription, see G. Dittenberger, *Sylloge Inscriptionum Graecarum*, 1125.

[20] The dominance of this motif in the midrash has been observed by C. Spicq, *L'Épître aux Hébreux*, 2. 197 and J. Cambier, 20.

[21] *Glaube*, 213.

[22] C. O. Cullmann, *The Christology of the New Testament*, 99. Cf. G. Schrenk, Ἀρχιερεύς, *TDNT* 3. 276.

Μένει, used in 7:3 for the τάξιν of Melchizedek, is used regularly in Hebrews for heavenly realities (cf. 1:11, διαμένει; 7:23; 10:34; 12:27; 13:14). Both in 7:3, 23 and 1:11 the term (or the related term διαμένει) has close affinities with the literature influenced by Plato. Philo regularly attributes immutability to the deity who is described as ὁ μένων and μονή (de Som. 2. 221). Μένειν is attributed by Philo to God and to the κόσμος νοητός, the intelligible world. Only the sage who leaves the unstable creation can achieve this stability (cf. de Post. Cain. 23) or receive a share of God's μονή (de Som. 2. 237). Similarly, in Plotinus and in the Hermetica, μένειν is regularly used for that which has no contact with the material creation.[23] Thus just as μένειν is used in Platonism for the immutability of the deity, it is used in Hebrews to show the immutability of Christ.

As an instrument for getting at this immutabilty of Christ, the permanence of the high priest now becomes a significant feature of the midrash. The section 7:4-10, introduced by θεωρεῖτε δὲ πηλίκος οὗτος, has as its purpose the contrasting of Melchizedek with Abraham (vv 4-7) and his descendants (vv 8-10). Just as the pericope in 1:1-13 is intended to show that Christ is "better" than angels, vv 4-10 show that the order of Melchizedek is superior to the levitical order (τὸ ἔλαττον ὑπὸ τοῦ κρείττονος εὐλογεῖται, 7:7). Melchizedek, in being the imparter of blessing to Abraham and in receiving tithes from him (7:6), is greater than the levitical priesthood. This greatness is also indicated by the contrast between the levitical priests and Melchizedek in 7:8, where the Levites are described as ἀποθνήσκοντες ἄνθρωποι who are contrasted to the one about whom it is said ὅτι ζῇ. Ζῇ is a comment on μήτε ἀρχὴν ἡμερῶν μήτε ζωῆς τέλος ἔχων in v 3. The term is used, as in 7:3, 25, as an exegetical comment on Ps 110:4, and is to be compared to ζωὴ ἀκαταλύτου in 7:16. Ἀποθνήσκοντες is to be compared with the author's view of θάνατος as the particular characteristic of the earthly sphere (2:14). This contrast between "life" and "death" is to be understood in a spatial framework as the distinction between two spheres. The levitical priesthood belongs to the sphere of death; because of the exaltation, Christ now is in the sphere of life. Just as the author distinguishes spatially between the earthly and heavenly cultus in 9:1, 11-14, 23, he distinguishes here between the sphere of life and the sphere of death.[24] This contrast between the spheres of "life" and of "death" is comparable with Philo's similar contrast between the

---

[23] On Corpus Hermeticum, cf. 11. 2-4; On Plotinus, cf. En. 5. 4. 1; 3. 7. 2. 13, 20; 3. 7. 3. 12; 6. 9. 9. 5-6. On μένειν, cf. above, page 51.

[24] F. J. Schierse (Verheissung und Heilsvollendung, 9-11) shows convincingly that the author's argumentation works within the framework of the dichotomy heavenly-earthly, and that the categories of "old covenant" and "new covenant" are subordinated to the contrast between the heavenly and earthly reality.

spheres of mortality and immortality. In *de Som*. 2. 231 Philo distinguishes between the θνητὸς γένος, which lives in the created world, and the ἀθάνατος γένος, which has no part in the material world. This distinction is also comparable with the distinction in the Hermetica between ἀθανασία, the characteristic of αἰών, and θάνατος, which belongs to the sphere of γένεσις (*CH* 11. 1-4). The εἰς τὸν αἰῶνα, which the author has read with his own metaphysical assumptions, is used to support the argument that Christ, now exalted to the heavenly world, abides. Such metaphysical assumptions show considerable affinities to the world of Philo and others influenced by Platonism.

The purpose of the section 7:11-28 is to indicate the ways in which the heavenly τάξις is superior to the earthly τάξις.[25] The author introduces this contrast through an exegetical device which is perhaps original to him. By playing off a quotation from the Writings against the quotation from the Law, he finds in Scripture a reference to the inadequacy of the old order (cf. 8:13). The difference between the two τάξεις is stated in parallel terms in 7:16. One is established κατὰ νόμον ἐντολῆς σαρκίνης, the other is established κατὰ δύναμιν ζωῆς ἀκαταλύτου. It is significant that the author thinks not only in terms of "old" and "new," but in terms of two different spheres.[26] The exaltation implies that Christ is removed from the sphere of the earthly σαρκίνη world where θάνατος rules.[27] The significance of ζωή has been indicated above. The important feature of this text is the alignment of adjectives which inform the argument in the contrast between σαρκίνη and ἀκατάλυτος. Σαρκίνη is always used in the NT with a negative connotation, usually in contrast with πνεῦμα(πνευματικός, cf. Rom 7:14; 1 Cor 3:1; 2 Cor 3:3). Σάρξ in Hebrews always has the meaning of that which is peculiar to the material world or the material aspect of human existence.[28] At

---

[25] Τάξις, which generally means "order" or "rank," refers in Hebrews to the entirely different nature of Christ's priesthood as compared with that of Aaron. Cf. BAG, 811. In Hebrews τάξις refers to two different spheres of existence. The use of this term to refer to a sphere of existence is parallel to the use which is made in Plotinus (*En*. 5. 6. 4) and the Gnostic Fourth Treatise of the Jung Codex (103:18), where there are two τάξεις τῶν ὄντων. One may compare Philo, *de Som*. 2. 229-231, where τάξις and γένος are terms used for a sphere of existence.

[26] Cf. 9:1, 11, where the ἅγιον κόσμικόν is contrasted with the temple οὐ χειροποίητος (cf. also 9:24). These texts show that the author thinks not only in terms of a horizontal time line, but in terms of spheres of reality.

[27] As 5:7 indicates, Jesus is considered a heavenly being whose earthly life as υἱός is only a fixed period. Thus αἷμα and σάρξ is what Jesus accepted (2:14). E. Schweizer has shown that σάρξ in Hebrews refers to the earthly sphere which is separated from the divine world. Σάρξ, *TDNT* 7. 143. In Hellenistic literature σάρξ frequently appears as a term for matter (Plutarch, *Mor*. 2. 745e; *Leg. All*. 3. 152). See E. Schweizer, "Die hellenistische Komponente im neutestamentlichen σάρξ Begriff," 242-253.

[28] Schweizer, *TDNT* 7. 143.

12:9 the author distinguishes between the fathers τῆς σαρκός and the father τῶν πνευματῶν. At 9:13-14, σάρξ belongs to the earthly aspect of man while συνείδησις belongs to man's heavenly existence.[29] The levitical system is composed of δικαιώματα σαρκός (9:10); i.e., it belongs to the sphere that is κοσμικός (9:1). Thus the νόμος ἐντολῆς σαρκίνης of Heb 7:16 is obviously understood in a spatial framework here. The assessment which is made of the angels (chap. 1) and of the earthly temple (9:1, 11-14) is the same as the assessment of the levitical priesthood here. It belongs to the earthly sphere, and is characterized by transitoriness.

This negative evaluation of σάρξ, suggested in Heb 7:16, finds analogies in Philo, for whom the flesh is a burden. Because God is a non-fleshly, non-corporeal being, those who come near to God lay aside the flesh (de Som. 2. 232).[30] Such a negative undersanding of the flesh is to be seen in the context of Philo's cosmic dualism, for in Philo flesh belongs to the lower sphere of existence.[31] Apparently the author of Hebrews is in agreement with Philo's assumption, for he argues that the τάξις which is "fleshly" is inferior (7:16).

Σαρκίνη is the opposite of ἀκατάλυτος, which means "indestructible" or "unending."[32] As a contrast to σαρκίνη the term is used in a spatial sense to refer to the sphere of the exalted Christ. The use of ἀκατάλυτος within a spatial framework is to be compared with Philo's use of the cognate word, καταλύειν. Philo (de Mut. Nom. 34) says of the terrestrial sphere, φθείρεται οὖν εἰκότως τὸ γεῶδες καὶ καταλύεται. Καταλύειν is thus the characteristic of the terrestrial world.[33] Ἀκατάλυτος of Heb 7:16 is used in a spatial framework to speak of the authentic life, which belongs to the heavenly world.[34] The point of the exaltation is, for the author, that Christ is now removed from the sphere of σάρξ and has the "indestructible" life of the heavenly sphere. This reflection is derived from the metaphysical assumptions with which the author has read his text, Ps 110:4.

The author's interest in the oath (ὁρκωμοσία) is derived from the ὤμωσεν of Ps 110:4 (7:20-22). The function of the oath, as 6:17-18 makes

---

[29] See above, p. 108. Cf. Schierse, Verheissung, 39: "Dem Gegensatz von Himmel und Erde entspricht also ein anthropologischer Dualismus von Fleisch und Gewissen."

[30] G. Theissen, Hebräerbrief, 31, "Fleischliche Gebote (7:16), Schwäche (7:18), und Sterblichkeit (7:23) sind Kennzeichen des Irdischen schlechthin."

[31] Schweizer, TDNT 7. 122.

[32] F. Büchsel, Ἀκατάλυτος, TDNT 4. 339.

[33] J. Cambier, Hellénisme, 20.

[34] Ibid. Cambier observes the correspondence between the "incorruptible life" in Heb 7:16 and Philo, Leg. All. 1. 32, where the latter describes the creation of man: ὁ δὲ νοῦς οὗτος γεῶδής ἐστι τῷ ὄντι καὶ φθαρτός, εἰ μὴ ὁ θεὸς ἐμπνεύσειεν αὐτῷ δύναμιν ἀληθινῆς ζωῆς. "Par la dernière expression ἀληθινῆς ζωῆς, il faut entendre, selon la pensée alexandrine, la vraie vie telle que Dieu la possède, telle qu'elle existe dans la sphère céleste."

clear, is to show God's unchangeability (ἀμετάθετος), and thus to ground ἐλπίς. The oath is of considerable significance to the author, as both 6:17-18 and 7:20-22 indicate. Indeed, the presence or absence of an oath is the author's criterion for evaluating the two covenants. Thus in 7:20-22 the author works out the contrast between Christ and the levitical priesthood as the contrast between οἱ μέν . . . χωρὶς ὁρκωμοσίας and ὁ δέ . . . μετὰ ὁρκωμοσίας. This same contrast is established in 7:28, where the author contrasts ὁ νόμος and ὁ λόγος τῆς ὁρκωμοσίας. The significance of the oath is to verify (cf. 6:16; εἰς βεβαίωσιν) the absolute reliability of the high priesthood of Christ. Thus the oath functions here to serve the parenetic needs of the community by giving grounds for βεβαίωσις. The oath shows that Christ, and not the earthly priesthood, is unfailing and εἰς τὸν αἰῶνα (7:21, 28).[35] Such an oath is intended to anchor the hopes of the Christian community (6:19-20).

It is likely, though not certain, that behind the author's interest in the function of the oath in providing certainty there are again metaphysical assumptions which are derived from Hellenistic metaphysics. That the divine oath provides certainty (βεβαίωσις) is a view which the author shares with Philo.[36] Indeed, the LXX reading of Ps 110:4, according to which God οὐ μεταμεληθήσεται (7:21), is reminiscent of Philo's claim that God, unlike men, never repents of what he says (*de Vit. Mos* 1. 283; *Deus Immut.* 26). Philo's argument concerning the oath is rooted in his metaphysical understanding of the immutability of God.[37] It is likely that the author of Hebrews, whose metaphysical assumptions lead him to affirm the immutability of Christ (1:10-12), shares with Philo the view that the immutability of God gives validity to his oath. God has sworn that the high priesthood of Jesus is εἰς τὸν αἰῶνα. Such an oath is intended to provide certainty for the community.

This oath is guaranteed by Jesus, the ἔγγυος (7:22). Just as his priesthood is "better" than the levitical priesthood (7:7), he is the guarantor that the new covenant is "better" than the old. Ἔγγυος is a term derived from Greek legal terminology,[38] signifying that which gives certainty to a contract or promise. In this text the use of the term corresponds to the author's

---

[35] O. Michel, (*Hebräer*, 274) observes that the oath brings to expression the importance of εἰς τὸν αἰῶνα.

[36] *Leg. All.* 3. 204; *de Sac. A.C.* 93.

[37] *Leg. All.* 2. 89. See O. Hofius, "Die Unabänderlichkeit des göttlichen Heilsratschlusses," 140. Hofius concedes the verbal similarity between Hebrews and Philo, but denies that Hebrews contains such an interest in the immutability of the deity. Hofius argues that the closest parallels to Hebrews' interest in the reliability of the oath are OT statements (Isa 40:8; 45:23; 31:2; Jer 4:28; Ezek 12:28) and rabbinic exegetical traditions on Num 23:19.

[38] H. Preisker, Ἔγγυος, *TDNT* 2. 329.

general interest in the certainty and stability that are present in the new covenant. God's oath is confirmed by his deed. Thus his deed in Jesus Christ is a confirmation of his oath. This fact is indicated in 6:16-20, where the author moves from the certainty provided by the oath to the hope which is established by the exaltation. Christ is, as 6:16-20 indicates, the ἔγγυος as a result of the events which culminated in the exaltation.[39]

That the one heavenly high priest guaranteed by God stands in contrast with the human levitical priests has been argued in 7:5, 8, 20. The very plurality of high priests for the author is a sign of incompleteness and imperfection (10:1-4), as the corresponding οἱ μέν (7:23) —ὁ δέ (7:24) clauses indicate.[40] In this contrast, the limitation of the levitical priests is that they are transitory: καὶ οἱ . . . ἱερεῖς διὰ τὸ θανάτῳ κωλύεσθαι παραμένειν. Παραμένειν is a strengthened form of μένειν, and is used here to mean "abide in office."[41] The author here, as in 7:8, understands mortality as signifying transitoriness. For him, θάνατος is the reality of the earthly sphere (cf. 2:14). Such a view is in contrast with the traditional belief that the priesthood did remain. One may compare, for instance, Josephus' claim (using παραμένειν) that the high priesthood did remain (Ant. 11. 309). But the author of Hebrews read his text with his own metaphysical assumptions, according to which earthly existence, the realm of θάνατος, σάρξ (7:16), and matter (12:18) are marked by transitoriness.

The characteristic of the exalted Christ, by contrast, is that he abides (ὁ δὲ διὰ τὸ μένειν αὐτὸν ἀπαράβατον ἔχει τὴν ἱερωσύνην). Because of the exaltation, Christ does not belong to the sphere of σάρξ that is marked by transitoriness. The author's text, read with his own metaphysical assumptions, signifies the abiding of the exalted one. Just as the author argues for Christ's superiority to angels on the basis of his "abiding," he argues for his superiority to the levitical priesthood on the same basis. Μένειν and ἀπαράβατος are used for that which is "incorruptible" or "immutable."[42] Just as the exalted Christ is "the same" (1:12, 13:8), he is here described as immutable.[43] This immutability is further indicated by μένειν (cf. 7:3), a verb which is used regularly in Hebrews for the immutability and stability of heavenly realities, and in specific contrast with the transitoriness of earthly existence. This spatial understanding, by which μένειν is used for the heavenly world, finds

[39] *Ibid.*

[40] Michel, *Hebräer*, 276.

[41] *Ibid.*

[42] J. Schneider, Ἀπαράβατος, *TDNT* 5. 742. Instead of the passive "unchangeable," many expositors have suggested the active meaning, "which cannot be transferred to another." Schneider correctly argues that this interpretation does not fit the context, as the contrast is not directed toward a transferable priesthood in 7:23. Cf. Michel, *Hebräer*, 276.

[43] Cf. J. Cambier, *Hellénisme*, 20.

its closest analogies in Platonism (*Tim.* 37D; *CH* 11. 4; Philo, *de Som.* 2. 221, 237). The author has, therefore, read his text (Ps 110:4) within a dualistic framework. Inasmuch as Psalm 110 is read christologically as an exaltation text, these assumptions inform his view of the exaltation of Christ.

It is not the purpose of this midrash to engage merely in metaphysical speculation, as the concluding remarks in 7:25-28 indicate. The motif of "abiding" provides the groundwork for parenetic statements. Ὅθεν designates a logical result in Hebrews (cf. 2:17; 3:1; 8:3; 9:18),[44] and is used to indicate the result of the christological reflections for the life of the community. This result is to solidify the hope of a community which has lacked certainty.[45] This hope is solidified in the knowledge of the finality and duration of Christ's work for his people. He is able to save his people εἰς τὸ παντελές, and he always (πάντοτε) intercedes. Both εἰς τὸ παντελές and πάντοτε resume and explicate the εἰς τὸν αἰῶνα of the psalm, as ὅθεν indicates. The accent is not on σώζειν or ἐντυγχάνειν, but on the duration and finality of Christ's work. Εἰς τὸ παντελές means "for all time."[46] Πάντοτε ζῶν signifies that the exalted Christ, unlike earthly beings, is "at all times" active for his people, an inference drawn from Ps 110:4. The once-for-all (ἐφάπαξ) character of Christ's death, contrasted with the repeated sacrifices of the levitical priests (καθ' ἡμέραν ἀνάγκη) is also an inference from the author's metaphysical understanding of Ps 110:4 (7:28). Because Christ is exalted, his work is final (εἰς τὸ παντελές) and therefore ἐφάπαξ.[47] The author hopes, by these turns in the argument, to anchor the hope of the Christian community. Christology and metaphysics in this midrash are made serviceable to the concrete needs of the community.[48] Because the exalted

[44] Ὅθεν is never used by Paul. It has the meaning, "from which reason" or "therefore." BAG, 557.

[45] O. Michel correctly summarizes a growing consensus in Hebrews scholarship: "die theologisch-didaktischen Teile des Briefes stehen also nicht auf sich selbst, sondern bilden die Voraussetzung für die Paränese" (59). Cf. Käsemann's view (*Gottesvolk*, 156) that the purpose of the high priestly language is to provide "Befestigung" for the hopes of the community.

[46] BAG, 613.

[47] The ἅπαξ/ἐφάπαξ idea in Hebrews, as a reference to Christ's death (9:12, 26), is derived from the author's two-sphere world view. That which is "heavenly" is completed, εἰς τὸ παντελές. The assumption which informs this usage of ἐφάπαξ is to be compared with the Platonic idea that a "once-for-allness" characterizes eternity, while time (and sense perception) is always in the process of "becoming" and is never completed. Plotinus takes up this view and elaborates it when he argues that all that exists within time is ἀτελές (3. 7. 6. 42); i.e., it is never complete. In contrast, all that exists in the intelligible world is forever completed. This kind of argumentation has probably influenced Hebrews in the development of the use of ἐφάπαξ. Levitical priests, who lived within the earthly sphere, were never finished (10:2-4). Christ, who offered himself in the heavenly sphere, has finished his task ἐφάπαξ.

[48] H. Braun, "Gewissheit," 322-324.

Christ has achieved a permanent status as the one who is "higher than the heavens" (7:26), he has provided the certainty which the community had lacked.

Such use of Scripture, with its dualistic reading of the OT and its emphasis on the stability of the deity, is at home in the environment of Philo. Both Philo and Hebrews share this dualistic reading of the OT and both agree that immutability comes in leaving this creation. Moreover, just as Philo argues that the immutable God provides βεβαίωσις for the man of God (de Post. Cain. 23; de Som. 2. 221-237), Hebrews argues that the immutability of the exalted Christ provides the ἄγκυραν . . . ἀσφαλῆ τε καὶ βεβαίαν (6:19). Thus the certainty which the author attempts to provide his community in 7:25-28 is grounded in the fact that Jesus belongs to the τάξις which is abiding.

Conclusion

The conceptual framework which is exhibited in Hebrews 7 finds its closest analogies in the work of Philo, as this study has shown. The arguments made about the order of Melchizedek have little in common with the interests that are developed in 11Q Melch. 11Q Melch does not argue from the "abiding" of this order of priesthood; nor does this document base its expectation on the dualistic reading of the OT which one finds in Hebrews. Conversely, Hebrews 7 has none of 11Q Melch's interest in Melchizedek as avenger and judge. The dualistic reading of the OT, the use of Hellenistic terminology in 7:3, and the focus on the abiding of the exalted one have their closest analogies in the work of Philo.

CHAPTER VIII

THE STRUCTURE AND PURPOSE OF THE CATENA IN HEBREWS 1:5-13*

Interpreters have been in general agreement that the catena of Scripture quotations in Heb 1:5-13 is employed to provide support for the affirmation which is made in Heb 1:1-4: that Jesus Christ, who sits at God's right hand, now has a dignity and status which make him "better than angels" (1:4). However, there has been no consensus on attempts to come to a more precise understanding of the place of the catena in the total argument of Hebrews, for this passage has continued to present exegetical difficulties. H. Windisch saw in the catena a polemic against some type of Gnosticizing angel worship.[1] O. Michel argues that the catena is an expanded commentary on the exaltation, presenting successive stages in the enthronement.[2] Similarly, E. Käsemann saw here a description of successive stages of the enthronement drama.[3] According to Käsemann, "Heb (aufweist) ein festes Schema der Christologie, in welchem die Offenbarung des Sohnes immer weitere Kreise zieht und verschiedene Akte umfasst." It is the purpose of this chapter to analyze this much-disputed passage in an attempt to ascertain the structure and purpose of the catena within the total argument of the epistle.

Because in the catena the author is quoting and using very little of his own language, the task of ascertaining his intention is especially difficult. Furthermore, the author tends to quote very fully and offers few exegetical comments of his own. The task of the interpreter, consequently, is to ascertain the thrust of individual citations against the background of the argumentation of the entire epistle. Careful attention must be given to words and phrases which appear to be recurring themes in the catena and which are significant elsewhere in the epistle. By focusing on motifs which are of importance for the author elsewhere in the epistle, one can ascertain more clearly the purpose for which individual citations are given as well as the purpose of the entire catena.

The catena must be understood in the light of the preceding section,

*Revised from an earlier article which appeared in *CBQ* 38 (1976)

[1] H. Windisch, *Der Hebräerbrief*, 14-15.
[2] O. Michel, *Der Brief an die Hebräer*, 109.
[3] E. Käsemann, *Gottesvolk*, 59.

1:1-4. Verse 3 is to be understood, as G. Bornkamm[4] and G. Deichgräber have shown, as a christological hymn which "Den ganzen Christusweg nachzeichnet,"[5] including the pre-existence, earthly life, and exaltation of Christ. It is probable that this hymn concluded with an affirmation of the exaltation of Christ, as is common in NT hymnic material (cf. 1 Tim 3:16; Phil 2:11). The author's interest in this hymn may derive from the presence of the exaltation motif in it, as the exaltation is of enormous importance to him.[6]

The exaltation is referred to, as is usual in the NT, through the allusion to Ps 110:1.[7] This text is important elsewhere in Hebrews for the understanding of Christ's heavenly existence (cf. 8:1; 10:12; 12:2). It is especially significant that Ps 110:1, used in the hymn in 1:3 and supplied by the author in 1:13, provides the framework to the citations. The important place given to Ps 110:1 indicates that the catena is to be understood as an interpretation of the exaltation, a reflection on the hymn in 1:1-3. Ἐν ὑψηλοῖς, added to the psalm quotation,[8] as is ἐν τοῖς οὐρανοῖς in 8:1, emphasizes the spatial aspect of the exaltation. That Christ is ἐν ὑψηλοῖς or ἐν τοῖς οὐρανοῖς is of great importance to the author of Hebrews, for a fundamental aspect of his argumentation is the spatial distinction between this creation (9:11, 23; 12:18, 22)

---

[4] G. Bornkamm, "Das Bekenntnis im Hebräerbrief," *Studien zu Antike und Christentum* (Munich: Kaiser, 1959) 2. 198.

[5] G. Deichgräber, *Gotteshymnus und Christushymnus in der frühen Christenheit* (SUNT; Göttingen: Vandenhoeck und Ruprecht, 1967) 137.

[6] O. Michel (*Hebräer*, 60-61) argues that the "Ausgangspunkt" for the author's thinking is the "Einsetzung in die Sohnschaft und das Hohepriestertum Christi" (Heb 1:1-4). A more precise way of describing the author's "Ausgangspunkt" it to say that the exaltation is the starting point for the author's reflections, for the author uses a variety of titles (ἀρχηγός, πρόδρομος, υἱός, ἀρχιερεύς) to describe Christ's work as the exalted one. Cf. U. Luck, "Himmlisches und irdisches Geschehen im Hebräerbrief," 208.

[7] Cf. F. Hahn, *Christologische Hoheitstitel*, 127. Cf. David M. Hay, *Glory at the Right Hand; Psalm 110 in Early Christianity* (SBLMS; New York: Abingdon, 1973) *passim*.

[8] One cannot be certain whether ἐν ὑψηλοῖς was originally a part of the hymn or has been supplied by the author. The phrase ἐν τοῖς οὐρανοῖς is added to the psalm citation in 8:1; similarly, ἐν τοῖς ἐπουρανίοις (οὐρανοῖς in B C pc) in Eph 1:20. Perhaps, as O. Michel (105) suggests, "wir (haben) mit einer alten christlichen Bekenntnisformel zu tun, die verschiedene griechische Gestalt angenommen . . . hat." If the author has taken the phrase over from an earlier tradition, its meaning for him would correspond to the meaning which he regularly gives to "heaven" or "the heavens" (cf. 8:1).

Ἐν ὑψηλοῖς, a phrase used by no other author in the NT, is a LXX expression (cf. Ps 92:4; 112:5). It is to be observed that the author employs no unified terminology for the heavenly world. He alternates, with no apparent change in meaning, between οὐρανός (9:24; 11:12), οὐρανοί (1:10; 4:14; 7:26; 9:23; 12:23, 25), and ἐπουρανία (8:5). "The heavens" can refer either to the transitory created order (1:10; 12:26) or to the eternal place of the exaltation (9:24). A. Cody rightly distinguishes between the "cosmologically" heavenly and the "axiologically" heavenly. Cf. *Heavenly Sanctuary and Heavenly Liturgy*, 77-80. Ἐν ὑψηλοῖς belongs to the axiologically heavenly sphere.

and the heavenly world of the exaltation. Indeed, it is precisely because the exaltation places Christ ἐν ὑψηλοῖς, beyond this creation (9:1), that his work is effective (9:11-14).⁹ Ἐν ὑψηλοῖς thus introduces the spatial category into the author's argument. The introduction of this category is of decisive importance in the catena for developing the author's understanding of the exaltation.

The significance of the exaltation is stated in 1:4. Christ has received a new name and is κρείττων τῶν ἀγγέλων. Inasmuch as these two motifs (the new name and superiority to angels) are commonly identified with the exaltation of Christ (cf. Phil 2:9; 1 Pet 3:22; Eph 1:20), it is probable that the author has taken them over from earlier tradition.¹⁰ Κρείττων is the author's word here (19 times in the NT, 13 times in Hebrews). The term is used to show that the exaltation has given Christ a status "better" and more exalted than the angels. Κρείττων, which is used frequently by the author in making value judgments, is often used to function in connection with the spatial contrast between the heavenly ("better") reality, and the earthly, inferior reality (see 9:23; 10:34; 12:24). Probably κρείττων functions in 1:4 in this spatial contrast to indicate that Christ, not the angels, is exalted to the heavenly world.

The Structure of the Catena

The catena which follows takes up the issue of Christ and the angels and is structured around that issue. Inasmuch as the basis of the claim for Christ's status is the exaltation (1:3=Ps 110:1), the catena is to be understood as assuming the exaltation of Christ. The author follows the NT tradition of taking texts out of their OT contexts and giving them a christological reference.¹¹ Ps 110:1, which the catena interprets, also serves as the concluding quotation of the catena, thus providing the framework of the citations. Within the catena the first three citations, of which the first two refer to the son and the third refers to the angels, are used as scriptural proof of what the author has said in 1:4: that Christ is "better" than the angels. The second section of the catena (1:7-12), in which there is one citation concerning the angels and two concerning the son, moves from affirmation to argument. In this section, the citations indicate the grounds on which the author argues

---

⁹ For the importance of the cosmological distinction between heaven and earth in the soteriology of Hebrews, see U. Luck, "Geschehen," 208-214.

¹⁰ Deichgräber, *Gotteshymnus*, 138. Hebrews does not refer to cosmic powers, as do Eph 1:20; 1 Pet 3:22. Implicit in the comparison in 1:4 is the early Christian combination of Pss 110 and 8 (cf. Eph 1:20-22; 1 Cor 15:27) which, when taken together, allow the interpretation that Christ is exalted above the angels.

¹¹ Michel, *Hebräer*, 107.

that Christ is "better." Verse 13 returns to Ps 110:1 and then verse 14 concludes with the author's exegetical observations concerning the inferior status of angels.[12] The three sections together function as an elaboration of the argument that is made at 1:4: the exaltation gives Christ a status superior to angels.

Christ as Exalted Son: 1:5-6

That the first two citations are to be understood as a reference to the exalted son is indicated by the connecting γάρ in 1:5. According to 1:4 the exalted one has received a new ὄνομα.In 1:5 this ὄνομα is identified as the title υἱός. Thus the significance of these texts, both of which are well-known messianic texts (Ps 2:7; 2 Sam 7:14),[13] lies in the presence of the title υἱός. That Jesus is υἱός is of considerable importance in Hebrews (cf. 1:2; 5:7-10; 7:3). Inasmuch as υἱός in 1:5 is apparently to be identified with ὄνομα in 1:4, and the line as a whole suggests the conferring of this "name," it is evident that the exaltation is viewed as the time at which the title υἱός was conferred.[14] One may compare 5:5, where the titles of high priest and son were both conferred at the same time (i.e., at the exaltation). For Hebrews, υἱός can have the meaning of a heavenly being, as 7:3 indicates. Hebrews follows here well-known Christian traditions in identifying the exaltation with the acquiring of a new status by Jesus (Acts 2:36; 13:13; Rom 1:3).[15] By demonstrating from Scripture that Jesus is υἱός, the author shows that he is "better than angels."[16]

That Christ is superior to angels is developed in 1:6 by a contrasting citation concerning angels: καὶ προσκυνησάτωσαν αὐτῷ πάντες ἄγγελοι

[12] For this understanding of the structure of the citations, cf. C. Spicq, L'Épître aux Hébreux, 15. This analysis of the structure is far more plausible than O. Michel's argument that several successive actions are envisioned in the catena (109).

[13] The two texts appear together in 4Q Testim, a fact which suggests that they circulated together. Ps 2:7 is one of the most important texts in early Christian apologetic for claiming that Jesus is υἱός. Cf. B. Lindars, New Testament Apologetic, 139-144.

[14] See E. Käsemann, Gottesvolk, 58. "Die Himmelfahrt reicht also dem Christus zugleich die Sohneswürde dar." Käsemann admits the apparent contradiction in Hebrews, according to which υἱός is used for the earthly Jesus (1:2; 5:8) as well as for the exalted Christ, but rightly considers the sayings about the earthly υἱός as proleptic.

[15] In Acts 2:36; 13:33; Rom 1:3, the new status is attained at the resurrection. However, inasmuch as the resurrection and exaltation are frequently, as in Hebrews, not separated, these passages are also to be regarded as exaltation texts.

[16] The frequent characterization of angels as "sons of God" (Gen 6:2; Ps 29:1; 89:7; Job 1:6) is probably the background for the author's selection of a text describing Jesus as υἱός to show that he is better than angels. Cf. Michel, Hebräer, 111. Windisch, Hebräerbrief, 15. James Moffatt, The Epistle to the Hebrews 10.

θεοῦ.[17] Christ is, as the introductory formula makes clear, the πρωτότοκος whom God "brought" εἰς τὴν οἰκουμένην.[18] Πρωτότοκος may be suggested by υἱός (or by γεγέννηκα, 1:5) in order to acclaim Christ as the "firstborn son."[19] Πρωτότοκος is used in connection with the resurrection in Col 1:18; Rev 1:5, and is here applied to the exaltation. This formula is an indication that the exaltation is the time of the angelic homage. Οἰκουμένη[20] refers to the heavenly world and is parallel to οἰκουμένην τὴν μέλλουσαν in 2:5. That οἰκουμένην refers to the heavenly world, as in 2:5, is indicated by the similarity of function in the two texts where οἰκουμένη is mentioned; in both instances the subjection of angels is involved. That angels pay homage to the heavenly Messiah is a familiar concept in Jewish literature (*Asc. Isa.* 11:23-25; Rev 5:8-10), a fact which indicates that the author has quoted a text which is intended to provide scriptural proof of the messianic dignity of Jesus in familiar terms. This argument carries special force in Hebrews, for it is axiomatic to the author that what is inferior renders homage to that which is superior (cf. 7:4-8). Thus the citation indicates that Christ is "better" (κρείττων, v. 4) than angels, inasmuch as he is worshipped by them.

Grounds for Argument: 1:7-12

The new section of the catena begins at 1:7 in which the author, having cited three texts to argue the superior dignity of the son, now provides the basis for the argument that Christ is "better" than the angels (vv 7-12). One may follow the citations in order to see how the author understands the

---

[17] The text, as cited in 1:6, appears to be a conflation of two LXX texts. The LXX of Ps 96:7 has προσκυνήσατε αὐτῷ, πάντες οἱ ἄγγελοι αὐτοῦ. The LXX of Deut 32:43 has, καὶ προσκυνησάτωσαν αὐτῷ πάντες υἱοὶ θεοῦ. It is possible that the author here quotes the text as it circulated in his time or that he quotes a liturgical tradition. Cf. F. Schröger, *Der Verfasser des Hebräerbriefes als Schriftausleger,* 49. However, the presence of υἱοὶ θεοῦ where the author has cited ἄγγελοι suggests that the author has deliberately conflated the texts himself in order to show that the one υἱός is worshipped by angelic beings who have no claim to the title.

[18] The introductory formula, ὅταν δὲ πάλιν εἰσαγάγῃ τὸν πρωτότοκον εἰς τὴν οἰκουμένην, is problematic. Πάλιν can be read with λέγει ("again he says," cf. 2:13; 4:5; 10:30), and thus be understood as parallel to the πάλιν of 1:5. However, it can be read with εἰσαγάγῃ to mean "when he again introduced him into the οἰκουμένη." The writer's preference for πάλιν to introduce citations makes likely the sense suggested by H. Windisch (*Hebräerbrief,* 15), "Again, however, he said." This view is more plausible than Michel's argument (113) that the author has in mind a "re-introduction" at the parousia.

[19] Πρωτότοκος in the introductory citation is obviously a reference to υἱός. Cf. πρωτότοκα (11:28; cf. Rom 8:29).

[20] Οἰκουμένη is used here and at 2:5 in an unusual sense. The word can have such meanings as "the inhabited earth," "mankind," or "the Roman Empire." Cf. BAG, 563. Cf. G. Johnston, "Οἰκουμένη and κόσμος in the New Testament," 352, for the view that οἰκουμένη is used for the "world of eschatological salvation."

exaltation and in what way Christ is "better" than angels. The first citation, from Ps 104:4, is intended to show the inferiority of angels:

ὁ ποιῶν τοὺς ἀγγέλους αὐτοῦ πνεύματα,
καὶ τοὺς λειτουργοὺς αὐτοῦ πυρὸς φλόγα.

This text, quoted from the LXX of Ps 104:4 with only a minor variation,[21] is used in a far different way from its usage in rabbinic tradition. Rabbinic tradition understood the text as meaning, "He who makes his angels into winds."[22] This text was often quoted in rabbinic literature to accent either the transcendence of God[23] or the might of the angels.[24] Hebrews uses the text, in contrast, to show the inferiority of angels. Ὁ ποιῶν is a reference to God's creative activity and the power over nature (1:2; cf. 12:27). The objects of his creative activity are τοὺς ἀγγέλους (τοὺς λειτουργούς). This text was quoted in rabbinic literature for a variety of reasons. Never, however, was it used to show the inferiority of angels. This inferiority comes, according to the present author, from the fact that angels are changeable.[25] They do not stand above the created order, as does the exalted son. As objects of God's creative activity, being made into πνεύματα[26] and πυρὸς φλόγα, they belong to the created order. One may compare πυρὸς φλόγα at 1:7 to the κεκαυμένον πῦρ at 12:18. The latter appears with a negative connotation as a representative of the material world (ψηλαφημένον) and is contrasted to the heavenly, non-material and non-transitory world. Comparison with 12:18-21 thus suggests that, in the author's view, πνεύματα and πυρὸς φλόγα[27] are terms for the material creation. The exalted Christ, unlike the angels, does not belong to the created order. Thus angels who are part of this material

[21] Hebrews has πυρὸς φλόγα in place of the LXX πῦρ φλέγον. This difference from the LXX is probably to be explained by supposing that the reading given in Hebrews corresponds to the LXX text which the author used.

[22] Both in Hebrew (עשה מלאכים רוחות) and Greek two meanings are possible: a) "He who makes his angels into winds," and b) "He who makes winds into angels." The former is more likely in Greek, where the definite noun is more likely to be the direct object.

[23] Cf. Ex.Rab. 25 (86a). God's power as "Lord of hosts" is indicated by his power to execute his deeds through his angels. They sit and stand at his will, and appear in the form of a woman or of a man, or even as wind and fire." Cited in Str-B 3. 678.

[24] Cf. Targ. to Ps 104:4, "Who makes his angels hasten as the wind, his servants mighty as glowing fire." Cited Ibid.

[25] O. Kuss, Der Brief an die Hebräer, 37; Michel, 117.

[26] Πνεύματα carries here, as does the Hebrew רוח, the meaning "wind." Cf. 1 Clem. 36:3 for a similar usage.

[27] It is an interesting fact that, whereas in the OT fire and wind are God's instruments for theophany, in Hebrews they stand in connection with a different set of assumptions. One may compare various Gnostic texts (e.g., CH 1. 4; 10. 16; Pistis Sophia 12-14; Ginza 73:10-15), where fire is the characteristic of the material, corruptible world. See F. Lang, Πῦρ, TDNT 6. 939-941.

world are denigrated in a way that rabbinic tradition never anticipated. Whereas the mutability of angels in rabbinic tradition is no sign of inferiority, in Hebrews their changeableness and connection with the material world marks them as inferior. Such a handling of the Scripture citation indicates that the author reads his text with his own metaphysical assumptions. He distinguishes spatially between what belongs to the created order (including angels) and what is above the creation. Because angels do not share in the exaltation, their existence is unstable.[28]

This understanding of the status of angels is unlike the views attested at Qumran and in other apocalyptic literature, where angels form a part of the heavenly entourage.[29] The suggestion that angels are not exalted to God's right hand has its closest analogies in the work of Philo and the Middle Platonists. For the Middle Platonists the transcendence of God and the heavenly world required the work of intermediate beings.[30] These beings, commonly described as *daimons* by the Middle Platonists, are equated with the angels by Philo (*de Gig.* 16). Philo follows the traditional Middle Platonic view that this level of being is the proper inhabitant of the air, serving as the agent and minister of the Creator (*de Gig.* 16; cf. Plutarch, *Def. Or.* 416-17; Apuleius in Varro apud Aug. *CD* 7.6). Consequently, as the story of Jacob's ladder suggests to Philo, angels "ascend and descend" (*de Som.* 1. 33) throughout the universe. They share the human characteristics of passion and change. Indeed some, because of their passions, turn to evil (*de Gig.* 17).

The Middle Platonist metaphysic, with its emphasis on transcendence, provided both Philo and Hebrews with a framework for placing angels within the intermediate world. Consequently, the author of Hebrews distinguishes between the place of Christ in the heavenly world and the place of angels in the physical world. Such a metaphysical distinction between the status of angels and the Messiah is not attested in the angelology of apocalyptic literature.

The description of angels in 1:7 is the background to a contrast to the son in 1:8. Whereas angels are transitory, the son is the θεός, whose throne is εἰς τὸν αἰῶνα τοῦ αἰῶνος. Undoubtedly one reason for the selection of this

---

[28] It is significant that such Christian Platonists as Basil of Caesarea and Gregory Nazianzen quoted this Psalm and argued that angels are substantial and corporeal. According to Gregory Nazianzen, πνεύματα and "flames of fire" are terms which cannot be applied to angels unless they are corporeal (*Orat.* 27. 31. 70. 3-7). Cf. Basil, *Hom. on Ps 48:8*. Cited in I. P. Sheldon-Williams, "The Greek Christian Platonist Tradition from the Cappadocians to Maximus and Eriugena," in A. H. Armstrong, ed., *The Cambridge History of Later Greek and Early Medieval Philosophy* (Cambridge: University Press, 1970) 435, 442-444.

[29] Cf. *1 En.* 15:2; 39:5; 47:2; 104:1; Rev 5:11.

[30] See John Dillon, *The Middle Platonists,* 216.

passage is the presence of the title θεός, which the author applies to Christ. Nevertheless, a major purpose in the citation is to press the phrase, εἰς τὸν αἰῶνα τοῦ αἰῶνος, which contrasts the son with the angels. The δέ in the introductory formula in 1:8 shows that the attribution of eternity to the son is intended to contrast him with the instability of angels. Εἰς τὸν αἰῶνα τοῦ αἰῶνος thus takes on the meaning of immutability. Christ is exalted ἐν ὑψηλοῖς, and is thus unchangeable. The phrase, εἰς τὸν αἰῶνα τοῦ αἰῶνος, is of tremendous importance to Hebrews (cf. 13:8), and is frequently used in reflections on Ps 110:4 (cf. 5:5; 6:20; 7:17, 21, 24, 28).[31] As 6:19-20; 7:3, 16 make clear, it is the heavenly existence of Christ which makes possible the unlimited duration of his existence. Earthly matters, including angels and cult (cf. 8:13), are transitory; but because of the exaltation Christ is eternal.[32] One may observe here the distinction between the author's understanding of eternity as a christological category and that view expressed in the traditional reflections on the Davidic Messiah. In Hebrews, Christ is eternal because he is a heavenly being; in the Jewish traditions of the OT and apocalyptic literature, the reign εἰς τὸν αἰῶνα (*Ps. Sol.* 17:4; *T. Jud.* 22) is attributed to an earthly being. The author's contrast between the eternal son and the changeable creation in this catena further indicates that the attribution of eternity to the son presupposes the spatial distinction between the heavenly and the earthly. Such an assumption is apparently indebted to Greek metaphysical speculations concerning eternity.

It is to be emphasized with regard to the texts used in 1:7-9 that the author cites them with a totally new content and thrust which differs greatly from what one usually finds in Jewish reflections on these texts. The author has come to his text with his own set of assumptions which inform his reading of these passages.

Similar assumptions are at work in the citation of Ps 102:26-28 in 1:10-12.[33] In this text, the son is set over against the created order with the implication that this creation is the dwelling place of angels.[34] Γῆ and οὐρανός both belong to the created order. It is likely that ἔργα τῶν χειρῶν σου is to be equated with χειροποίητος at 9:11, 24 and signifies the earthly

---

[31] Cf. εἰς τὸ διηνεκές in Heb 7:3; 10:12, 14.

[32] Cf. 9:12, where the "eternal" redemption is effected by the heavenly existence of Jesus.

[33] Several variations from the LXX text are to be observed in the author's citation. Σύ stands before κατ' ἀρχάς as a deliberate attempt to bring the citation into line with 12c. Διαμενεῖς in the LXX is altered to the present διαμένεις in Hebrews in order to express more adequately the timeless-eternal quality of Christ's work (cf. 7:3 for μένει). In v. 12 Hebrews has ἑλίξεις in place of the LXX ἀλλάξεις. Hebrews repeats at 12b ὡς ἱμάτιον before καὶ ἀλλαγήσονται.

[34] O. Michel, *Hebräer*, 121.

κτίσις (9:11) in contrast with the heavenly world of the exaltation. The terms in which this relationship of the exalted Christ to the creation is spelled out (cf. 1:2) are well known in the Hellenistic Age, where the problems of defining God's relationship to the world had occasioned the increasing interest in a hypostasis who creates and sustains the world.[35] Jewish wisdom speculations, which play an important role in the development of NT christology, speak of Wisdom's relation to the world (Prov 8:22; cf. John 1:1-3; 1 Cor 1:24; Col 1:15-20). Similarly, the Hermetica hypostasizes the Platonic category αἰών and affirms that αἰών (11. 2) made the world. Such speculations are undoubtedly a presupposition of the author of Hebrews when he affirms that the creation is the work of Christ.

Hebrews 1:11 shows the reason behind the utilization of Psalm 102 to introduce the category of transitoriness-eternity into the argument, as the author cites the words, αὐτοὶ ἀπολοῦνται, σὺ δὲ διαμένεις. Because of the importance of this category elsewhere in Hebrews, it is probable that the author has selected this particular text because he found there what he wanted to accent: the contrast between the changeable creation and the immutable creator.[36] The transitoriness of the creation is indicated by the subsequent phrases which reinforce 1:11a. The text cited uses the image of clothes to convey the transitoriness of the cosmos. Thus the author quotes, ὡς ἱμάτιον παλαιωθήσονται. Παλαιόω, which means "to grow old" or "become obsolete,"[37] is theologically significant for the author. At 8:13 he uses the term in his critique of the cultus in order to show that the transitory cult lacks ultimate validity. The change from ἀλλάσσω to ἑλίσσω suggests the image of rolling up of a cloak, thus providing another image of changeableness.[38] Ἀλλάσσω, meaning "change," is to be understood, in view of the added ὡς ἱμάτιον, as a change of clothes.[39] Thus the characteristic of the created order (and implicitly, of angels) is made on the basis of its mutability. The author has no intent, as A. Vögtle rightly argues,[40] to develop a

---

[35] For an illuminating treatment of this problem, see M. Nilsson, *Geschichte der griechischen Religion* 2. 706.

[36] F. Schröger, *Schriftausleger*, 69.

[37] H. Seesemann, Παλαιόω, *TDNT* 5. 720.

[38] W. Bauer cites significant texts which speak of the "rolling up" of heaven (Hymn to Apollo) or of earth. Such traditions provide the background to the author's alteration of the LXX. I understand, against *D*, ἑλίσσω to be the best reading, as the ἀλλάξεις of *D* is likely an attempt to bring the text into line with the LXX.

[39] Ἀλάσσω is important in many apocalyptic writings for the descriptions of the transformation of the cosmos at the last day. Cf. *Barn.* 15:5; *Sib. Or.* 3. 638; 5. 273. That, however, is not the intent of ἀλλάσσω here, where the author thinks in terms of a change of clothes. Ἀλλάσσω serves to point to the mutability of the cosmos in contrast to the eternal existence of Christ.

[40] *Das Neue Testament und die Zukunft des Kosmos*, 96. O. Hofius (*Katapausis*, 258)

thoroughgoing thesis concerning the world conflagration; his purpose is to provide the contrast to the one who is exalted above the created order and thus remains. That the author is bringing to his text his specific assumptions about the world is indicated by comparison with 12:25-28, where the transitory nature of the world is contrasted to the eternity of the stable possession.[41] It is not necessary to see in 1:10-11 the announcement of an eschatological catastrophe, as O. Michel understands the text (cf. p. 58). The author's interest is to distinguish radically between the changeable creation and the immutable Christ. The argument is parallel to 1:7-8, where the mutability of angels is contrasted to the eternity of Christ.

The distinction between the change which is inherent in the cosmos and the abiding of the deity was already present in the author's text Ps 102:26-28. But for the psalmist there is no essential metaphysical intent; the psalmist indicates only that God outlasts the creation. By using this psalm as an exaltation text, the author has introduced the spatial framework into the argument. His argument is reminiscent of the Platonic view in which the "becoming" (γένεσις) in this creation is distinguished from the eternal world of forms.[42] One may compare Philo's argument that this world is subject to dissolution (*Leg. All.* 3. 101, αἱ γὰρ ἐν γενητοῖς ἐμφάσεις διαλύονται) in contrast to those things above the creation which are μόνιμοι καὶ βέβαιοι καὶ ἀΐδιοι. Whereas such representatives of Platonism as the Hermetica, Plutarch,[43] and Philo speak of the mutability of the perceptible world, Hebrews speaks of the change inherent in angels (1:7) and in the creation. It is probable, therefore, that the author has read Ps 102:26-28 with Platonic assumptions in order to interpret the exaltation and to demonstrate the

incorrectly cited Heb 1:10-12 as evidence that the author shares with *4 Ezra* the expectation of a world transformation. The author's distance from the apocalyptic understanding of the eschaton becomes clear in his comments on the eschatological tradition in 12:27-28.

It is admittedly difficult to establish the author's intent in such a passage as 1:10-12, inasmuch as the author cites the text of Ps 102:26-28 without giving an exegetical comment. In the absence of any exegetical comment, the interpretative key to 1:10-12 must be the parallel passage, 12:26-28, where the author comments on his tradition. This fact has been observed by Vögtle, *Zukunft*, 96.

41 See the discussion in Chapter III.

42 *Tim.* 37D; Plutarch, *Quaest. Plat.* 8. 4. 7; Philo, *De Post. Cain.* 30; *CH* 11. 2. Plato never argued that the earth will be destroyed. However, in Middle Platonism and in Gnosticism, both of which owe much to Plato in their views of the structure of the world, the Platonic distinction between the intelligible world and the perceptible world was pushed further, so that the destruction of the world was accepted by many. Cf. Philo, *de Decal.* 58, καὶ γὰρ γέγονε, γένεσις δὲ φθορᾶς ἀρχή.

43 In Plutarch (*The E at Delphi*, c 19), μεταβάσεις καὶ παραλλήξεις (cf. ἀλλαγήσονται, Heb 1:12) are attributed to the perceptible world and are contrasted with God's abiding nature. Cf. *CH* 11. 4, where μεταβολή is attributed to the world of sense perception.

precise way in which Christ is "better" than angels.[44]

What the exaltation means to the author can be ascertained from two of the phrases of Psalm 102 which are of special christological significance for him. Σὺ δὲ διαμένεις serves to contrast the abiding of the exalted son with the transitory nature of the creation. That Christ is the one who "remains" is of central importance to Hebrews (7:3, 24; cf. 13:8). Furthermore, the author regularly uses μένειν in theologically significant texts for a Christian possession which "abides." In each instance, forms of μένειν are used exclusively for a heavenly reality. The use of μένειν regularly in Hebrews indicates that the author has chosen this text precisely because of the presence of διαμένεις in it. The author has altered the future διαμενεῖς of his LXX text to the present διαμένεις in order to emphasize the timeless and eternal nature of the exalted Christ.

The use of διαμένεις in a text where Christ is contrasted with the created order indicates that διαμένεις here betrays the author's metaphysical understanding. One may compare the use of μένειν in Plato (*Tim.* 37D), Plotinus (3. 7), Philo (*de Som.* 2. 221), and the Hermetica, where (δια)μένει is regularly used in a spatial framework to contrast the immutability of the intelligible world with the change which exists in the sphere of γένεσις. This metaphysical understanding had come to play an important role in the piety of the Hellenistic Age. Of special importance as a parallel to Hebrews is Philo's view that the σοφός who leaves τὰ ἐν γενέσει (*Leg. All.* 2. 54) is able to share in the μονή of God (*de Som.* 2. 237). Similarly, in the Hermetic literature αἰών is a hypostasis in the intelligible world who διαμένει (11:4). Thus just as the Hermetica attributes διαμονή to the αἰών of the intelligible world, Hebrews says that the exalted Christ διαμένει.

As a parallel to διαμένεις the author cites further from his text the words, σὺ δὲ ὁ αὐτός. That "sameness" is an important christological category for the author is evident at 13:8. The term reflects also a dependence on Greek metaphysics. Philo says that God is ὁ αὐτός (*de Post. Cain.* 19). Similarly, the Hermetica speaks of αἰών as that which is διαμένουσα τῇ ταυτότητι (11. 4). In the tractate *Asclepius*, αἰών is identified with God and declared immutable (*semperque similiter*), in contrast to the world of sense perception. For the author of Hebrews, the fact that Jesus is ἐν ὑψηλοῖς means that he is now immutable. This understanding of the exaltation shows a definite point of contact with the literature influenced by Plato. Just as the Hermetica attributes "sameness" to the αἰών of the intelligible world,

---

[44] The possibility of reading Platonic assumptions into Ps 102:26-28 is apparent in Eusebius' *Preparatio Evangelium* 11. 10. 15 (233) where Eusebius argues that Plutarch's εἰ formula is a commentary on the OT expression ἐγώ εἰμι ὁ ὤν and σὺ δὲ ὁ αὐτὸς εἰ (Ps 102:28). Cited in E. Norden, *Agnostos Theos*, 231-232.

Hebrews attributes the same quality to the exalted Christ who is ἐν ὑψηλοῖς.

Having demonstrated through the careful selection of texts that Christ, as the abiding son (1:7-12), is "better than angels," the author returns in 1:13 to Ps 110:1, the text which provided the starting point for the reflections contained in the catena. The δέ of 1:13 correlates this verse to the preceding argument and to the reflections concerning Christ and the angels. The messianic understanding of this psalm is well known in the NT[45] and of great importance to Hebrews.[46] The setting of this citation at 1:13 indicates that the author uses it to recapitulate all that has been argued in 1:3-12: the angels do not share in the exaltation, and thus they are inferior. Because they are cosmologically subordinate (ὑποπόδιον τῶν ποδῶν σου, 1:13), they have an inferior status (1:14).

The δέ of 1:13 reinforces the argument which is made in 1:7: that because angels do not share in the exaltation to the heavenly world, they do not abide. Δέ serves in this context to distinguish between the abiding of the son and the changeableness of the angels. This usage indicates further the assumptions with which the author approaches his text, Ps 110:1. Such a reading of Psalm 110 is quite different from both the rabbinic and early Christian use of this text and can only be explained by supposing that the author's metaphysical assumptions influenced his reading of the text. The significance of the exaltation is that Christ "initiert . . . die Ewigkeitsbejahung."[47] A dualistic reading of the OT is the basis of the author's argumentation.

The close connection between the argument from the superiority of Christ over the angels and the parenesis in 2:1-4 indicates that the argument in 1:5-13 serves as the basis for the parenesis. Διὰ τοῦτο in 2:1 connects the warning in 2:1-4 with the theological statement in chap. 1. The author has shown on metaphysical grounds that Christ is greater than the angels. This fact means for the community that the word of Christ is to be taken more seriously.[48] The author's metaphysical argument thus serves the needs of parenesis.

Conclusion

Comparison of the argumentation within the catena with the author's

---

[45] F. Hahn, *Hoheitstitel*, 113-116; Hay, *passim*. Hay's treatment of Psalm 110 shows the shifts in the early Christian understanding of the psalm.

[46] 1:3; 5:6, 10; 6:20; 7:3, 11, 15, 17, 21, 24, 28; 10:12-13; 12:2.

[47] H. Braun, "Die Gewinnung der Gewissheit in dem Hebräerbrief," 330.

[48] *Ibid.*, 325. For the similar use of the warning following the affirmation of the superiority of the Christian possession, cf. 12:25. In other cases the author follows the theological statement with encouragement (cf. 4:16; 10:19-25). "Die Überlegenheit Jesu gewährt eine überlegene Gewissheit, aber auch eine überhöhte Gefährdung."

use of similar themes in the epistle reveals the purpose of the catena. The author intends neither to combat a definite heresy nor to present various stages of the enthronement. In the catena the author presents a meditation on the exaltation. As in other places in Hebrews (cf. 6:19-20; 7:3, 16, 25-28; 12:27-28; 13:8), the author's intent is to demonstrate that Christ is the one who abides. By handling his texts with metaphysical assumptions which were very much at home in the Platonic tradition, the author is able to show that the exalted Christ is εἰς τὸν αἰῶνα τοῦ αἰῶνος (1:8), that he διαμένει (1:11), and that he is ὁ αὐτός (1:12). This argument, given on metaphysical grounds, provides the basis for the parenesis in 2:1-4.

CHAPTER IX

Outside the Camp: A Study of Heb 13:9-14*

Heb 13:9-14 is one of the most complex passages in Hebrews, if not in the entire NT. Two major problems have made this text a source of exegetical difficulty. On the one hand, the passage is characterized by an extraordinary number of references which seem to stand alone in Hebrews, and are thus difficult to interpret in the context of the rest of the epistle. There is a continuing debate, for instance, over the meanings of several of these references: "the strange and diverse teachings," the "foods," the Christian "altar," and the place "outside the camp." As F.J. Schierse has said, "There is scarcely a concept . . . in verses 9-14 which can be reduced to a clear, generally recognized view."[1] On the other hand, there is the added difficulty of ascertaining how these references form a coherent argument. It is obvious from the repeated connectives (*gar*, vv 9, 11, 14; *dio*, v 12, *toinun*, v 13) that this section is intended to form a coherent piece.[2] Yet the connection between these verses remains a matter of debate. It is the intention of this chapter to clarify both the individual references and the place of the entire argument in the context of Hebrews.

The history of exegesis reveals a considerable number of alternative attempts to deal with the many exegetical enigmas of this passage. It has been widely interpreted, for instance, as a polemic against Judaism and Jewish food laws.[3] In contrast with this interpretation, there is a view, widely held from Chrysostom until now, that this passage is a summons to the community to leave, not Judaism, but the material world.[4] There is, in addition, the continuing controversy over the reference to "foods." The reference has been interpreted as an allusion to ascetic food regulations, on the analogy of Col 2:16 or Rom 14:1.[5] It has also been interpreted as a warning

---

*This chapter appeared originally in *CBQ* 40 (1978).

[1] See F.J. Schierse, *Verheissung und Heilsvollendung*, 184.

[2] *Ibid.*

[3] H. Strathmann, *Der Brief an die Hebräer*, 55; cf. J. Jeremias, Πυλή, *TDNT* 6. 922; G. Bornkamm, "Das Bekenntnis im Hebräerbrief," *Studien zu Antike und Christentum* (Munich: Kaiser, 1970) 195.

[4] *Hom. Heb.* 33; see J. Cambier, *Eschatologie ou Hellénisme dans l'Épître aux Hébreux*, 15-18.

[5] O. Michel, *Der Brief an die Hebräer*, 495.

against either a sacramental view of the eucharist[6] or syncretistic cultic meals.[7] Those who understand this passage as a polemic connect the warning against "strange teachings" with the reference to "foods" and view the summons to "go out" (13:13) as an exhortation to give up the heresy which is envisioned in the interpretation.

The problem with such attempts to understand this passage is that these interpretations do not account adequately for the unpolemical character of the rest of the epistle. Indeed, in some instances these interpretations can be advanced only if 13:9-14 is the lens through which the rest of the book is viewed.[8] The epistle employs a variety of motifs, especially cultic in nature, to serve the needs of parenesis.[9] It is thus not polemical in character. This unpolemical nature of the book makes highly improbable a polemical interpretation of this passage. It is thus the argument of this chapter that any interpretation of this passage must be derived from the dynamics of the epistle.

This passage can best be understood within the dynamics of the epistle if we observe that it conforms to the author's customary parenetic form. It begins with the imperative (μὴ παραφέρεσθε), which is then supported by two statements in the indicative ("We have an altar"; "Jesus . . . suffered outside the camp," 13:10, 12). This indicative is followed by an exhortation in the hortatory subjunctive (ἐξερχώμεθα πρὸς αὐτόν), which is then grounded in an additional statement in the indicative (13:14). Comparison of this passage with other parenetic sections indicates that the author regularly employs a parenetic form by which he interweaves the indicative (usually with ἔχω used in a creedal formulation) with both the imperative and the hortatory subjunctive (cf. 4:14; 10:19; 12:2). In this parenetic form, the indicative ordinarily contains a christological statement about Jesus' exaltation and high priestly work. This affirmation serves as a basis for the summons, in the hortatory subjunctive, to follow Jesus in the Christian pilgrimage. Although the pareneses may vary in length and completeness, such a form with these elements is remarkably consistent (cf. 4:14-16; 10:19-23; 12:1-3). Inasmuch as Heb 13:9-14 shares the parenetic form with other sections of the epistle, it is probable that careful comparison of this passage with the other pareneses will clarify some of the obscurities of this passage.

---

[6] H. Koester, "Outside the Camp," 315. Cf. G. Theissen, *Untersuchungen zum Hebräerbrief*, 77.

[7] H. Windisch, *Der Hebräerbrief*, 117; J. Behm, Βρῶμα, *TDNT* 1. 643.

[8] See O. Kuss, *Der Brief an die Hebräer*, 22.

[9] For the decisive role of parenesis as a criterion for determining the intention of the epistle, see Schierse, *Verheissung*, 206; O. Michel, *Hebräer*, 59: "The theological-didactic parts of the epistle do not stand on their own, but rather form the presuppositions for parenesis."

The Context

The pericope appears in the context of closing exhortations which give the final chapter the formal appearance of an epistolary ending. The exhortations in 13:1-6 are loosely placed here, and bear no relation to the rest of the epistle. There is a shift in the instruction at 13:7, for beginning here the author returns to the theological issues which he has developed previously. The imperative of 13:7 is a summons to maintain the same endurance which was exhibited by the original leaders. Apparently the confessional statement of 13:8, with its emphasis on the "sameness" of Christ, is intended to demonstrate that the readers, who are now weary in their pilgrimage, can rely on the stability of their faith. In contrast with the original leaders (ἡγούμενοι), who died, Christ remains ὁ αὐτός. This fact is intended to support the author's summons for the readers to endure. This summons to endure, a frequent subject of the epistle, provides the context to 13:9-14.

The Exhortation

The imperative μὴ παραφέρεσθε links 13:9-14 to the preceding imperatives in the parenesis. The concern of 13:9, with the contrasting μὴ παραφέρεσθε . . . βεβαιοῦσθαι, suggests the close connection between this parenesis and other parenetic sections in the epistle. Παραφέρεσθε suggests the image of one who, without an anchor (cf. 6:19), is "carried away" by the winds. The term can be used for those who become a prey to strange ideas because they have no place to stand (Jude 12; Plato, *Phaedrus* 265b). One may compare it with the author's use of other terms which indicate his fears for the community: παραρυῶμεν (2:1), ὑστερηκέναι (4:1), ἀποβάλητε (10:35), and ἀποστῆναι (3:12). All of these verbs suggest the author's concern lest the community fail to hold on. They suggest that the author's major concern is with the endurance of the community, and not with a specific heresy. These verbs provide the context within which παραφέρεσθε is to be understood. The verb suggests the author's concern lest the weary community fail because it is insufficiently anchored in the instruction which has been communicated by the past teachers (13:7; cf. 2:1-4).[10] It is important that the community be secured in the teaching of the one who is "the same" (13:8), and not "carried away."

Because Christ is unchangeable (13:8), the teaching should also be unchanged.[11] A church that is not firmly anchored is vulnerable to "diverse and strange teachings" (διδαχαῖς ποικίλαις καὶ ξέναις). The author does not identify such "diverse" teachings. Indeed, the general absence of references

---

[10] Kuss, *Hebräer*, 221. "The appearances of paralysis make the church vulnerable."
[11] H. Windisch, *Hebräerbrief*, 106.

to heresy in the epistle make it unlikely that the author has a specific heresy in mind.[12] The reference is very general. Ποικίλος, meaning "diversified,"[13] is not the word one would have expected if the author had been combatting a specific heresy.

The alternative to being "carried away" is the contrasting statement in 13:9b, as the connecting γάρ indicates. Instead of being carried away, καλὸν . . . χάριτι βεβαιοῦσθαι τὴν καρδίαν. Βεβαιοῦσθαι, which is contrasted to παραφέρεσθε, links this pericope to the other pareneses of Hebrews. The author has a special fondness for forms of βεβαι- and other words for steadfastness and stability. He has already shown that, because of the exaltation of Christ, the church has an ἄγκυραν . . . ἀσφαλῆ τε καὶ βεβαίαν (6:19). His interest for his weary community is that it develop "firmness" (3:6, 14).[14] The pericope in 13:9-14 is thus closely related in content and intention to the other pareneses of Hebrews.

In order that the community not be "carried away," καλὸν . . . χάριτι βεβαιοῦσθαι τὴν καρδίαν, οὐ βρώμασιν, ἐν οἷς οὐκ ὠφελήθησαν οἱ περιπατοῦντες (13:9). Comparison of ὠφελήθησαν with the author's use of cognate forms of ὠφελεῖν in 4:2; 7:18 (ἀνωφελές) suggests that the "benefit" which "foods" do not provide is the eschatological salvation.[15] "Foods," like the levitical priesthood in 7:18, are "useless" in providing the church with the hope which will strengthen the heart.

What does the author have in mind when he refers to foods which do not "strengthen the heart?" The answer is suggested by his use of βρῶμα/βρῶσις elsewhere in the epistle. The term is used in 9:10 and 12:16. In 9:10 the author contrast the gifts and sacrifices offered in the levitical cultus with the sacrifice of Christ in the heavenly sanctuary. The levitical sacrifices, which deal with "foods and drinks and baptisms" (μόνον ἐπὶ βρώμασιν καὶ πόμασιν καὶ διαφόροις βαπτισμοῖς), are only δικαιώματα σαρκός. That is, they purify the flesh (9:13), but not the conscience, which is purified by

---

[12] The "strange teachings" have been commonly identified with the reference to "foods " in 13:9. Such an interpretation has difficulties, however. The reference in 13:9 is far too indefinite to allow us to see here a reference to a specific heresy, as a survey of the many interpretations of this passage indicates. We must recall also that the author's reference to "foods" elsewhere does not appear to be directed against a specific heresy (cf. 9:10). Just as it is unacceptable to argue that the author is polemicizing against many specific heresies in the book (i.e., an angel-heresy in chaps. 1-2, a Moses heresy in 3:1-6, a cult heresy in 7:1-10:18), it is not necessary to connect the "strange teachings" with a heresy about food laws.

[13] BAG 690.

[14] See H. Braun, "Die Gewinnung der Gewissheit," 321, for the importance of βεβαι- in Hebrews. Cf. pp. 95-96 and 117 for the importance of βεβαι- in Hebrews.

[15] G. Theissen (*Untersuchungen*, 76) has shown that ὠφελεῖν, used in the absolute sense in Hebrews, consistently refers to the eschatological salvation.

Christ (9:14) in the heavenly sanctuary. The author works with a dualistic anthropology, according to which there is a sphere of σάρξ and a sphere of συνείδησις.[16] His critique of all cultic activities of the levitical system has been within this dualistic framework. The levitical system, according to 7:18, is ἀνωφελές; it belongs to the sphere of σάρξ.[17] Similarly, according to 9:10, food regulations are δικαιώματα σαρκός. This perspective can also be observed in 12:16, where the "food" which distracted Esau from his inheritance appears to be a term for worldliness in general.[18] Esau's worldly behavior is thus to be contrasted with the behavior of the men of faith who gave up earthly assurances in favor of the heavenly reward (cf. 11:7, 10, 14).

Comparison of this passage with similar passages in the epistle suggests that one need not see in the reference to "foods" a specific threat to the community. Thus the author is referring neither to a sacramental view of the eucharist nor to ascetic food laws. The epistle regularly uses aspects of the levitical cultus as a foil or "parable" (9:9) for contrasting the heavenly work of Christ. The reference to "foods" in 13:9, as in 9:10, is intended to suggest that the church will not find its stability in any earthly assurances. Just as the high priesthood of Christ gives the church a παρρησία not offered by the earthly cult (10:19), so the church in 13:9 must find its strength in something greater than earthly assurances.

The alternative to "foods" is that the heart be strengthened by grace (καλὸν γὰρ χάριτι βεβαιοῦσθαι τὴν καρδίαν). Βεβαιοῦσθαι τὴν καρδίαν is equivalent to κατὰ συνείδησιν τελειῶσαι τὸν λατρεύοντα in 9:9. Καρδία and συνείδησις are to be understood as equivalent terms for the "higher" aspect of man's existence (cf. 9:13-14), which can be "purified" (9:14) only by the work of Christ in the heavenly sanctuary. The author's word for the benefits of Christ in the heavenly sanctuary is χάρις. Christ has brought the church to the "throne of grace" (4:16), so that they may "find grace in time of

---

[16] For the author's dualistic anthropology, see R. Völkl, *Christ und Welt nach dem Neuen Testament*, 345. Cf. Schierse, *Verheissung*, 119. In 12:9, the author distinguishes between "fathers of the flesh" and the "fathers of the spirit." In 13:3 the author compares the life ἐν σώματι to imprisonment.

[17] A critique similar to 9:1-14 is made in 7:16, where the levitical priesthood is characterized by σάρξ. E. Schweizer has shown that σάρξ in Hebrews refers to the earthly sphere which is separated from the divine world. Cf. *TDNT* 7. 143. The term is thus parallel to the other terms which the author uses within a dualistic framework to describe earthly institutions (χειροποίητος, 9:11; κοσμικός, 9:1; ψηλαφημένος, 12:18). In Hellenistic literature σάρξ frequently appears as a term for matter (Plutarch, *Mor.* 2. 745e; Philo, *Leg. All.* 3. 152). See E. Schweizer, "Die hellenistische Komponente im neutestamentlichen σάρξ Begriff," 242-253.

[18] Esau, who threw away his reward for the sake of food, is in Jewish literature an example of the worldly man who chose this world as his part because he wanted to enjoy life here and now (*Gen. R.* 63; 65; *Targ. Jer.* 1 Gen 25:32, 34). Cited in R. Völkl, *Christ und Welt*, 352. Cf. Chapter III, note 13.

need" (4:16) or "have grace" (12:28). Such heavenly benefits of salvation are the only answer to a weary community.

The content of this χάρις is specific in 13:10. Indeed, the confessional statement in 13:10, ἔχομεν θυσιαστήριον,[19] appears to be the author's elaboration of χάρις. Although he does not use θυσιαστήριον for the work of Christ in Hebrews, the regular use of cultic language in connection with Christ is analogous to the language of 13:10. At 8:1-5 he argues that the work of levitical priests is a shadow of heavenly things. Christ is the heavenly high priest who carries on priestly activities. According to 9:11-14, the work of Christ is done in the heavenly sanctuary. To intepret the altar as the eucharist is to ignore the connection between ἔχομεν θυσιαστήριον (13:10) and other credal formulations in the epistle. Ἔχομεν θυσιαστήριον is the equivalent of ἔχομεν ἀρχιερέα (8:1; cf. 4:14).[20] It is Christ's work in the heavenly sanctuary which provides the anchor (6:19) and allows the church to be "unwavering" (10:23) in holding its commitment. This heavenly work of Christ is the χάρις which strengthens the heart.

If the author uses θυσιαστήριον for the heavenly sanctuary, who are those τῇ σκηνῇ λατρεύοντες? Attempts have been made to identify these people as Christians who insist on ascetic food laws, or as a reference to those who insist on a sacramental view of the eucharist.[21] However, the reference should be compared to other texts in Hebrews. For instance, 8:4, 5 speaks of those who ὑποδείγματι καὶ σκιᾷ λατρεύουσιν. Similarly, 9:9 (cf. 10:1) speaks of gifts and sacrifices offered (προσφέρονται) which are not able to perfect the conscience of the one who serves (τὸν λατρεύοντα). The author's frequent use of the present tense to describe cultic activities of the OT is the background for the understanding of the reference to "those who serve in the tent" in 13:10. These cultic activities only serve as a "parable" of the present age (9:9). The author's understanding of these activities is a "book knowledge," not a reference to occurrences in his milieu. Thus "those who serve in the tent" is parallel to "those who serve in a copy and shadow" (8:5) of the true tent. The author is referring to no specific heresy. He is suggesting, as he has throughout the epistle, that the heavenly sanctuary of Christ is far more beneficial than cultic activities which belong in the sphere of σάρξ.

The connecting γάρ in 13:11 indicates that the following christological argument is intended to support the affirmation about the Christian altar in

---

[19] For the credal use of ἔχειν, cf. 4:14; 8:1, 10:19. Cf. Bornkamm, "Bekenntnis," 182-203.

[20] The close relationship between the credal formulations in 8:1 and 13:10 suggests that the altar is the heavenly sanctuary, not the earthly Golgotha. Cf. H. Koester, "Outside the Camp," 312, for the equation of Golgotha and θυσιαστήριον.

[21] Cf. H. Koester, "Outside the Camp," 315. Michel, *Hebräer*, 495.

13:10. The author refers to the practice in the levitical cultus, whereby σώματα of sacrificial animals were burned ἔξω τῆς παρεμβολῆς after the blood had been poured out at the altar. The author sees here a correspondence between this activity of the levitical cultus and the fact that Jesus ἔξω τῆς πύλης ἔπαθεν (13:12). Such an interpretation corresponds to the author's regular interpretation of the levitical cultus as a prototype of the work of Christ. It is here at the Christian altar that the church has been sanctified by the blood of Christ (ἵνα ἁγιάσῃ διὰ τοῦ ἰδίου αἵματος τὸν λαόν). The author is not concerned that his typological correspondence breaks down, inasmuch as the blood of Jesus, unlike that of sacrificial animals, is shed "outside." His concern is to show that the Christian altar is ἔξω τῆς πύλης.

Helmut Koester has correctly argued that ἔξω τῆς πύλης is to be identified with the Christian θυσιαστήριον and that the θυσιαστήριον is here contrasted to the cultic activities as exemplified in βρώματα.[22] But Koester argues incorrectly that the author identifies ἔξω τῆς πύλης with the "uncleanness of the world." The distinction in Hebrews is not, as Koester argues, between "sacred" and "profane." The distinction in Hebrews 13:10-13 is between the sphere of σάρξ, as exemplified by the reference to "foods," and the heavenly sphere of the Christian altar. This distinction between heaven and earth is the basis of the author's argumentation throughout the epistle.[23] The work of Christ at the heavenly altar, or "outside the camp," is more effective than any earthly means of providing βεβαίωσις. His work does not take place in an earthly sanctuary (8:1-5; 9:1, 11-14, 23), and thus it is effective. Thus when the author says that Jesus died "outside the camp," he shows that the Christian altar is not in the earthly sphere.

Undoubtedly ἔξω τῆς πύλης contains an implicit reference to Jesus' death outside the gates of Jerusalem.[24] The author's interest is not, however, in mere historical information. He is interested in showing that Jesus fulfills the levitical requirements and that his death took place at the heavenly altar. This argument does not suggest that the author denies the reality of the suffering of Christ. Indeed ἔπαθεν here is used in Hebrews only for the suffering of Christ (5:8; 9:26). Nevertheless, the death and exaltation of Christ are regularly brought together in Hebrews. The καταπέτασμα separating heaven and earth is the σάρξ of Jesus (10:20). The blood of Christ was

---

[22] Koester, pp. 305-306.

[23] In chapter 1, the contrast is between the exalted son and the angels who belong to the lower sphere, and are thus mutable (1:7; cf. Chapter VIII). In 7:1-10:18 the contrast is between the heavenly work of Christ and the inferior cultic activity on earth. For this dualistic reading of the OT, see Braun, "Gewissheit," 321-324.

[24] John 19:20. Cf. E. Grässer, "Der historische Jesus im Hebräerbrief," 82.

offered in the heavenly sanctuary (9:19). Consistently the author brings together the death and exaltation of Christ (1:3; 5:8-9; 12:1-2), as though they form one event.[25] Although the death involved shame (αἰσχύνη, 12:2), the death was the last stage, the leaving of the sphere of σάρξ (10:20), before the exaltation. Thus ἔξω τῆς πύλης refers not merely to Calvary; it refers to the sacrifice of Christ in the heavenly sanctuary. It is the heavenly character of Jesus' death which gives stability to the heart (13:9; cf. 6:19).

The author's understanding of the LXX ἔξω τῆς παρεμβολῆς is to be compared with Philo's understanding of the same phrase. Philo interprets Exod 33:7 ("so too Moses pitched his tent outside the camp") to mean that "Moses left the whole array of bodily things" (οὕτως καὶ Μωυσῆς ἔξω τῆς παρεμβολῆς καὶ τοῦ σωματικοῦ παντὸς στρατοπέδου πήξας τὴν ἑαυτοῦ σκήνην).[26] Similarly in *de Ebrietate* 25, commenting on Ex 33:7, he explains that by ἐν τῷ στρατοπέδῳ (=ἐν τῇ παρεμβολῇ), Moses means ἐν τῷ μετὰ σώματος βίῳ. Thus for both Philo and Hebrews, "outside the camp" means outside the earthly sphere. For Hebrews, Christ's offering was in the heavenly sanctuary.

In Hebrews, the place of the community is to follow the ἀρχηγός (cf. 2:10; 12:2). The hortatory subjunctive is frequently used by the author where he makes parenetic use of his theological arguments. In many instances, the credal ἔχομεν/ἔχοντες is followed by the hortatory summons. Thus the community has been encouraged, on the basis of the heavenly work of Christ, to "draw near" (προσερχώμεθα, 4:16; 12:22), to "make every effort" (σπουδάσωμεν, 4:11) to reach the heavenly rest, and to "run" (τρέχωμεν) the race (12:1). Christ has opened the way into the heavenly world (10:19-23), and now it is the task of the church to follow. Thus the church is summoned, τοίνυν ἐξερχώμεξα πρὸς αὐτὸν ἔξω τῆς παρεμβολῆς. "Outside the camp" means neither "outside Judaism," nor "outside Jerusalem." Christian existence is a matter of "going out" in the direction of the ἀρχηγός (cf. 11:8, 15). To "go out" is to give up earthly securities (11:8) and to accept the style of life of the pilgrim people. The many references to the pilgrim existence of the faithful ones in chapter 11 (11:9, 13, 29, 38) serve as paradigms for the Christian community, for Christians still live as "strangers and pilgrims" (11:13). To live "outside" may involve bearing the "shame" (τὸν ὀνειδισμὸν αὐτοῦ φέροντες) of Christ, just as the pilgrim people in the

---

[25] See U. Luck, "Himmlisches und irdisches Geschehen im Hebräerbrief," 211. "The historical suffering of Jesus is closely connected . . . with the heavenly sanctuary. It would be correct to say that, for Hebrews, the suffering of Jesus is already his service in the heavenly sanctuary." Cf. E. Käsemann, *Gottesvolk*, 148: "The sacrificial death of Jesus, by which he offers his fleshly body, is . . . at the same time the *eisodos* into heaven."

[26] *Leg. All.* 2. 54-55; 3. 46; *Quod Det. Pot.* 160.

past endured shame for his sake (11:26). There is a sense, therefore, in which the pilgrim existence involves the renunciation of all securities in the earthly sphere.[27]

When we compare the hortatory subjunctive with the content of the other pareneses, we observe that the exhortation is parallel with προσερ-χώμεθα . . . τῷ θρόνῳ τῆς χάριτος (4:16); σπουδάσωμεν οὖν εἰσελθεῖν εἰς ἐκείνην τὴν κατάπαυσιν (4:11); and προσερχώμεθα . . . ἐν πληροφορίᾳ πίστεως (10:22). Thus to "go out" from earthly securities is at the same time to "enter" the heavenly world. The summons to the church is similar to that of 2 Clement 5:1, καὶ μὴ φοβηθῶμεν ἐξελθεῖν ἐκ τοῦ κόσμου.[28]

The exhortation to "go out" is grounded in the indicative with the credal ἔχω, as in 13:10. The church can take the risk of going out from visible securities because it has an invisible one: οὐ γὰρ ἔχομεν ὧδε μένουσαν πόλιν, ἀλλὰ τὴν μέλλουσαν ἐπιζήτουμεν. The pilgrim existence can be maintained only by those who have a city (11:9-10, 16). It is the "invisible" reality (11:27) that empowers the community to endure without any earthly securities. According to 13:14, the μένουσα πόλις is not "here" (ὧδε) in this sphere. The abiding city belongs to the heavenly world, and will become a reality to the community in the future. The church thus lives, as did the men of faith (ch. 11), with the security that rests only in having a "city" (11:10, 16; cf. 11:14).

The "abiding city" corresponds to the "altar" (13:10) which the church possesses. It is this possession which gives βεβαίωσις to the community (cf. 13:9), and enables it to "go out" on its pilgrimage. The author has regularly grounded the church's capacity to endure in its possession of the transcendent possession made possible by Christ. Thus it is because of Christ's exaltation that the church has a "firm anchor" (6:19). It is because the church receives the "unshakable kingdom" that it can "have grace" (12:28). The "abiding possession" in 10:34 gives the church the capacity to endure (10:34-36), and the entrance of Christ into the heavenly world allows the church to be "unwavering" (ἀκλινής, 10:23). In the same way, the possession of the "abiding city" serves in 13:9-14 to "strengthen the heart."

Comparison with 12:22 indicates that the πόλις is the author's word for

---

[27] E.Grässer (*Glaube*, 114) has shown the close similarity between Hebrews and Philo in this understanding of the pilgrim existence. The heavenly world is, for Philo, the true city and fatherland (*de Conf. Ling.* 79-82; *de Cher.* 120-122) while one exists on earth as a stranger. See also the discussion on pp. 59-60 and 75-77.

[28] I understand the form of this withdrawal to mean that the church does not rely on any material assurances of stability, as the references to "ordinances of the flesh" (9:10) suggest. The church continues to offer its "sacrifice of praise" (13:15), which is the unworldly existence not dependent on material observance.

the transcendent possession made available by Christ.[29] This city does not belong to the earthly sphere.[30] It is thus equivalent, in the author's view, to the other terms for transcendence: κατάπαυσις (chaps. 3-4), βασιλεία ἀσάλευτος (12:28), τὰ μὴ σαλευόμενα (12:27), and τὰ μὴ βλεπόμενα (11:1).[31] Because it is a transcendent reality, the *polis* can be described by the participle μένουσα. Μένειν is used here, as in 12:27, for the stability of the heavenly world. Such a use of μένειν is to be found regularly in the Platonic literature for the stability of those things which are above the world of sense perception.[32] Such an abiding city is not "here" (ὧδε) in this sphere. Indeed it remains a future prospect. Nevertheless, the stability of this heavenly possession can "strengthen the heart" in the present.

We may observe that the author's manner of stabilizing the hearts of the members of the community bears many similarities to the perspective of Philo, whose writings exhibit a concern with the process by which one finds stability. For Philo, God is immutable, while the creation is unstable. Those who remain identified with the earth and the material things will remain unstable. On the other hand, proximity to something stable produces stability in man.[33] Thus those sages who leave τὰ ἐν γενέσει are able to share in the stability of God. Such an argument has points of contact with 13:9-14 and the other pareneses of Hebrews, for it is the author's consistent argument that the church's possession of the heavenly and abiding gift made accessible by Christ now gives it the stability of heart (13:9; cf. 10:23; 6:19) to continue the Christian pilgrimage. Such a possession is grounds for their maintenance of a life of worship and good works (13:15-16).

Conclusion

Careful comparison of the form and structure of 13:9-14 with the other pareneses of Hebrews suggests that this difficult passage is not to be understood as a polemic against heretical teachings about which we could only speculate. This passage, like the major sections of the book, employs references to levitical customs to use as a foil for the author's contrast between

---

[29] For the author's use of *polis*, cf. 11:10, 16; 12:22.

[30] In 12:22, the *polis* is distinguished from Mount Sinai, which is categorized as tangible (ψηλαφημένος). See the discussion in Chapter III.

[31] E. Grässer, *Glaube*, 174.

[32] Plato, *Timaeus* 37D; Philo, *de Som.*2. 221, 237; Plotinus, *On Time and Eternity* 3. 7. E.Grässer (*Glaube*, 174) has said that μένειν in Hebrews regularly accents not only the duration of things, but also their stability.

[33] *Leg. All.* 2. 54; *de Som.* 2. 237.

earthly assurances and the better possession which the church now "has" (ἔχειν, 13:10, 14). Such a confessional statement serves here, as in the other pareneses, as the grounds for the community to find the "stability" necessary to continue the Christian pilgrimage.

CHAPTER X

CONCLUSION: THE TRANSITION TO CHRISTIAN PHILOSOPHY

"Nothing is harder to disentangle," Emile Brehier has pointed out, "than the history of intellectual thought" in the first two Christian centuries.[1] These centuries witnessed the brilliant resurgence of the Stoic movement under Seneca, Epictetus, and Marcus Aurelius. This era also witnessed the rebirth of Athenian idealism as it had existed in the systems of Plato and Aristotle. This rebirth is to be seen in the work of Plutarch, Albinus, Antiochus, and many others. At the same time a Pythagorean literature, impregnated with Platonism, came into existence.[2] Alongside the philosophical schools, there were other trends in this era, including the apocalyptic and Gnostic movements, which achieved a great following.

The history of Christianity, as W. Jaeger and others have shown,[3] follows a path toward accommodation with the philosophy of the Greeks. This accommodation became inevitable with the Christians' communication in the Greek language. In the Pauline literature and in Luke-Acts, traces of the impact of philosophy have been shown. Such traces are to be found also in the Apostolic Fathers.[4] It is not until the Apologists that Christians both employ philosophical categories and self-consciously cite the Greek philosophers.[5] Henry Chadwick has referred to Justin as the first Christian philosopher.[6] Justin's attempt to defend and describe the faith within the categories of philosophy were, despite the objections of many contemporaries, continued by his successors, especially in the Eastern church.

The philosophy which was accepted as an instrument for explaining the faith was primarily Middle Platonism, which was both popular and easily set

---

[1] *The History of Philosophy: The Hellenistic and Roman Age*, cited in H.B. Timothy, *The Early Christian Apologists and Greek Philosophy* 1.

[2] Timothy, *Apologists*, 1-2.

[3] W. Jaeger, *Early Christianity and Greek Paideia*, passim. H. Chadwick, *Early Christian Thought and the Classical Tradition*. H. Wolfson, *The Philosophy of the Church Fathers*.

[4] Jaeger, *Paideia*, 12-13.

[5] See J.H. Waszink, "Bermerkungen zum Einfluss des Platonismus im frühem Christentum," *VC* 19 (1965) 129. Cf. R.P. Daniélou, *Le Message chrétienne et la Pensée grecque au IIᵉ Siècle*.

[6] H. Chadwick, "Philo and the Beginnings of Christian Thought," in A.H. Armstrong, ed., *The Cambridge History of Later Greek and Early Medieval Philosophy*, 161.

within a Christian framework. Philo of Alexandria had already seen the possibilities for using the Platonic metaphysic to explain the biblical faith. Indeed, his heirs are to be found among Christian writers, as Philo is unknown to the subsequent Jewish tradition.[7] His work had a strong influence on the exegesis of Clement, Origen, Gregory of Nyssa, and others in the eastern Mediterranean.[8] The extraordinary impact of Philo of Alexandria on later Christian thought is reflected in the legend that Philo had been converted to Christianity during his stay in Rome.[9]

Research into the relationship between Philo and Hebrews has too often ignored the fact that Philo was a part of a larger tradition of Jewish scholarship in Alexandria. Although he was a major figure in Alexandrian Judaism, his work did not stand alone. There were predecessors and contemporaries of Philo who also were influenced by the contemporary philosophy of Alexandria. Some were less thoroughly indebted to philosophy and allegory than Philo, while others were more committed to the allegorical method.[10] This fact suggests that there was an Alexandrian tradition of biblical exegesis within the framework of Greek philosophy which both precedes and follows Philo. Thus when Henry Chadwick ironically calls Philo the originator of Christian philosophy,[11] there is reason for caution, as Philo was only one among many who interpreted the Bible with the assumptions and standards of Greek philosophy.

When early Christianity turned to philosophy for a metaphysical foundation, there was a remarkable consistency in the work of the Apologists and their successors at Alexandria. The metaphysical foundation had been provided by the tradition of Alexandrian Judaism. The apocalyptic world view had become obviously inadequate for a church which no longer anticipated an imminent eschaton. In the place of the apocalyptic world view, the early church turned to Platonism. Justin was convinced that, with a few necessary qualifications and corrections, Plato and Christianity could be reconciled.[12] He, along with later Christian Platonists, could find harmony between the Platonists' insistence on the transcendence of the deity and the God of the Bible.[13] Christian Platonists were able to reconcile the account of the crea-

---

[7] Chadwick, "Philo," 137.

[8] Cf. W. Bousset, *Jüdisch-christlicher Schulbetrieb in Alexandria und Rom.* Cf. R.P. Daniélou, "Philon et Grégoire de Nysse," in *Philon d'Alexandrie* (Colloque National de la Recherche Scientifique, 1967).

[9] Cited in Eusebius, *H.E.*, 2. 17. 1.

[10] See Birger Pearson, "Friedländer Revisited. Alexandrian Judaism and Gnostic Origins," *Studia Philonica* 2 (1973) 24.

[11] H. Chadwick, "Philo," 137.

[12] Chadwick, "Philo," 161.

[13] Chadwick, "Philo," 156, 161; cf. Daniélou, *Message*, 18-19.

tion in Genesis and Plato's Timaeus.[14] They could also find a harmony between the Platonic insistence that the "inner man" belongs to another world and the biblical view of man and salvation.[15] Clement is certain that the heaven of the Bible is the Platonic *kosmos noētos*.[16] Thus Platonism offered a distinct world view which enabled Christians to replace the apocalyptic categories.[17]

The acceptance of Platonic categories does not mean that a Platonic system was totally and uncritically accepted by Christian writers. J.H. Waszink has shown that the Platonic elements, which were taken over by Christian writers because of their usefulness, were often "foreign elements" in the Christian literature. The use of a Platonic *terminus technicus* did not imply a systematic use of the Platonic world view.[18] The biblical revelation remained the criterion of judgment for assessing what is true and false in philosophy. Justin says, for example, that Platonists are right about the transcendence of God but wrong about the doctrine of the soul's immortality and transmigration.[19]

The variety of ways in which Platonic categories were taken over is important for our understanding of the thought world of Hebrews, for this fact is a reminder that the presence of Platonic elements does not mean that an author is a systematic Platonic philosopher. The thought world of Hebrews is therefore as difficult to disentangle as the literature of antiquity in general. The author of Hebrews has inherited various traditions which he has interpreted within his own world view.

In a very important sense the author of Hebrews is the heir of Christian predecessors who were shaped by the thought world and categories of Jewish apocalyptic literature. He has inherited the traditional doctrine of the two ages (1:2; 6:5) and the hope for a second coming (9:27; cf. 12:25-28). In addition, one can see in Hebrews' exegetical work important connections with the work of his Christian predecessors. The texts which he chooses for discussion are largely those which earlier Christian teachers had employed (i.e., Ps 2:7; 110:1; Jer 33:33). The author, like other early Christian writers, gave these texts an eschatological and Christological interpretation. R. Williamson has correctly shown that Philo and Hebrews base their discussions on an entirely different sets of texts from the OT.[20]

---

[14] Daniélou, 20. See Justin's citation of *Tim.* 28c in *Apol.* 2. 10. 7.
[15] Chadwick, *Early Christian Thought*, 3.
[16] *Strom.* 5. 6. 34, 7.
[17] H.B. Timothy, *Apologists*, 81.
[18] J.H. Waszink, 137.
[19] Chadwick, "Philo," 161.
[20] R. Williamson, *Philo and the Epistle to the Hebrews*, 498-503.

While there is continuity between Hebrews and previous Christian teachers in the use of the OT, there is also a totally new approach in Hebrews. The strangeness of Hebrews consists in the unique method of argumentation and set of assumptions that one finds in the author's interpretation of the OT. Indeed, this method of argumentation, which is found throughout the diverse materials of Hebrews, gives the book an underlying unity.

This unity is most apparent in the exhortations which appear regularly at the conclusion of the major theological statements of the book. These pareneses, which normally follow the author's midrashic reflection over a section of Scripture, provide the author with the occasion of applying the midrash to the needs of the audience (2:1-4; 3:6, 14; 5:11-6:9; 10:19-39; 12:28; 13:13-14). The major concern of these exhortations is the problem of encouraging a weary church to "hold fast" to its original confession (cf. 3:6, 14). Indeed, a striking feature of the exhortations is the consistent use of terms for stability. The author fears that his community will "drift away" (2:1), be "carried away" (13:9), and fail to "hold firm" to the end (3:14). The intention of the author is to demonstrate to his readers that they have a "sure and steadfast anchor of the soul" (6:20), and that the readers can "hold on without wavering" (10:23). The imagery of stability, as suggested by forms of *bebai-*, is a unifying theme of the paraeneses.

This unifying element now allows us to understand the function of the author's major theological sections. These sections cover a variety of themes and texts from the OT, leaving the impression that Hebrews is only a collection of unconnected midrashim. Closer observation, however, suggests that the unity of Hebrews is to be found in the themes and categories which are found in each section. The consistent feature of this diverse material is the dualistic reading of the OT and the emphasis on the transcendence of the Christian possession. The "great salvation" (2:3) has a metaphysical superiority to the word delivered by angels. The prior revelation dealt only with the sphere of the tangible (12:18), the worldly (9:1), and the "handmade" (9:11). Christian experience includes sharing in the heavenly call (3:1), access to God's heavenly sanctuary (10:19-22), and access to the unseen world (11:13).

Although Hebrews is composed of diverse exegetical traditions, the unifying feature is the emphasis on transcendence. Hebrews is a series of comparisons between Jesus Christ (and his word) and the "word" delivered by angels (cf. 2:2). The verdict given in each instance is that Christ is "better" (cf. 1:4; 3:3; 6:9; 7:4, 22; 9:11). In most instances, the superiority of Christ is established on metaphysical grounds, for the institutions of the OT are connected with this creation; Christ is the exalted one who sits at the right hand of God in the heavenly world.

The function of these comparisons is to be seen in the pareneses which follow, for the theological sections provide the background for the author's appeal to his community. The theological sections are not intended to combat a specific heresy within the community; they are intended to demonstrate to the readers the greatness of the Christian faith on metaphysical terms.

The connection between the theological and the parenetic sections is particularly apparent in the author's consistent emphasis on the stability of this transcendent possession made available by the exaltation of Christ. While earlier Christian literature emphasized the exaltation of Christ and his place in the heavenly world, only Hebrews emphasizes the "sameness" (1:12; 13:8) and the abiding (1:11; 7:3, 24) of the exalted one. In addition, the transcendent possession of the community is characterized by its unshakability (12:27-28) and by its abiding quality (*menein*, 10:34; 12:27; 13:14). These categories are employed within a definite metaphysical dualism. Stability is the characteristic of the unseen and intangible world.

The stability of the Christian possession has an importance in the life of the community, as the pareneses indicate. The church's anchor is provided by the exalted status of Christ (6:19-20). The existence of the abiding possession (10:34) gives the church the stability to accept the role of alien in this world (cf. 11:13-16) and to follow its pioneer "outside the camp" (13:13). The access to the heavenly sanctuary provides the church with the capacity to "hold on without wavering" (10:23). The consistent metaphysical dualism of Hebrews functions to provide certainty for a wavering community.

The strangeness of the method of argumentation employed in Hebrews consists of the dualistic assumptions which support the author's emphasis on transcendence and stability. Although Hebrews has inherited much from apocalyptic thinking, this feature does not come from apocalyptic literature. Indeed, the author's assumptions are most apparent where he has himself interpreted apocalyptic traditions and shifted the emphasis to stability, as in 12:25-28 (see Chapter III).

Scholarship on Hebrews has often attempted to account for the metaphysical dualism of Hebrews by suggesting the importance of Philo as a background to the book. This issue has largely been confused by the whole question of literary dependence and by the difficult problem of defining what is involved when one speaks of a Philonic influence. Differences between the two writers are probably great enough to exclude a literary dependence of Hebrews on Philo. The author does not cite the same texts as Philo; nor does he have the same preoccupation with philosophical questions. One has no difficulty, therefore, in showing differences between the two writers. Indeed, the difference in size and genre between Philo and Hebrews will make it inevitable that one will find many issues discussed by Philo that are not in Hebrews. In addition, the place of Hebrews within the Christian tradition involves obvious convictions that are not found in Philo.

The fact that one is able to point to differences between the two writers does not mean that there is no Philonic influence or that the parallels are only "formal," as Williamson attempts to show.[21] This monograph has shown that the two writers share a common set of categories and a metaphysic that is similar. Both read the OT with dualistic assumptions. Such categories as "motherless" and "without genealogy" are shared by the two writers. There are similarities in the two writers' views on faith, rest, and theophanies of the OT, the efficacy of material sacrifices, and of the levels of education. While Hebrews seldom demonstrates extensive knowledge of discrete traditions which are found in Philo, it shares many of the latter's categories and assumptions.

A pervasive theme in Philo is the motif of stability, which is rooted in his distinction between the unstable creation and the unshakable heavenly world. His belief that mortals can share in the stability of the deity by refusing to place their trust in the creation is frequently stated. Indeed, Philo appeals to his readers to attain the same stability which the sages had found at God's side. He employs the nautical image of "tossing" to describe the existence of those who place their trust in this creation (*de Post. Cain.* 22).

It is against this background that one can understand the role of the stability motif in Hebrews. The author shares with Philo the conviction that access to a stable possession confers stability (cf. *de Post. Cain.* 23). Both writers assume that one's anchor is found in a relationship to the heavenly world, and that one otherwise "wavers." Thus while the author of Hebrews is not dependent directly on Philo's works, he belongs largely to the same conceptual world.

These categories of transcendence and stability are not limited to Philo and Hebrews. Philo was himself a representative of a broader stream of thought, as he reflects a combination of Platonism, Stoicism, and Pythagoreanism. His emphasis on the stability of the heavenly world was a major motif of Middle Platonism. The Middle Platonist view of the structure of the world was widely accepted in antiquity. It was adopted both by Gnostics and by "orthodox" Christians in the eastern church.[22] In fact, as I have shown, this understanding of transcendence was one feature of Middle Platonism which was particularly useful to Christian thinkers. Thus the similarities

---

[21] Williamson, *Philo*, 133.

[22] See H. Krämer, *Der Ursprung der Geistmetaphysik*, 232. I have also shown in my unpublished dissertation, "*That Which Abides*": *Some Metaphysical Assumptions in the Epistle to the Hebrews* (Vanderbilt University, 1974), the consistent way in which Gnostic texts appropriate the Platonic stability motif. Cf. E. Baert, "La thème de la vision de Dieu," 467. According to the Simonians, God is the stable one (*Strom.* 2. 52. 2). According to Numenius (Fr. 24), the highest deity is characterized by his stability.

between Philo and Hebrews do not suggest a literary relationship between the two writers. It is more likely that both writers have accepted a common set of assumptions from the environment. Hebrews thus represents a preliminary stage in the church's adoption of a Platonic metaphysic.

An examination of Alexandrian Judaism suggests that there were many ways in which Platonic elements could be used to interpret the biblical faith. Indeed Philo appears to have stood in the middle between those who were more thoroughgoing in their use of Platonism and those who were less dependent on Platonic categories. Thus Hebrews' less extensive use of Platonic categories may indicate that the author is more comfortable with the models offered by Aristobulos and other Alexandrian Jews than with the more extensive Platonism of Philo. Nevertheless there was a tradition in Alexandria of appropriating Platonic elements into biblical exegesis, and one may assume that many of Philo's categories belong to that tradition. The author of Hebrews is also acquainted with these categories.

While the author of Hebrews is not a philosopher, it is undeniable that the book is the work of a skilled rhetorician. The extraordinary vocabulary (140 hapax legomena), with a large number of words attested nowhere else in biblical literature but common in secular literature, point to the educational level and rhetorical ability of the author. The word plays, careful syntactical constructions, and well-constructed parallelisms all point to a level of training that was recognized in the ancient church as exceptional.[23] R. Williamson describes the vocabulary as "unique in the New Testament for its richness and variety," and as the product of a remarkable early Christian theologian.[24]

E.A. Judge has said that philosophy in the strict sense was a matter only for a few. However, there was a certain acquaintance with philosophical ideas which one can assume for the educated people of the period.[25] The education of a rhetorician, for example, included an elementary introduction to philosophy.[26] Therefore the Middle Platonism of the period, which we meet in the work of Philo, Plutarch, and others, was known widely among rhetoricians of the period. Thus while the author of Hebrews was not a philosopher, his level of education suggests that he would have been the recipient of the secondary education, which would have included instruction in philosophy. It is naive to argue that he employed a highly sophisticated vocabulary without also being aware of some of the philosophical associations which the language suggested.

Henry Chadwick says of Clement of Alexandria what Plotinus once

---

[23] See E. Norden, *Die antike Kunstprosa* (Leipzig and Berlin, 1909) 2. 499.
[24] Williamson, *Philo*, 13.
[25] E. A. Judge, "St. Paul and Classical Society," 32.
[26] Waszink, "Einfluss," 145.

said of Longinus, that he is more a man of letters than a philosopher.[27] One can make the same affirmation for the author of Hebrews. While he is not a philosopher, there are in his work statements and propositions that implicitly point toward metaphysical positions.[28] The work is thus a transition to Christian philosophy.

A final argument for Hebrews as a transition toward Christian philosophy is the fact that this work was first accepted and regarded as canonical in the Alexandrian church. Franz Overbeck pointed to an irony in the fact that Hebrews is first cited in the West,[29] but was regarded as apostolic and canonical in Alexandria. While it is not certain that the citation in 1 Clement is taken directly from Hebrews, it is certain that Clement of Alexandria and Origen demonstrated a special appreciation for Hebrews. Indeed, it is because of the eastern church that Hebrews was finally accepted in the canon.[30]

Overbeck argued that Clement of Alexandria's appreciation of Hebrews is a sign of the book's congeniality to a Christian Platonist. The "Alexandrianism" of the book, including its metaphysic and allegorization, made Hebrews particularly acceptable in Alexandria.[31] In fact, both Clement and Origen were uneasy with the ascription of Pauline authorship to Hebrews, but attempted to maintain the connection between Paul and Hebrews.[32] This fact suggests the acceptability of Hebrews to the Alexandrians.

The congeniality of Hebrews to Clement is indicated by the extraordinary number of citations of Hebrews which appear in Clement's work. Clement cites the introduction of Hebrews on numerous occasions.[33] He also has a special interest in the *katapausis* motif of Hebrews 3-4.[34] Like Philo, Clement is particularly interested in an allegorical interpretation of the high priest's entry into the holy of holies.[35] Thus he interprets the *hagia* in

---

[27] Chadwick, "Philo," 181.

[28] Chadwick ("Philo," 158) says, "Christian philosophy does not strictly begin in the New Testament, but even at this stage it is easy to discern statements and propositions that implicitly and indirectly point towards certain metaphysical positions."

[29] F. Overbeck, *Zur Geschichte des Kanons*, 68-70. Overbeck refers to *1 Clem.* 36:1.

[30] Overbeck, 69-70.

[31] Overbeck, 19n, 69.

[32] Overbeck, 18. On Origen, cf. Eusebius, *H.E.* 6. 25. 11-13. On Clement, see Eusebius, *H.E.* 6. 14. 4. Both writers apparently were aware that the Pauline authorship was doubted in their own time. Thus Hebrews is commonly cited as Pauline, but both writers recognized a difference in style. Nevertheless the value they placed on it is evident in their defense of its apostolicity.

[33] *Paed.* 3. 8. 43; *Strom.* 1. 3. 27, 1; 5. 6. 35, 1; 6. 4. 39, 3; 6. 7. 58, 2; 6. 10. 81, 6; 6. 12. 106, 4; 7. 17. 95, 13.

[34] *Prot.* 9. 84. 3-85; *Strom.* 2. 22. 134, 4; 7. 16. 93.

[35] *Strom.* 3. 6. 59, 4; 5. 6. 34, 7-8; 7. 7. 40, 1.

Heb 9:25 as the *noētē ousia* and the tent of Heb 9:11 as the *kosmos noētos*.[36] As a Christian Platonist, Clement was much concerned with defining faith in a way that could employ the categories of Greek philosophy.[37] Consequently, he cites Hebrews 11 on several occasions in order to give his interpretation of the relationship between faith and knowledge.[38] Hebrews was, therefore, a particularly important work for Clement.

Rowan Greer has shown that Origen cited Hebrews with even greater frequency than Clement.[39] Origen seizes on several themes of Hebrews and fashions them into the larger framework of the Christian faith. Like Clement before him, Origen was particularly interested in developing an allegorical interpretation of the tabernacle (*Hom. Ex.* 9. 2. *GCS*). The Platonizing language of Heb 8:5; 10:1 is brought within Origen's framework in several instances (cf. *Hom. Num.* 3. 3, *GCS* 7, 16). Hebrews 11 and 5:11-14 are also employed in Origen's view of the Christian life.[40] Origen is particularly interested in the latter passage as a justification for his view of the Christian life as a progress toward perfection in which the deeper, allegorical interpretation of Scripture plays a role.[41] In fact, practically every chapter of Hebrews is brought within Origen's framework of Christian Platonism.

The "strangeness" of Hebrews within the canon is probably the very feature which made it useful to Clement and Origen. This strangeness consists of assumptions and categories which had been developed at Alexandria and perhaps elsewhere in the eastern Mediterranean. Hebrews is thus distinguished from other early Christian literature by a consistent metaphysic that was commonly known in educated circles. While the author is not a philosopher, his work is a transition to Christian philosophy.

Hebrews and the Canon

Both Herbert Braun and R. Williamson argue that a dependence on metaphysics and philosophical categories would mean that Hebrews is outside the center of canonical literature.[42] The denial of a philosophical background, according to Williamson, "invites us to think of the Epistle to the Hebrews as in the central stream of early Christian theology, not as some-

---

[36] *Strom.* 7. 7. 40, 1; 5. 6. 34, 7.

[37] S. Lilla, *Clement of Alexandria*, 118.

[38] *Strom.* 2. 2. 9, 1; 2. 4. 12, 1-14, 3; 4. 16. 103, 1-3.

[39] R. Greer, *The Captain of our Salvation*, 7.

[40] Greer, 34-42.

[41] Greer, 41.

[42] H. Braun, "Die Gewinnung der Gewissheit im Hebräerbrief," 321-330. Cf. Braun, "Das himmlische Vaterland bei Philon und im Hebräerbrief," 319-327.

how off-centre, deflected from the central stream of early Christian thinking by extraneous philosophical doctrines."[43] H. Braun points to the metaphysical character of Hebrews, among other features as an argument that Hebrews has left the Pauline doctrine of justification.

E. Grässer has shown that the place of Hebrews in the canon does not rest on the question of whether the author repeats the phrases and categories of Paul. The question is, rather, whether Hebrews communicates the Christian message of salvation in a historically changed situation.[45] The issue before the author is not the salvation of Gentiles; it is "intellectual laziness" (5:11) and withdrawal (10:25, 39). Thus the author attempts to provide certainty, "knowledge of the truth" (10:26), and a stable basis for the community's endurance. He provides this through a word that is "hard to understand" (5:11).

The use of metaphysical categories does not totally separate Hebrews from other NT literature. Indeed, metaphysical reflection was a natural development from the use of Ps 110:1 in early Christianity. The early Christian claim that "Jesus is Lord" was based on the conviction of his metaphysical dignity. The Pauline reflections in Rom 8:28-39 offer hope to the church on the basis of the exalted status of Christ. Similarly, Eph 1:19-23 is an example of the way Psalm 110 was used in early Christian cosmological reflections. The distinctiveness of Hebrews is to be seen in the direction which is taken with the author's metaphysical assumptions.

E. Grässer has correctly shown that the Pauline doctrine of justification has not been lost. Because the issue of Gentile salvation no longer stands at the center, the radical character of Paul's doctrine of justification of the godless has diminished.[46] This change was inevitable. However, while the category of *dikaiosynē* does not stand at the center of Hebrews, the cultic terminology of *katharismos/katharismeō* is central. By the use of this category the author insists as clearly as does Paul on the inadequacy of all human activity for salvation.[47] That the death of Christ is "for us" is affirmed not only by Paul and the pre-Pauline tradition; it is also affirmed in Hebrews (9:24).[48] The scandal of the cross is a motif shared by both Paul and Hebrews

[43] Williamson, 580.

[44] For Braun's view of the canon within the canon, see *Gesammelte Studien zum Neuen Testament*, 229.

[45] E. Grässer, "Zur Christologie des Hebräerbriefes," 199. Idem, "Rechtfertigung im Hebräerbrief."

[46] "Rechtfertigung," 83.

[47] "Rechtfertigung," 87.

[48] Cf. Peter Stuhlmacher, *Vom Verstehen des Neuen Testaments*, 236-244. The doctrine of the cross as God's "Versöhnung," according to Stuhlmacher, belongs to the "Mitte der Schrift."

(1 Cor 1:18-25; Heb 13:9-13). The use of metaphysical arguments has thus not diminished the claim that the drama of the historical events of the incarnation and cross is the turn of the ages, allowing a new participation in the "powers of the age to come" (6:4-6).

BIBLIOGRAPHY

I. Primary Sources

Arnim, J. von. *Stoicorum Veterum Fragmenta.* Leipzig: Teubner, 1921.

Babbit, Frank Cole, ed. *Plutarch's Moralia.* 15 Vols. LCL. London: Wm. Heinemann, 1962.

Bury, J. B. *Plato, with an English Translation.* LCL. London: Wm. Heinemann, 1925.

Colson, F. H. and G. H. Whitaker. *Philo, with an English Translation.* 10 Vols. LCL. London: Wm. Heinemann, 1941.

Edelstein, L. and I. G. Kidd. *Posidonius: Vol. I, The Fragments.* Cambridge: University Press, 1972.

Festugière, A.-J. *Corpus Hermeticum.* Paris: Société d'Édition, 1960.

Mutschmann, H. *Sexti Empirici Opera.* Leipzig: Teubner, 1958.

Nauck, A. *Porphyrii Philosophi Platonici.* Leipzig. Teubner, 1886.

Oldfather, W. A. *Epictetus, with an English Translation.* LCL. London: Wm. Heinemann, 1961.

Schmidt, C. and W. Till. *Koptisch-gnostische Schriften.* Berlin: Akademie Verlag, 1954.

Stählin, O. *Clemens Alexandrinus. Die griechischen christlichen Shriftsteller der erste drei Jahrhunderte.* Leipzig: J. C. Hinrichs, 1905.

II. Concordances

Hatch, Edwin and Henry A. Redpath, eds. *Concordance to the Septuagint.* 2 Vols. Oxford: Clarendon Press, 1897.

Mayer, Günther. *Index Philoneus.* Berlin: Walter de Gruyter, 1974.

Moulton, W. F. and A. S. Geden, eds. *A Concordance to the Greek New Testament.* 4th ed. Edinburgh: T & T Clark, 1963.

III. Lexica

Bauer, W. *A Greek-English Lexicon of the New Testament and Other Early Christian Literature.* Translated by W. F. Arndt and F. W. Gingrich. Chicago: University of Chicago Press, 1957. [BAG]

Liddell, H. G. and Robert Scott. *A Greek-English Lexicon.* Oxford: University Press, repr. 1968. [LSJ]

IV. Journal Articles

Andriessen, Paul. "Das grössere und vollkommenere Zelt." *BZ* N.F. 15 (1971).

————. "La communauté des 'Hébreux': Était-elle tombée dans le Relachement?" *NRT* 96 (1974).

————, and A. Lenglet. "Quelques passages difficiles de l'Épître aux Hébreux (5:7.11; 10-20; 12:2)." *Bib* 51 (1970).

Baert, E. "La thème de la vision de Dieu chez Justin, Clement d' Alexandrie et S. Grégoire de Nysse." *Freiburger Zeitschrift für Philosophie und Theologie* 12 (1965).

Braun, H. "Die Gewinnung der Gewissheit in dem Hebräerbrief." *TLZ* 96 (1971).

Dautzenberg, G. "Der Glaube im Hebräerbrief." *BZ* N.F. 17 (1973).

Fiorenza, E. S. "Cultic Language in Qumran and in the New Testament." *CBQ* 38 (1976).

Grässer, E. "Der Hebräerbrief 1938-1963." *TRu* N.F. 30 (1964).

————. "Der historische Jesus im Hebräerbrief." *ZNW* 56 (1965).

Hofius, O. "Die Unabänderlichkeit des göttlichen Heilsratschlusses." *ZNW* 64 (1973).

Johnston, G. "Οἰκουμένη and κόσμος in the New Testament." *NTS* 10 (1964).

Judge, E. A. "St. Paul and Classical Society." *JAC* 15 (1972).

Koester, H. "Outside the Camp." *HTR* 55 (1962).

Loewenich, W. von. "Zum Verständis des Opfergedankens im Hb." *TBL* 12 (1933).

Luck, U. "Himmlisches und irdisches Geschehen im Hebräerbrief." *NovT* 6 (1963).

Lührmann, D. "Pistis im Judentum." *ZNW* 64 (1973).

Luz. U. "Der alte und der neue Bund bei Paulus und im Hebräerbrief." *EvT* 6 (1967).

Nikiprowetzky, V. "La Spiritualisation des Sacrifices et le Cult Sacrificiel au Temple de Jérusalem chez Philon d'Alexandrie." *Sem* 17 (1967).

Owen, H. P. "The 'Stages of Ascent' in Hebrews V. 11 - VI. 3." *NTS* 3 (1957).

Ramaroson, L. "Contre les 'Temples Faits de Main d'Homme.'" *Revue de Philologie de Littérature et d'Histoire Anciennes* 43 (1969).

Rusche, H. "Die Gestalt des Melchisedek." *MTZ* 6 (1955).

Schmidt, K. L. "Jerusalem als Urbild und Abbild." *Eranos Jahrbuch* 18 (1950).

Schweizer, E. "Die hellenistische Komponente im neutestamentlichen σάρξ Begriff." *ZNW* 48 (1957).

Swetnam, J. "The Greater and More Perfect Tent." *Bib* 47 (1966).

Wallis, R. "The Idea of Conscience in Philo of Alexandria." *Studia Philonica* 3 (1974-75).

Waszink, J. H. "Bemerkungen zum Einfluss des Platonismus im frühen Christentum." *VC* 19 (1965).

Young, F. M. "The Idea of Sacrifice in Neoplatonic and Patristic Texts." *Studia Patristica* 11 (1967).

————. "Temple Cult and Law in Early Christianity." *NTS* 19 (1973).

V. Books

Armstrong, A. H., ed. *The Cambridge History of Later Greek and Early Medieval Philosophy.* Cambridge: University Press, 1970.

Bartelink, G. J. *Quelques Observations sur Παρρησία dans la Littérature Paléo-Chrétienne.* Supplementa. Nijmegen: Oekker and Van de Vegt, 1970.

Bianchi, U., ed. *Le Origini dello Gnosticismo.* Leiden: Brill, 1967.

Bonhöffer, A. *Epiktetus und das Neue Testament.* Giessen: A. Töpelmann, 1911.

Bornkamm, G. *Studien zu Antike und Christentum.* Munich: Kaiser, 1959.

Bousset, W. *Jüdisch-christlicher Schulbetrieb in Alexandria und Rom.* Göttingen: Vandenhoeck und Ruprecht, 1915.

Braun, H. *Gesammelte Studien zum Neuen Testament.* Tübingen: Mohr, 1967.

Brehier, E. *The History of Philosophy: The Hellenistic and Roman Age.* Trans. by W. Baskin. Chicago and London, 1965.

_____. *Les Idées Philosophiques et Religieuses de Philon d'Alexandrie.* Paris: Librairie Philosophique, 1925.

Breitenstein, U. *Beobachtungen zu Sprache, Stil und Gedankengut des vierten Makkabäerbuchs.* Basel: Schwabe, 1976.

Brown, J. R. *Temple and Sacrifice in Rabbinic Judaism.* Evanston: Seabury Western Theological Seminary, 1963.

Büchler, A. *Studies in Sin and Atonement.* London: Oxford University Press, 1928.

Cambier, J. *Eschatologie ou Hellénisme dans l'Épître aux Hébreux.* Louvain: Nauwelaerts, 1949.

Chadwick, H. *Early Christian Thought and the Classical Tradition.* Oxford: Clarendon Press, 1966.

Christen, J. *Bildung und Gesellschaft; Erträge der Erforschung.* Darmstadt: Wissenschaftliche Buchgesellschaft, 1975.

Cody, A. *Heavenly Sanctuary and Heavenly Liturgy.* St. Meinrad: St. Meinrad Press, 1961.

Cullmann, O. *The Christology of the New Testament.* Philadelphia: Westminster, 1959.

Daniélou, R. P. *Le Message chrétienne et la Pensée grecque au IIe Siècle.* Paris: Institut Catholique, 1961.

Deichgräber, G. *Gotteshymnus und Christushymnus in der frühen Christenheit.* Studien zur Umwelt des Neuen Testaments. Göttingen: Vandenhoeck und Ruprecht, 1967.

Deissman, A. *Licht vom Osten.* Tübingen: Mohr, 1909.

Dey, L. K. K. *The Intermediary World and Patterns of Perfection in Philo and Hebrews.* Missoula: Scholars Press, 1975.

Dibelius, M. *Die Formgeschichte des Evangeliums.* Tübingen: Mohr, 1933.

Dillon, J. *The Middle Platonists.* London: Duckworth, 1977.

Dittenberger, G. *Sylloge Inscriptionum Graecarum.* Leipzig: Hirzelium, 1920.

Dodds, E. R. *Pagan and Christian in an Age of Anxiety.* New York: Norton, 1965.

Festugière, A. J. *Contemplation et vie contemplative selon Platon.* Paris: Librarie Philosophique, 1950.

Geffcken, J. *Zwei griechischen Apologeten.* Berlin: Teubner, 1907.

Giversen, S. *Apocryphon Johannis.* Copenhagen: Prostant apud Munksgaard, 1963.

Grässer, E. *Der Glaube im Hebräerbrief.* Marburger Theologische Studien. Marburg: N. G. Elwert, 1965.

————. *Texte und Situation.* Gütersloh: Gerd Mohn, 1973.

Greer, R. A. *The Captain of Our Salvation.* Tübingen: Mohr, 1973.

Haenchen, E. *Die Botschaft des Thomas-Evangeliums.* Berlin: Töpelmann, 1961.

Hahn, F. *Christologische Hoheitstitel.* FRLANT 83. Göttingen: Vandenhoeck und Ruprecht, 1966.

Harnack, A. *Kritik des Neuen Testaments von einem griechischen Philosophen des 3. Jahrhunderts.* Leipzig: J. C. Hindrichs, 1911.

Hegermann, H. *Die Vorstellung vom Schöpfungsmittler im hellenistischen Judentum.* Berlin: 1961.

Hofius. O. *Katapausis; Die Vorstellung von endzeitlichen Ruheort im Hebräerbrief.* WUNT 2. Tübingen: Mohr, 1970.

————. *Der Vorhang vor dem Thron Gottes.* WUNT. Tübingen: Mohr, 1972.

Jaeger, W. *Early Christianity and Greek Paideia.* Cambridge: Harvard University Press, 1965.

Johann, H. T., ed. *Erziehung und Bildung in der heidnischen und christlichen Antike.* Darmstadt: Wissenschaftliche Buchgesellschaft, 1976.

Jonas, H. *Die Gnosis und der spätantiker Geist.* FRLANT 51. Göttingen: Vandenhoeck und Ruprecht, 1934.

Käsemann, E. *Das wandernde Gottesvolk.* FRLANT 55. Göttingen: Vandenhoeck und Ruprecht, 1938.

Klappert, B. *Die Eschatologie des Hebräerbriefs.* Munich: Kaiser, 1969.

Klinzing, G. *Die Umdeutung des Kultus in der Qumrangemeinde und im Neuen Testament.* SUNT 7. Göttingen: Vandenhoeck und Ruprecht, 1971.

Krämer, H. *Der Ursprung der Geistmetaphysik.* Amsterdam: Grüner, 1967.

Kuss, O. *Der Brief an die Hebräer.* RNT. Regensburg: Friedrich Pustet, 1966.

Lilla, S. R. C. *Clement of Alexandria.* Oxford: University Press, 1971.

Lindars, B. *New Testament Apologetic.* London: SCM, 1961.

Michel, O. *Der Brief an die Hebräer.* KEKNT. Göttingen: Vandenhoeck und Ruprecht, 12. Auflage, 1966.

Moffatt, J. *A Critical and Exegetical Commentary on the Epistle to the Hebrews.* ICC. Edinburgh: T. and T. Clark, 1924.

Moore, G. F. *Judaism in the First Centuries of the Christian Era.* Cambridge: Harvard, repr. 1966.

Nikiprowetzky, V. *Le Commentaire de l'Écriture chez Philon d'Alexandrie.* Leiden: E. J. Brill, 1977.

Nilsson, M. *Geschichte der griechischen Religion.* Munich: C. H. Beck, 1961.

Norden, E. *Agnostos Theos.* Darmstadt: Wissenschaftliche Buchgesellschaft, 5. Auflage, 1971.

Overbeck, F. *Zur Geschichte des Kanons.* Chemnitz: Schmeitzner, 1880.

Pascher, J. 'Η Βασιλικὴ ὁδός; Der Königsweg zur Wiedergeburt und Vergöttung bei Philon von Alexandria. Paderborn: Schöningh, 1931.

Peisker, M. Der Glaubensbegriff bei Philon. diss. Breslaus, 1936.

Rad, G. v. Gesammelte Studien zum Alten Testament. Munich: Kaiser, 1958.

Rad, G. v. Old Testament Theology. New York: Harper and Row, 1965.

Schierse, F. J. Verheissung und Heilsvollendung: Zur theologischen Grundfrage des Hebräerbriefs. MTS 9. Munich: Zink, 1955.

Schmidt, C. Koptisch-gnostische Schriften. GCS. Leipzig, 1905.

Schröger, F. Der Verfasser des Hebräerbriefs als Schriftausleger. Regensburg: Friedrich Pustet, 1968.

Seeberg, A. Der Kathechismus der Urchristenheit. Leipzig: A. Deichert, 1903.

Smith, A. Porphyry's Place in the Neoplatonic Tradition. The Hague: Martinus Nijhoff, 1974.

Sowers, S. The Hermeneutics of Philo and Hebrews. Richmond: John Knox, 1965.

Spicq, C. L'Épître aux Hébreux. Paris: Librairie Lecoffre, 1952.

Strack, H. and P. Billerbeck, Kommentar zum Neuen Tesament aus Talmud und Midrasch. Munich: Beck, 1926. [Str-B]

Strathmann, H. Der Brief an die Hebräer. NTD. Göttingen: Vandenhoeck und Ruprecht, 1936.

Stuhlmacher, P. Vom Verstehen des Neuen Testaments. Göttingen: Vandenhoeck und Ruprecht, 1979.

Theiler, W. Die Vorbereitung des Neuplatonismus. Berlin: Weidmannsche, 1930.

Theissen, G. Untersuchungen zum Hebräerbrief. Gütersloh: Gerd Mohn, 1969.

Thyen, H. Der Stil der judisch-hellenistischen Homilie. FRLANT. Göttingen: Vandenhoeck und Ruprecht, 1955.

Timothy, H. B. The Early Christian Apologists and Greek Philosophy. Assen: Van Gorcum, 1973.

Vielhauer, P. Aufsätze zum Neuen Testament. Munich: Kaiser, 1965.

Vögtle, A. Das Neue Testament und die Zukunft des Kosmos. Dusseldorf: Patmos Verlag, 1970.

Völker, W. Fortschritt und Vollendung bei Philon von Alexandrien. Leipzig: J. C. Hinrichs, 1938.

Völkl, R. Christ und die Welt nach dem Neuen Testament. Würzburg: Echter, 1961.

Walter, N. Der Thoraausleger Aristobulos. Berlin: Akademie, 1964.

Walzer, R. Galen on Jews and Christians. Oxford: University Press, 1949.

Wendland, P. Die urchristlichen Literaturformen. Tübingen: Mohr, 1912.

Wenschkewitz, H. Die Spiritualisierung der Kultusbegriff. Leipzig: Eduard Pfeiffer, 1932.

Williamson, R. Philo and the Epistle to the Hebrews. ALGHJ. Leiden: E. J. Brill, 1970.

Windisch, H. Der Hebräerbrief. HNT. Tübingen: Mohr, 2. Auflage, 1931.

Witt, R. E. Albinus and the History of Middle Platonism. Amsterdam: Kakkut, repr. 1937.

Wolfson, H. *The Philosophy of the Church Fathers.* Cambridge: Harvard University Press, 1956.

Wrede, W. *Das literarische Rätsel des Hebräerbriefs.* FRLANT. Göttingen: Vandenhoeck und Ruprecht, 1906.

Zimmerman, H. *Die Hohepriester-Christologie des Hebräerbriefs.* Paderborn: Ferdinand Schöningh, 1964.

VI. Articles in Festschriften

Barrett, C. K. "The Eschatology of the Epistle to the Hebrews," in *Background of the New Testament and its Eschatology*, ed. by W. D. Davies and D. Daube. Cambridge: University Press, 1956.

Braun, H. "Das himmlische Vaterland bei Philo und im Hebräerbrief," in *Verborum Veritas*, fs. G. Stählin, ed. by. O. Böcher and K. Haacker. Wuppertal: Brockhaus, 1970.

Grässer, E. "Das Heil als Wort," in *Neues Testament und Geschichte*, fs. O. Cullmann, ed. H. Baltensweiler and Bo Reicke. Tübingen: Mohr, 1972.

_____. "Rechtfertigung im Hebräerbrief," in *Rechtfertigung*, fs. E. Käsemann, ed. J. Friedrich, W. Pöhlmann, and P. Stuhlmacher. Tübingen: Mohr, 1976.

_____. "Zur Christologie des Hebräerbriefes," in *Neues Testament und Christliche Existenz*, fs. H. Braun, ed. H. D. Betz and L. Schottroff. Tübingen: Mohr, 1973.

Héring, J. "Eschatologie biblique et idéalisme platonicien," in *Background of the New Testament and its Eschatology*, ed. by W. D. Davies and D. Daube. Cambridge: University Press, 1956.

Sandmel, S. "Virtue and Reward in Philo," in *Essays in Old Testament Ethics*, ed. James L. Crenshaw and John T. Willis. New York: KTAV, 1974.

Schenke, H.-M. "Erwägungen zum Rätsel des Hebraerbriefes," in *Neues Testament und christliches Existenz*, ed. by H. D. Betz and L. Schottroff. Tübingen: Mohr, 1973.

VII. Dictionary Articles

Behm, J. Βρῶμα. *TDNT* 1.

Braumann, G. "Kind." *Theologisches Begriffslexikon zum Neuen Testament.* II. Ed. L. Coenen, E. Beyreuther, and H. Bietenhard. Wuppertertal: Brockhaus, 1972.

Braun, H. Ποιέω. *TDNT* 6.

Büchsel, F. Ἀκατάλυτος. *TDNT* 4.

_____. Ἔλεγχος. *TDNT* 2.

Bultmann, R. Πίστις. *TDNT* 6.

Colpe, C. "Philo." *RGG³* 5.

Delling. G. Αἰσθητήριον. *TDNT* 1.

Fuchs, H. "Enkkyklios Paideia." *RAC* 5.

Hanse, H. Κατέχω. *TDNT* 2.

_____. Μετέχω. *TDNT* 2.

Hauck, F. Ὑπομένω. *TDNT* 5.

Jeremias, J. Πυλή. *TDNT* 6.

Kittel, G. Θέατρον. *TDNT* 3.

Klauser, T. "Auswendiglernen." *RAC* 1.

Köster, H. Ὑπόστασις. *TDNT* 8.

Lang, F. Πύρ. *TDNT* 6.

Lohse, E. Χειροποίητος. *TDNT* 9.

Maurer, C. Συνείδησις. *TDNT* 7.

Michaelis, W. Ὁρατός. *TDNT* 5.

Michel, O. "Glaube." *Theologisches Begriffslexikon.* I.

Preisker, H. Ἔγγυος. *TDNT* 2.

―――――. Νωθρός. *TDNT* 4.

Sasse, H. Κόσμος. *TDNT* 3.

Schlier. H. Παρρησία. *TDNT* 6.

Schneider, C. "Anapausis." *RAC* 1.

Schneider, J. Ἀκατάλυτος. *TDNT* 4.

―――――. Ἀπαράβατος. *TDNT* 5.

Schniewind, J. and G. Friedrich. Ἐπαγγελία. *TDNT* 2.

Schrenk, G. Ἀπάτωρ. *TDNT* 5.

―――――. Ἀρχιερεύς. *TDNT* 3.

Schweizer, E. Σάρξ. *TDNT* 7.

Seesemann, H. Παλαιόω. *TDNT* 5.

Stählin, G. Προκοπή. *TDNT* 6.

Strathmann, H. Λατρεία. *TDNT* 4.

Würthwein, E. Μισθός. *TDNT* 5.

INDEX

APOCALYPTIC LITERATURE

1.32	123
1.43	79
1.80	24, 67
1.98	24, 37, 63
1.108	76
2.33	57
2.34	79
2.54-55	148
2.54	138
2.67	93
2.83	25, 34, 57
2.89	49
2.221-237	127
3.14	37, 63
3.29	77
3.36	24
3.39	77
3.40-44	67
3.46	148
3.48	77
3.71	77
3.72	63
3.79-82	119
3.83	59
3.97-100	49
3.101	137
3.103	93
3.152	145
3.201	64, 78
3.203-233	58
3.203	67
3.204	57, 93, 124
3.210	36
3.226-233	58
3.228	58
3.244	23

de Cher.

3	22
6	22
57	45
73	45
78	63
80-81	34, 36, 63, 78
90	57
120-121	60

120-122	148

Sac. A.C.

7	22
44	23
70-71	77
78	23
85	24, 32
85-86	24
91	25
93	124
129	66

Quod. Det. Pot.

20	114
21	113
41	22-25, 35
48	118
64	24
69	24
85	32
107	113
115	25
136	66
145-146	114
157	66
160	71, 148
166	23
171	23

de Post. Cain.

12	96
15	60
19	138
19-29	49
20	45
22-23	95, 157
23	25, 34, 50, 57, 66, 85, 86, 121, 127, 157
28	84, 86
28-29	84
30	137
142	77
163	77
168	65

CLASSICAL SOURCES

TOPICS